Web Resources for Future Millionaires

Save typing! Every Web address in this book can be clicked from
www.MillionsOnTheInternet.com!

Picking and Getting Domain Names

URL	Contents
www.networksolutions.com/help/general.html	Basic information on domain names
www.uspto.gov/web/offices/tac/notices/guide299.htm	Domain trademark information
www.nametrade.com	Naming consultant with advice
www.metaphorname.com	Another naming consultant
www.uspto.gov/tmdb	Trademark lookup
www.QWho.com	Domain availability check
Namesecure.com	Domain registration and forwarding
registerfree.com	Discount domain registration
NetworkSolutions.com	U.S. and international registration
idNames.com	International registration service

Web Site Design Resources

URL	Contents
WebDevelopersJournal.com	Magazine for Web site creators
NetStudio.com	Web graphics design program
SpinFrenzy.com	Online Web design package
geocities.yahoo.com	Free Web space
www.tripod.com	Free Web space
www.TRUSTe.org	Web privacy certification
www.freemerchant.com	Free Web merchant site provider
www.eCongo.com	Free Web merchant site provider
www.Bigstep.com	Free Web merchant site provider
www.iCat.com	Fee-based merchant site provider
store.yahoo.com	Fee-based merchant site provider
www.VirtualSpin.com	Fee-based merchant site provider

Web Site Promotion Resources

URL	Contents
www.bcentral.com/?leindex	Web advertising and promotion tools
websitegarage.netscape.com	Web promotion tools
www.DoubleClick.net	Web advertising
www.refer-it.com	Affiliate program guide
www.press-release-writing.com	How to write a press release
E-Releases.com	Press release distributor

tear here

Content Sources and Services

URL	Contents
www.ultimatebb.com	Bulletin board system
www.unitedmedia.com/info/ufs.html	Newspaper feature–style content
www.creators.com/featurewire/	Comics and columns
www.tms.tribune.com	TV and movie listings, and more
www.iSyndicate.com	Syndicated content (some free)
businesswire.com	Press releases

Employment Resources

URL	Contents
Monster.com	Database of jobs and job-seekers
HotJobs.com	Database of jobs and job-seekers
Jobsearch.com	Database of jobs and job-seekers
Internetjobs.com	Internet-specific jobs site

Startup Financing Resources

URL	Contents
eCompanies.com	Incubator
nbia.org	Information on incubators
www.mercurycenter.com/svtech/	Venture capital news
adventurecapital.com	Venture capital advertising
www.nasbic.org	Organization of investors
www.nasbic.org/links.html	Links to investors
wasatchvc.com	Wasatch Venture Fund (investor)
firstcapitalgroup.com	First Capital Group (investor)
seacoastcapital.com/intro.html	Seacoast Capital (investor)
sba.gov/INV/	Investments from U.S. government
Garage.com	Venture capital matchmaker

Business Resources

URL	Contents
ClickZ.com	Online business information
AllEC.com	Business news and information
TheStandard.com	Internet business magazine
WebMarketingToday.com	Daily Internet business news source
Builder.com	e-Business articles and links

Save typing! Every Web address in this book can be clicked from
www.MillionsOnTheInternet.com!

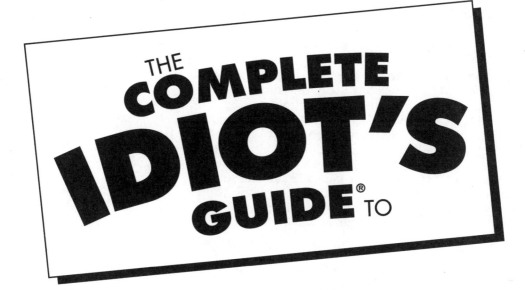

Making Millions
on the Internet

Nat Gertler and Rod Underhill

A Division of Macmillan USA
201 West 103rd Street, Indianapolis, Indiana 46290

Trademarks

Warning and Disclaimer

Associate Publisher
Greg Wiegand

Acquisitions Editor
Angelina Ward

Development Editor
Sarah Robbins

Managing Editor
Thomas F. Hayes

Project Editor
Tricia A. Sterling

Copy Editor
Kay Hoskin

Indexers
Deborah Hittel
Erika Millen
Mary SeRine

Proofreader
Jeanne Clark

Technical Editor
Robert Patrick

Illustrator
Judd Winick

Team Coordinator
Sharry Gregory

Interior Designer
Nathan Clement

Cover Designer
Michael Freeland

Copywriter
Eric Borgert

Production
Gloria Schurick
Mark Walchle

Contents at a Glance

Contents

Part 2: Ready, Set, Startup   67

6 Building Your Team   69

7 Jumping on Someone's Team   83

20 Little Bitty Pieces of Company: Stock and Stock Options 255

21 Sell Your Cake and Eat It, Too: Going Public 271

Foreword by Stan Lee

Let me tell you how great Rod and Nat are. Even though I've already got a Web site of my own, after reading their *The Complete Idiot's Guide to Making Millions on the Internet* I felt like rushing out and creating another one!

What a book it is! It tells you straight on how much wealth is waiting on the Web for those who know how to find it. It makes you want to drop everything and get yourself a Web site while the getting's good. Then, it wastes no time in showing you what to do, why to do it, and—most important of all—how it's done. As if that's not enough, it manages to present this passionate plethora of priceless pointers in a style that's breezy, fun, and easy to understand.

If ever there was a right book for the right time, Rod and Nat's *Idiot's Guide* has to be it. Never has anything snowballed as quickly as the public's burgeoning interest in the Internet. It's almost hard to remember a time when most of the new addresses you learned didn't have a "dot com" or "dot net" attached to them. What's more, there's hardly any product or service that can't be found on the Web with an "e" in front of it. The Internet has become the place to go for anything and everything that anyone could ever want. And think of the advertising dollars that are starting to pour in.

Okay, what does that tell us?

It tells us there's money, big money, to be made on the Internet. While still in its infancy, it's growing and expanding at a breathtaking pace. But, it can be a jungle if you tackle it without a map, without knowing your way. Which is why this book is such a necessity. It guides you through the perils and pitfalls and does it entertainingly.

But I mustn't detain you any longer. The good stuff's waiting on the pages ahead. Remember, there are fortunes to be made in cyberspace. One of them could be yours!

Excelsior!

Stan Lee

Stan Lee

In the 1960s, Stan Lee and some talented comic book artists created the Silver Age Marvel Comics Universe, including Spider-Man, the Incredible Hulk, the X-Men, and many more. In 1999, Stan founded Stan Lee Media, a company based at the stanlee.net *Web site. Stan is the Chief Creative Officer, creating new characters for use on the site and for licensing out to other media. Stan Lee Media stock trades under the symbol SLEE.*

About the Authors

Rod Underhill is a lawyer, a musician, and a writer. He is also one of the founders of MP3.com, the mega-successful Web site offering free music over the Internet. Rod still serves as music director of MP3.com.

Nat Gertler has written or co-written more than a dozen computer books, including *The Complete Idiot's Guide to MP3* (co-authored with Rod). He is also the founder and owner of Aaugh.com, serving information and retail sales to comic strip readers.

Judd Winick, illustrator, is the creator of the acclaimed comic *The Adventures of Barry Ween, Boy Genius*, currently optioned for animated television. He is also a former star of MTV's *The Real World*. For more information, visit his Web site, www.BarryWeen.com.

Dedication

This book is dedicated to the dreamers, the schemers, the innovators, and those who help and support them against the legions of naysayers. —Nat

I would like to dedicate this to my beloved family, especially to my wife. I would also like to thank the former members of the San Diego Juvenile Court Dependency Panel. I hope your new careers turn out as well as mine did. —Rod

Tell Us What You Think!

As the reader of this book, *you* are our most important critic and commentator. We value your opinion and want to know what we're doing right, what we could do better, what areas you'd like to see us publish in, and any other words of wisdom you're willing to pass our way.

As an Associate Publisher for Que, I welcome your comments. You can fax, email, or write me directly to let me know what you did or didn't like about this book—as well as what we can do to make our books stronger.

Please note that I cannot help you with technical problems related to the topic of this book, and that due to the high volume of mail I receive, I might not be able to reply to every message.

When you write, please be sure to include this book's title and author as well as your name and phone or fax number. I will carefully review your comments and share them with the author and editors who worked on the book.

Fax: 317-581-4666

Email: consumer@mcp.com

Mail: Greg Wiegand, Associate Publisher
           Que
           201 West 103rd Street
           Indianapolis, IN 46290 USA

Introduction

The growth of the Internet has created perhaps the greatest opportunity for creating individual wealth since the patent ran out on that *sliced bread* idea. The Internet isn't just one new business like those little Fotomat-style huts where they sell you over-priced coffee. It is a tool that will change the way almost everyone does business. The last change of this scale may have been the telephone, or it may have been the introduction of paved roadways across the nation—however, neither of those spread nearly so quickly.

In the hundreds of pages, thousands of words, and occasional snide comments in this book, we hope to point you to the road to using that tool to make yourself a lot of money. You'll get an overview of how people are making money off of the Internet, with the steps that they've used to achieve that success.

What This Book Isn't

This book is not a sure-fire get-rich-quick scheme. Striving to become an Internet millionaire is a matter of investing your time, energy, ideas, and maybe even money in the hopes that it will work out. There are plenty of talented, ambitious people who have tried to do the same and it just didn't work out. You can get involved in a company that finds a way to download raspberry danish right to the Web user, and the effort can still fail because suddenly nobody feels like a raspberry danish. Or because a competitor comes out with a raspberry danish download site just before yours. Or because the people you work with are brilliant technicians but lack the marketing skills needed to sell umbrellas in a rain forest.

This book is also not likely to be the last reference you ever need, particularly if you are choosing to start your own Internet company (as opposed to joining on with someone else's). Starting a business is a complex task. We do, however, steer you toward publications and Web sites that will help you gain more information.

Conventions Used in This Book

We've used the following text styles to help make it easier to recognize certain things in this book:

➤ Web page addresses (URLs) are presented `like this`. For example, if we mention `www.aaugh.com`, then you can type that into the address field of your Web browser to see the site we're discussing. To save you a lot of typing, we've set up a special Web site with links to all the URLs mentioned in this book. Head on over to `www.MillionsOnTheInternet.com` and you can travel to all the relevant Web sites with just a click!

➤ New terms are presented in *italicized text*; pay close attention to these terms.

We've also used some sidebars and margin notes to provide you with bits of info you might not find anywhere else.

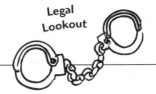

Legal Lookout

Realities of the Law

Throughout this book, Legal Lookout sidebars will give you tips and warnings related to the law. For example, here's an important one:

This book is built around American corporations, American markets, and American laws. As such, much of this book might not apply in other countries. Additionally, remember that the U.S. Congress is basically a team of people whose job it is to change the law when you least expect it. As such, legal changes that could affect you may have taken place after this book was written. In all legal matters, consult your lawyer. Your lawyer is your friend. (It's others people's lawyers who are the enemy.)

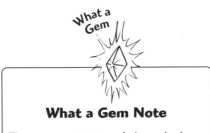

What a Gem

What a Gem Note

These notes, scattered through the book, give you quick tips toward building your success.

Wealth of Knowledge

Wealth of Knowledge Note

Through the book, you'll find Wealth of Knowledge notes giving you some in-depth information about a given topic.

Heroic Histories

In each chapter, you'll find two case studies of existing Internet successes, explaining what their business is and how they achieved success.

Rod Says a Bit

The opinions marked Rod Says are written by Rod Underhill, co-founder of MP3.com and the lead author on the more businessy sections of this book.

Nat Says Too Much

When Nat Gertler (seasoned computer book author and lead writer of the more Internet-oriented sections of this book) wants to spout off with his opinion, you'll see a Nat Says note.

The Sections of This Book

The main text of this book is divided into five parts, each with a different focus:

> ➤ **Part 1: The Big Idea** talks about coming up with an idea for a new Web site or Internet service.

> ➤ **Part 2: Ready, Set, Startup** deals with bringing together a team of people who can turn your idea into a reality, with information for you whether you're the person with the idea or someone who wants to be on the team.

> ➤ **Part 3: Building the Business** shows you how to go from having a company to having an actual online product.

> ➤ **Part 4: Growing the Business** helps you take your online offering and turn it into a popular one.

> ➤ **Part 5: The Big Payoff** shows you how your participation in this company, even if it's not a profitable one, can lead to millions of dollars for you.

Part 1
The Big Idea

Build a better mousetrap, *we are told,* and the mice will beat a path to your door and steal all your mail.

These days, the mousetraps (or is the plural of mousetrap micetrap?) that people are building are designed to lure the users of computer mice to clicking to their Web site. And if you can think up that better mousetrap, or even hook up with a dreamer who has already dreamed it up, then you are well on your way toward gathering some of that World Wide Wealth that you desire!

Chapter 1

Dot Commerce Creates WWWealth! Welcome to the World of e-Commerce

---

In This Chapter

➤ What is e-commerce?

➤ Examples of e-commerce

➤ Benefits of conducting e-commerce

➤ Customer concerns

What Is e-Commerce?

e-Commerce doesn't stand for anything more exotic than *electronic commerce*. Essentially, e-commerce simply means doing economic business on the Internet.

All the traditional types of business that you might expect to find in any traditional business community exist on the Internet. Do you want to buy a pair of socks? You can do that on the Internet. How about some shares of stock? Sure! Just like the business world that exists independently of cyberspace, you can buy, sell, or trade goods on the Internet.

Marketing has also made a home in the exciting new world of e-commerce. The famed, and highly lucrative, motion picture *The Blair Witch Project* launched a very successful publicity campaign from their spooky Internet Web site. The Blair Witch Project Web site, like the movie, is somewhat "low budget" but does the promotional job that often a multimillion-dollar television campaign fails to do. Bottom line: Their pre-release Web site ensured the movie's commercial success.

Some companies use the Internet to advertise the existence of their goods or services where the business transactions exist only offline, away from the Internet. Perhaps your Uncle Louie uses a home page on the World Wide Web simply to advertise the location of his car repair shop, his days and hours of operation, and the types of autos that he performs his repairs on.

Uncle Louie's Web site would be an example of a very basic way of using the Internet for e-commerce. Many e-businesses (see how e-easy it is to pick up this catchy e-lingo?) are really real-world outfits that are using the Internet to attract or educate potential and ongoing customers.

Uncle Louie could take his business one step further by offering to sell used car parts. This new addition could be performed very simply by Louie merely keeping an updated listing of his used parts somewhere on his Web page. Or he could get really high tech by allowing customers to order the car parts right there on his Web page, with the customers typing in their credit card numbers, shipping addresses, and requested part. This is one possible example of a traditional business expanding sales via the Internet. In Uncle Louie's case, by adding the sale of car parts on the Internet, his possible customer base has jumped from people in his own town, with broken-down cars, to all the millions of Internet e-shoppers who need a particular used car part.

In fact, Louie's first Internet car part sale might be to some lucky fellow in Germany who needs an original, but used, gear shift knob for his prized 1965 Ford Mustang. Such is the magic of doing e-commerce on the Internet. The world is your customer base—at least, the huge portion of the world who hang out on the Internet.

Another Type of e-Business

While some traditional, real-world businesses use the Internet to enlarge their customer base, other Internet businesses exist only on the Internet. This is one of the main reasons that the Internet has created such a stir in the business world. No business could exist solely on the Internet until the Internet had been invented, right?

Amazon.com exists only on the Internet. You've probably heard of Amazon.com, the company that sells South American real estate? Wait! I'm wrong! The real estate company is probably called BookStore.com. Amazon.com sells books (and other neat things) on the Internet, but only on the Internet. You won't find an Amazon.com bookstore in your town, my town, or even in anybody else's town. That's because it exists in the world's largest town, that all language speakin', all country existin', and mighty fine e-town called the Internet. And this particular e-town amounts to nothing less than the whole wide world.

By the way, they really should have called The World Wide Web the *Whole Wide World*, but they didn't check with me first or I would have told them.

Anyway, here's something to ponder for a moment. Why is the Internet like Las Vegas, Nevada? (Ponder, ponder, ponder.) Because it never closes. Yup! The Internet is open all night, every night, and never even closes on my birthday. (Although I've written several letters of complaint about that.)

Heroic History

Yahoo!: A Little Bit of Everything

Web site name: Yahoo.com

Founded: 1994

Service provided: Yahoo! is the definitive Internet portal.

Business model: Yahoo! started in the relatively early days of the Web as an online list of the existing Web sites. As the Web grew, such organization was needed. Yahoo! became a popular stopping site on your way to where you really wanted to be. It became an attractive site for advertisers, as a surfer who was specifically looking for a clothing site could be presented with a targeted ad for just such a site. In the interest of generating more visitors and keeping them there (rather than letting them surf on by), Yahoo! expanded to be a full portal, offering eyeball-catching information such as news and stock quotes; free services such as email, chat, and games; and directly profitable services such as an online travel agency (via cooperation with travelocity.com) and online auctions.

Where the money came from: Yahoo! went public in April 1996, with an IPO price of $26/share. After a series of stock splits broke each original share into 12 shares, the stock was trading on December 17, 1999 at just under $345 per share. The total market capitalization at that price is more than $90 billion. The stock trades under the symbol YHOO on the Nasdaq exchange.

The Three Magic Things About e-Commerce

We've already touched on two of them, but they deserve to be looked at more closely. Let's yell out the first one together and really bug the neighbors! Okay, here we go: *"The Internet reaches the Whole Wide World!"* (Wow, you really yelled that one out loud. If you get kicked out of your apartment don't blame me, I was only kidding about the yelling thing.)

Okay, let's yell out the second magic thing about e-commerce! (Wait, you look sort of cross right now. Was it something I said?) Alright, here we go! *"The Internet never closes!"* Of course, if your major Internet business's Web site crashes and goes offline because somebody kicks a glass of milk on your major computer machinery (resulting in what my little brother used to call *frying your computer's cookies*), well, that is one of the most major embarrassments that your e-business can suffer.

So, what's the third magic thing about doing business on the Internet? By being a computer-based business, you can really, really, cut down on overhead costs. Clever computer engineers who work for all the major e-commerce sites are always looking at ways to design automatic features that reduce the need for actual, living employees. Allow me to explain something to you. A Billion Dollar Company in the real world has a a lot more employees than a Billion Dollar Company that exists only on the Internet. It wouldn't be out of line for an Internet Company to gain a market valuation of more than a billion dollars with less than 500 actual living employees (and a whole bunch of computers quietly blinking in the background.) Plus, because you're based on the Internet, you don't have to pay those high mall rents, or provide parking spaces for your customers. Although the computer and Internet service costs won't be trivial, you can make up for it by setting up shop in the middle of nowhere. As long as you have access to the Internet and to an *uninterruptable power supply* (UPS), the customer won't care where you are.

Based on my studies, and my reading of tea leaves, here's a rough estimate of what an e-business saves by doing its commerce online. Let's assume that it costs a traditional business about a dollar a customer when that customer is served in a traditional real-world store, okay? Hang on to your hat. It could cost a successful e-business about one tenth of one cent to serve the same customer on the Internet.

Wait! I Forgot About the Fourth Magic Thing!

Silly me. I nearly forgot the existence of a fourth magic thing about creating an e-commerce business, particularly an e-business that exists solely on the Internet.

Some e-businesses can get very wealthy, very quickly. For example, the famed online music company MP3.com went from pennies of value to billions of dollars of value in less than two years.

My cautious co-author, Nat, would no doubt point out that such quick and incredible successes are the rare exception rather than the rule. He'd be right, too. Still and all, the fact of the matter is that such speedy successes are possible in the mighty world of e-commerce, although certainly not the norm by any means.

But, before we move on, let's talk (or rather, I'll type and you'll read) about something we Internet professionals call *Internet Time*. No, this isn't a new TV show about the Internet, but the concept that things seem to change much faster on the World Wide Web than they do in the so-called real world.

Nat Speaks

He's Right

I would tell you that multibillion-dollar successes are the small but visible exception. Still, with its phenomenal rate of growth and its short history, e-commerce has easily become one of the fastest generators of new wealth ever.

And, things can change very quickly on the Internet. New innovations seem to spring up quickly. New ways to do business seem to develop almost overnight. In reality, six months of real time is a very long time on the Internet when it comes to business. The importance of this is that Internet Time is a two-edged sword. Just as a business can quickly build itself on the Internet, a business can just as quickly fall behind if a red-hot Internet rival figures out a way to do your business better than you do. No Internet company, no matter how successful, can afford to rest on its laurels.

Uh, Boss, There's 100 Million Potential Customers at the Front Door!

Yup. That's the best estimate of the number of people using the Internet at the beginning of the year 2000. Out of those people using the Internet, I'd estimate that about 20–25 million of them actually made a purchase of some sort online. I base my numbers on a survey conducted by Nielsen Media Research a year or so ago, and my own estimations based on the research that I've conducted. While perhaps 20% of the Internet surfers out there have stopped their surfing long enough to make a purchase of some sort, the rest of them do a lot of reading on the Internet. When they read the advertisements on your site, you still have a way to make a buck, right?

That's a lot of customers or readers of advertising, and the numbers of people using the Internet are growing every day.

Where Did This Internet Come From, Anyway?

Its history is in the Cold War. A real James Bond sort of thing. The RAND Corporation, the famous think tank, wanted to figure out a way to transfer computer information from one city to another in the event of a nuclear war. No, really, I'm not making this up. This sounded good to the X-File sorts in our government, so a government-funded agency called *Advanced Research Projects Agency (ARPA)* thought about a way to send computer information between agencies (such as military bases, top-secret defense contractors, and certain university scientists) not only in case of a war, but just for ease of transfer of data. This led to ARPAnet, which was a mini-Internet that sent data across the USA in a more limited way than today's global Net that is the World Wide Web. All this stuff was happening by the mid 1970s.

Various improvements in technology came about that allowed different types of computers to communicate with each other, including personal computers such as the one that you have in your home or office—or, even, on your lap. By the 1980s the ARPAnet had become less of a government secret and more of a University playground. When I first became involved with what was then called the Internet, you had to enter via a University connection of some sort. It didn't take too long for things to open up and almost over night, as modems and computers became faster and stronger, the Internet exploded into what it is today.

Why e-Customers Love e-Shopping

Well, for one thing, it's easy. Why drive down to your local CD store in the middle of a snowstorm to pick up a copy of that best-selling duet by Underhill and Gertler when you can order it via your computer on the Internet? Or even just download the song from a Web site? Sheesh! Just the thought of scraping the ice off my windshield with a credit card makes me shiver to the bone. Plus, I can make much better use of my credit card by shopping online. (I really need to buy one of those neat windshield ice scrapers, park my car indoors, or move to a warmer climate.)

Shopping online can be cheaper than shopping offline! How come? Because the e-businesses can save a ton of money by doing their business on the Internet, they generally pass some of the savings on to consumers. Sure, you still have to be a careful shopper and all, but you should be able to at least match the prices found in real-world stores.

Oh, by the way, Internet pros usually call real-world stores *brick-and-mortar* businesses.

Things That Bother e-Customers

Nothing is perfect, not even the Internet. Some customers have some serious concerns about various aspects of doing business via the Internet.

One of the major areas of concern surrounds the safety of using a credit card to make an online purchase. The general fear is that some clever e-criminal will manage to snag your credit card information as it travels along the Internet's electronic byways.

Of course, such criminal activity has happened in the past. I don't know that using a credit card on the Internet is actually any more risky than using it at your local shopping mall. After all, a dishonest store clerk could jot down your credit card number, expiration date, and name, and promptly use it to send flowers to his parole officer, right? Anyway, many e-commerce businesses have rushed to provide *encryption* for their credit card–using customers. Sounds sort of James Bondish again, huh? In a way it is, I guess. Encryption is a high-tech way of disguising the data relating to your credit card via different ways of encoding your credit card information before it leaves your computer. Then, the e-business deciphers the credit card information after the data travels over the Internet.

The ever-increasing use of encryption seems to be easing the concerns of most Internet credit card users. And using a credit card sure beats mailing a check.

Besides, checks can be stolen in the mail, too. I had a check stolen once, and before you knew it my identity was swiped as well. Some evil doer was going across town writing rubber

Cookies: They Don't Come with Chocolate Chips

A *cookie* is a piece of information that a Web site can store on a Web surfer's computer. Many Web sites use a cookie stored on your computer to recognize who you are each time you visit; in that way, they can keep track of pages you've looked at in the past, what you've ordered from them before, and so on. This information on your surfing and purchasing habits can be very valuable to a company who deals in selling such information, or who uses the information to design its business model. Many Internet users don't care for cookies on their computers (but they might like them in the cookie jars). Your favorite Internet browser will have an Internet Security function where you can disable your cookies, if you want.

checks in my name. All he needed was one of my checks, and the next thing I knew I was getting some pretty angry telephone calls from various collection agencies concerning checks that I had never written at stores I had never ever even entered. (Brrrr. The Internet sounds a lot safer to me than the real world, now that I think about it.)

Some Things People Might Not Want to Buy Online

It is one thing to buy a compact disc at CDNow.com. It is quite another thing to buy a sofa on the Internet. Wouldn't you want to feel it, sit on it, and generally kick its tires? Wait! That's what you do when you buy a car, right? And people are actually starting to buy cars via the Internet.

Some e-businesses make it easy to shop for the best value in a particular car. You can pick the model and color, and tell the company what you are willing to pay. Then, the e-business helps you find the car of your dreams, hopefully located at a dealership near you. So, maybe buying a sofa online wouldn't be that odd, after all.

I've heard some people say that they would never buy clothing via the Internet. Why? Because they can't try the clothing on and so on. But people have been ordering clothing though the mail for years. Certainly, The Land's End clothing people have been doing business by mail for years. So has Victoria's Secret, which sells unmentionables, so I better not mention them. (Although I don't know how they expect to keep it a secret when they send everyone catalogs!)

It might turn out that there are few things that can't be sold, or at least marketed, via the Internet. Time will tell.

The Future of e-Commerce

This is the fun part, where I get to become something like a science fiction writer. But, then, today's Internet would have seemed like so much science fiction back in the 1980s.

Imagine a 'fridge that automatically ordered food via the Internet as you used it. Orange juice, steaks, ice cream, and more showing up at your front door according to preset wishes that you programmed into the minicomputer located inside your big, white refrigerator—all for no extra delivery charge or fees. You could easily order whatever type of food you wanted, beside the staples of your diet. (And if you've ever tried to eat staples, I wouldn't advise it.)

As a matter of fact, ordering food in this way appears to be just around the corner.

What about having your measurements taken and then logging that data into your computer? You could then order custom-tailored apparel without ever leaving your home, and they would fit perfectly. Instead of wearing size 34 pants when you are really size 34.3, you'd get exactly the correct size just as if little magic elves had made the pants for you. This would be done easily enough after the clothing manufacturers create *just in time* manufacturing—that is, making clothing one at a time via the use of computers.

Heroic History

GeoCities: Free Web Space

Web site name: geocities.Yahoo.com

Founded: 1994

Service provided: Free Web space

Business model: The explosion of access to the World Wide Web created a vast increase in the number of people who wanted to put up their own Web page to inform the world about one thing or another. Many of these people, however, did not have free Web space provided by their service provider. GeoCities simply gave Web space away; their profit came from placing advertising on each Web page, and charging advertisers. Where other ad-based sites were paying for content and then working to promote it, the GeoCities members were providing free content and promoting their own Web pages, causing GeoCities to be, at one point, the third most-visited Web site. To make it easier for new users to create Web pages, GeoCities provided easy-to-use Web design and publishing tools.

As browser technology grew more sophisticated, so did the ads, which went from being simple banners at the top of the page to including new pop-up advertising windows and floating GeoCities links as a part of the page.

Where the money came from: GeoCities was bought out by Web portal Yahoo! in May, 1999, so that Yahoo! could integrate the free Web page service and the large existing body of Web content. This was performed via a stock swap, with Yahoo! providing more than 21 million shares of stock in addition to converting millions of stock options. Total value of the deal at completion exceeded three billion.

Wow. Neat, huh? I suspect that the only thing that the Internet won't be able to someday provide is the food court found in your local mall.

The Least You Need to Know

➤ e-Commerce is changing how the world does business. Millions of customers are shopping on the Internet every day.

➤ Traditional businesses can market their wares and services online to the world at large. Meanwhile, it is possible to establish a business that exists only on the Internet.

➤ The Internet business world changes very quickly, and some very successful businesses can be created in very brief periods of time.

The Great Geniuses of Money and Nontraditional Thinking

In This Chapter

➤ How great Internet successes come about

➤ Get to know viral marketing

➤ Examples of big Internet successes

➤ What you need to know about nontraditional thinking

In the Beginning, There Was You

Stop what you are doing, hold up your hands, and take a look at them. (Oops! You dropped this book. I should have told you first to set the book down. Sorry, it won't happen again.) Anyway, gaze for a moment at your hands. Do you know what those are? Those are the hands of a potential Internet billionaire, millionaire, or even simply a (future) happily employed Internet professional.

Why? Because nearly anyone, with the right combination of ambition, skill, and determination, can join the ever increasing ranks of Internet pros and earn a living. Just how good that living might be depends on you, some luck, and a lot of planning and preparation. The world of e-commerce has a lot to offer the right person.

This is where Nat and I come in. We intend to help you become the *right person.* (All *left persons* don't have to leave, as we believe in offering our assistance to everyone. It's only the right thing to do.)

In Chapter 1, "Dot Commerce Creates WWWealth! Welcome to the World of e-Commerce," we gave you some basic information about what e-commerce is. In the following chapters, Nat and I will give you a great deal of information about how you can do things such as start your own e-business, join a preexisting company, or join a just-starting Internet company for fun and profit.

In this chapter I will discuss what it takes to have the right stuff to be a great success being the captain of your own Internet Business. In particular, I will discuss what it takes to become that very rare animal: The Internet Billionaire CEO of a Major Internet Company.

Later we provide more details on how you actually start your own Internet business, if that is your plan of action.

Starting your own business can be very risky. Leave your job and go for broke with your own Internet business? That can be scary. For some, however, it has worked out very well.

Failure Often Precedes Success

The mighty ones who make it in business understand this. Oh, they don't like failure any more than you do, but great successes often come only after years of failures. This is true for Internet billionaires as well as all the incredible business superstars of the pre-Internet Era. Nobody knew that better than a very successful man who died decades before the Internet became a household word: Walt Disney.

Consider, for a moment, just how successful Walt Disney was. Disney's cartoon hero Mickey Mouse is recognized all over the world. Families everywhere have come to equate the Disney brand with wholesome family entertainment. Walt Disney created a business that ensured his own immortality: The world remembers this great man, and smiles. And that, my friend, is true and lasting success. Walter Elias Disney made it as big as you can make it. (Well, okay, Microsoft CEO Bill Gates might have earned more money than Walt but at least Disney, Inc. was never nailed by the Feds for being a monopoly.)

However, as successful as Disney is, ol' Walt flopped on his face before he ever had his first real success. In 1919 as a very young man, Disney started his own business of creating short animated films, called Laugh-O-Grams. Disney managed to get these little cartoons into several Kansas City movie theaters. His business started out well enough. He hired a handful of animators and even incorporated his business. He was on his way to becoming the King of Animated Cartoons, right? Wrong.

Heroic History

Nullsoft: We Are Your Stereo

Web site name: Winamp.com

Founded: 1997

Service provided: Winamp, a downloadable program used to play music distributed over the Internet.

Business model: Winamp began as a shareware software product, which means that it was free to download and try. Users were on the honor system to pay for it if they continued to use it. As advanced versions of Winamp came out, they incorporated features which would allow building of commerce links into the player. For example, someone listening to a song by the group Moxy Fruvous could click to go directly to a search for their CDs at Amazon.com. Because of these other profit venues, it became worthwhile to distribute the player as freeware, no cost involved. Winamp was also designed to make it easy for programmers anywhere to design new features for the product (called *plug-ins*) or new visual appearances (*skins*). This not only allowed the product to become functional at no cost to Nullsoft, it also helped to make Winamp.com a recurring destination site for Winamp users.

Where the money came from: Nullsoft was bought out by popular Internet service America Online as part of a larger transaction in which AOL also acquired Spinner.com, an online broadcasting site. The transactions were stock-for-stock trades with a total value estimated at $400 million.

Disney Falls on His Face

Walt Disney wasn't the only gifted member of the Disney family. His brother Roy was quite bright, especially at managing money. For a while Roy was helping guide Walt's little cartoon business. Sadly, illness forced Roy to leave the Midwest for the warmer West Coast and Walt was left to run the business without his brother's much-needed business smarts. Laugh-O-Grams started to suffer, and at one point Walt was so down and out that he couldn't afford a pair of shoes. Man, he was broke. In short order, Walt Disney's company declared bankruptcy. He had failed and failed utterly.

Walt ended up moving out to California and once more started his own cartoon business. Brother Roy encouraged him to take a second stab at creating cartoons. Walt had really wanted to be a movie director but he couldn't land a job in Hollywood doing that, so he and Roy started a new company: Disney Brothers Studios. Eventually this would become the famous Walt Disney Company.

Their new business had a shaky start for a while, too, but eventually Walt and crew created Mickey Mouse and the rest, as they say, is history.

What Is True for the Real World Is Also True for the Internet

Michael Robertson, the young billionaire of the Internet who started MP3.com, is much like Disney. His first two attempts at creating a successful Internet business failed. His third attempt ended up being one of the Internet's most lauded financial successes. He became a prince of Wall Street.

Failure, as I've said, often follows success and vice versa. If you intend to start your own Internet business, you must free yourself from fear of failure or at least learn to ignore it. You must be willing to throw yourself head on into a full-time business without any guarantee of success if you want to become another Walt Disney or, more appropriately, another Michael Robertson or any other type of Internet business superstar.

Of course, such risk taking isn't for everybody. Starting a successful Internet business can't be a part-time affair. You have to be willing to put in long hours and work seven days a week. In short, you have to be absolutely driven to reach your ultimate goal.

This isn't the sort of thing that is for everyone, of course. Those of us with a family, for example, might be less inclined to take such risks. Only you can answer this question: Do you think you have the skills, the ideas, the luck, and the guts to start your own successful Internet business? If the answer is yes, well, Nat and I are both pulling for you.

And somehow I feel that dear old Walt Disney, who turned bitter failure into bright success, is pulling for you as well.

Walt Disney, Viral Marketing, and the Internet

Another bit of the real world that was successfully transplanted to the Internet is *viral marketing*. Walt Disney understood the importance of this concept, back before it became a popular phrase among Internet business gurus. You will also need to understand this very important way of reaching out to a world full of potential customers.

Think of a flu virus. It travels happily throughout the world, touching many of us with its nasty little powers and bringing us to our sneezing, coughing knees. Yes, those nasty little germs touch the lives of millions without having to pay for any print, radio, or television commercials. Instead, viruses come into our lives by being spread throughout Planet Earth one person at a time until millions are rushing to Amazon.com to purchase a copy of *The Complete Idiot's Guide to Getting Over a Cold or Flu* (which probably isn't actually one of our books but should be; the last cold I had was a really nasty little devil).

So, viral marketing really means spreading the joyful word of your business by word of mouth, from one happy fan to another. "Hey, have you heard about this cool new thing on the Internet?" If millions of people are talking about your business, that, my friend, is a successful marketing campaign and one that is often free of cost.

Some people try to give viral marketing a kick-start by spending millions of dollars on advertising. I'm sure you've seen national television commercials touting Internet businesses that you've never heard of. Sometimes major ad campaigns work well and people start talking about the business. Of course, this doesn't always work.

Ford Motor Company really pushed their automobile the Edsel back in the middle of the twentieth century. People were unimpressed to the max and the car failed to catch on. Still and all, when Ford brought out the Mustang in the 1960s, it became one of the most popular cars that they ever made. Why? Because the car was cool and millions of people were talking about it. Viral marketing sort of takes off by itself (if you are lucky), although a major ad campaign can certainly jump-start it.

So, let's turn our attention back to the late, great Walt Disney for a moment. He knew the power of viral marketing, even though he probably just called it *free publicity*. During the 1950s he began to design and construct Disneyland in Southern California. He convinced ABC television to put on a weekly program of the same name, and he gave frequent, brief updates on the progress of the theme park prior to running the show's primary content. By the time the park was open, people all over the country knew about Disneyland, the amusement park, and when Disneyland opened in 1955, it was a hit.

Think about how many times you've heard about something cool from a friend. Maybe it was about a great CD, a movie, or some other type of entertainment. That unpaid plug from your friend is the best type of advertising that any product can ever get. I recall, as a young boy, hearing about the Beatles the first time, not because I saw them on the Ed Sullivan Show (a popular national television program at the time) where they made their first American splash, but from several school friends who had seen the show themselves. Viral marketing, sure as heck.

Some Successful Internet Geniuses Find Viruses Early On

One of the ways to make it really big in the Internet is to be an early adopter of something that is going to be really popular in the future. Here's an example, although fictitious, of how this can work.

What if someone invented *XERP* (short for *XERP Eludes Reasonable Parsing)*, a hot new way of sending home videos over the Internet very quickly? In just a few moments, you could upload your cherished digital home movies of your family, and send them quickly and easily to Grandmother, though she lives far away in Lake Havasu City, Arizona. And, better still, what if the XERP technology was released to the world by its creator as a *free format*? That is, what if the wily genius who invented XERP decided to let everybody in the world use the XERP technology for personal use at no charge, but established that anyone who made XERP equipment, such as XERP-ready cameras or XERP-based computer software, would have to pay him a licensing fee?

That would be cool, huh? It would be even cooler if you learned about XERP early on, so you could run out and grab XERP.com as a domain name before anyone else did. Oh, you might discover that Joe E. Xerp of Waldo, Texas, had already nabbed XERP.com for some unknown reason, but maybe you could buy the Web address from him for a thousand bucks or so, if he didn't mind. Especially, if he hadn't heard of XERP home movie technology, of course.

If you launched XERP.com before millions of people started talking about XERP and using it en masse, that would be a good thing. The coolest thing would be to get in on the XERP mania *before* it became a mania. Getting in on something important early can be the key to fantastic success. Really, you want to be the first person who does something, not the second, if at all possible.

If XERP turned out to be a monster hit among the public, having ownership of XERP.com could be a very good thing. If XERP.com turned out to be a giant financial success, starting a copycat company, such as ME-TOO-XERP.com would probably not be quite as good. The big winners of the Internet are usually the people who are the first ones to get involved with something breathtakingly new. Bottom line: Strive to innovate, not to imitate, whenever possible.

Disneyland became very popular in part because it was the first of its kind. Walt Disney enjoyed amusement parks a great deal, but felt that they were, well, a bit seedy, at least in the days prior to 1955. So, he built a grand amusement park that families could enjoy. Disneyland has been such an outstanding financial success that others were built in Florida, Japan, and Europe, with a fifth one currently being constructed in Hong Kong. As for the ABC television network, which broadcast the Disneyland television show, the Disney Corporation purchased it a few years ago.

So, what have we learned from this? That being the first to build a certain e-business on the Internet can lead to great success, especially if it is built around a concept that will ultimately become a very popular one.

Nontraditional Thinking: One of the Keys to Success

Walt Disney was very nontraditional in his thinking. Many business geniuses are ridiculed early in their careers. (I know I was when I started Edible Shoes, Inc.) Shortly before Disneyland opened, the local press dubbed it "Disney's Folly." I guess the press thought Disneyland wasn't going to work out.

If you have a hot idea about an Internet business and tell it to your friends, I would expect many of them to laugh at you (although, perhaps, not to your face). Imagine if you told your friends and family "I think I'll start a business on the Internet where I give everything away for free."

They'd probably look at you as if you were crazy, huh? Yet, that is one of the more popular business concepts on the Internet today. Take, for example, Hotmail, the business that gives people free email accounts.

Hotmail was the world's first Web-based email provider. Why was that good? Because people who use Hotmail's email service can send and receive messages from any computer connected to the Internet, instead of having to use their computer at home or work. Dropping by a friend's house, and want to send an email message? No problem with Hotmail.

So, consider this: Hotmail was the first to provide a Web-based email service. But, as neat as being first to do this was, there was another distinct advantage that Hotmail had going for itself: It is a free service, has always been a free service, and always will be a free service.

People seem to like free stuff, especially valuable free stuff. Hotmail is a well-designed service. It is easy and dependable to use. Free, dependable, popular, yup, Hotmail ended up being a real winner for the folks who created it—so successful that the ultrasuccessful folks at Microsoft felt the need to buy them out.

Today's Big Internet Business Concept Might Not Be for You Because It Might Be Too Late

Hotmail understood one of the Internet's most innovative business concepts: Figure out what people are paying for on the Internet and give it away for free.

And people had been paying for email, through various Internet service providers. Then along came Hotmail, which gave away a much better email service for free.

How could Hotmail afford to give it away for free? Easy! It put ads on its Web site. The "Find what people are paying for on the Internet and give it away for free" concept is still a good one, too. However, remember that to be really successful you might have to come up with your own great idea before anybody else does.

Runner-Up Ain't Bad

Rod is right when he suggests that the innovator has an advantage, but you shouldn't rule out just trying to do something a little better or a little differently. Microsoft didn't invent the operating system, they just turned out a slightly better one for a new computer that need one. Henry Ford didn't invent the car, he just had a better way of manufacturing them—and following his basic method has been the source for a fair amount of success for Freddy Volkswagen and Sophie BMW.

Tomorrow's hottest Internet concept might have nothing to do with giving services away for free, but something that nobody has thought of yet. Are you the one to think of it? Once again, Nat and I are pulling for you.

The Great Geniuses of Nontraditional Thinking

To be the first at something, it would help if you tried to look at things from a different angle. Remember, if you are trying to start a business by doing what everybody else is doing, that really makes you sort of a lemming. Lemmings are, well, losers. Being either the first to do something, or sometimes, the first to do something the best way possible, can lead to success.

Thomas Alva Edison, the great inventor, was always thinking of new ways to do things. From the phonograph to improving electric lighting, Edison was right on top of doing things in a nontraditional way. In America, inventors can be awarded patents for both inventing something new, and for inventing a substantial improvement for something that is patented.

Henry Ford came up with a greatly improved assembly line process for manufacturing automobiles, which made him really rich. He didn't invent the assembly line, but he sure improved it by coming up with the first moving automobile assembly line in history in 1913. (Okay, he ran for the U.S. Senate in 1918 and lost, but nobody's perfect.)

The Internet offers similar opportunities for people who can come up with new ways of doing old things. Garage sales and auctions are nothing new. But putting garage sales on the Internet, and combining them with the concept of auctions, led to eBay.com where there are more than two thousand categories of stuff you can buy or sell, and where more than 2.5 million auctions are held each day. Two old concepts put together as one on the Internet led to an amazing success for eBay.com.

Heroic History

EMusic: Charging for Bits

Web site name: www.EMusic.com

Founded: January 1998

Service provided: Downloadable music for sale

Business model: The explosion of the popular downloadable music format MP3 was at first fueled by free, illegally distributed tracks by popular artists. Then the folks at MP3.com made a big thing of free, legally distributed tracks by unknown artists. In 1998, EMusic (then working under the name GoodNoise) made a push for legally selling downloads of MP3 files of known artists. Due to the reluctance of the major labels to be involved in the MP3 scene, EMusic has had to content themselves with a relatively small fraction of the known musical acts, relying heavily on those signed with independent labels (often those who have passed their career peak). The charge is 99 cents for a single track of music, or $8.99 for a full album. They do face the problem that downloading an album, even with MP3 compression, is difficult and slow over dial-up lines. This system should become more viable as more users acquire high-speed Internet access.

Where the money came from: GoodNoise merged with publicly traded Atlantis Ventures in March of 1998, which was effectively a buyout but retained the GoodNoise name. GoodNoise then bought out an existing site, which held the EMusic.com domain name, and assumed this name for the GoodNoise site and the corporation. EMusic.com, Inc. is publicly traded under the stock symbol EMUS on the Nasdaq exchange. As of December 17, 1999, its market capitalization was approximately $474 million.

The Netscape Story: Not First, But Still a Winner

Another Internet company, Netscape, was launched in 1994. At the time, it was the best Internet browser. A *browser* is a computer program that allows you to view the pictures, listen to the sounds, and read the text of the World Wide Web sites with ease. At the time, the best browser available was called Mosaic. A man named Jim Clark had left the first company he had started, Silicon Graphics. Teaming up with another computer guru called Marc Andreessen, who led the team who had created the Mosaic browser, the two decided to form a company to create and distribute an even better browser: Netscape.

How Much Money Does It Take to Start Up a Billion-Dollar Internet Company?

The answer, of course, is "I dunno." But I can give you two examples. Michael Robertson, CEO of the very successful MP3.com, began with $20,000 in the bank. Marc Andreessen and Jim Clark of the once highly successful Netscape Company were backed by the 15 million dollars that Mr. Clark had on hand at the time they created Netscape. The history of every highly successful Internet company seems to provide a different answer to this question.

The Netscape browser was a fantastic success, which led to one of the most successful stock market smashes in Internet history when Netscape took its business to Wall Street and offered the world a chance to buy stock in its company.

Improving on something that previously exists can lead to great success. See, you don't always have to be the first to win, after all!

However, even great successes can be (somewhat) fleeting. In Netscape's case, the giant company Microsoft took it on in the marketplace, bundling its own Web browser with its Windows software. This competition eventually became a major blow to Netscape and the company was eventually purchased by America Online.

The world of e-commerce is every bit as harsh as the world of offline business. Remember this always, and keep it close to your heart (and pocketbook).

What Is the Secret of Nontraditional Thinking?

I'm not sure. But it seems to come naturally to some people. They seem to doubt and distrust automatically the way things have always been done and instead look for ways to differ themselves and their products or businesses from the norm. Maybe this is why geniuses sometimes seem almost crazy to many people.

Albert Einstein, the great scientist, usually never wore socks and was seen as sort of wacky to a lot of people. Of course, some of his work lead to a great new invention, the Atomic Bomb. (Oh, thanks a lot, Albert.) But, another great idea that he had never took off. After that Atomic Bomb thing worked out so well (every nation seemed to want several) he came up with the idea of a one-world government. He reasoned that there would be no wars if there was only one government and suggested to several world leaders that they use the threat of the Atomic Bomb to create one worldwide government. The idea never caught on. Sometimes you can be too innovative, I guess.

The basic rule is this: Try to look at possible businesses from all the many angles that you can think of. Approach your ideas with a great deal of scrutiny. How can one particular existing business be improved? By providing a better product? By giving it away for free and building a business model around advertising? By getting involved with a new craze before anyone else does? By inventing a new product that nobody realizes doesn't yet exist?

Only you can answer these questions, but the answers are out there, if you look for them, on the great Internet.

Some Final Comments

Remember, you don't have to be the one who ends up as the CEO of a massive, multibillion-dollar Internet company in order to be happy in life. I know several people in their early twenties who are multimillionaires because they joined what would end up being a successful Internet company early on.

Although there are few billionaire Internet CEOs, there are actually a lot more Internet millionaires, such as people who have joined successful Internet companies at some process in their existence. That's not the easiest thing in the world to do, either, but something that we will discuss in detail in Chapter 7, "Jumping on Someone's Team." And, remember, even though your Internet business might not end up making you wealthy beyond your wildest imagination, you still could end up making a decent living, and that's far from being a failure.

The Least You Need to Know

➤ All businesses entail a certain degree of risk, and failure is always a possibility.

➤ Traditional businesses and Internet business share the same problems, such as competition, poor planning, and financial issues that can lead to failure.

➤ You should always be on the lookout for a new or better way to do business on the Internet rather than copy other people's business ideas unless you can significantly improve on them.

➤ There is always room for another truly innovative business idea on the Internet.

Chapter 3

Blockbuster Brilliance: Getting the Idea

In This Chapter

➤ Finding a new Web site idea

➤ Finding a new Internet service idea

➤ Finding an old idea and putting it on the Web

You can put anything you want on the Internet. However, if you're the only one who wants it, you won't go very far. You'll certainly do better if you put what other people are going to want. Figuring out what they will want in an Internet service is no small feat. Picking the right purpose for your Web site makes all the difference between founding CheapTickets.com or founding HowToHiccup.com.

Giving People What They Will Want

The first, most basic advice that people teach about business is that you should give the public what they want. All too often, this is taken to mean that you should give the people more of what they're already getting. While that can be a very profitable thing to do (witness the success of *Friday the Thirteenth Part 37: Jason Realizes That Saturday Has Come At Last*), it does cause you to compete in an already crowded field. The biggest successes are those that come as a surprise, making people want something that they never thought about before.

This doesn't mean that you should rule out going the tried-and-true route, but realize that when you see a success that you want to copy, there will already be others looking to copy it. Sometimes, however, you can find something that isn't a success but could be, if it was done better in some other way. That's a good opportunity.

Doesn't Need to Be Profitable

One of the curiosities of creating something on the Web these days is that you don't have to generate a profit to be successful. If you can come up with an idea that will bring hundreds of thousands of people to your Web site every day, but you can't figure out how to make a penny out of it, don't worry. At this point, only a very small portion of the popular Web sites are actually profitable. There are two considerations that let you judge an unprofitable Web site as a success:

➤ While the number of people on the Internet has already grown by leaps and bounds over the past few years, there is every reason to believe that it will continue to grow for years to come. A site or service that is popular now can grow further as the Internet grows, and have that much more opportunity to generate profits.

➤ Just because you haven't figured out a way to make a profit doesn't mean that someone else won't come up with a way later. If you can gather the audience or the attention, you can bet someone will come up with a plan to turn a profit off of it. Odds are they'll be willing to pay you big bucks for the chance to try.

Give 'Em What They Already Buy, Only Free!

People like free things. If you went on the street corner and started passing out free aglet tighteners, people would line up to take them from you. This is true even if the same people would never think of paying for an aglet tightener, and didn't even know what a aglet was or why it needed tightening. And, if you told them that aglet tighteners usually cost two bucks, they would feel proud of having scored one for free. Some would even start keeping an eye open for stores that sell aglets, because it would be a shame to let such a valuable tightener go to waste.

If you started handing out something that people were actually willing to buy, then they would stand in line for a long time to get it. A friend of mine once came to work half an hour late because he stood in line to get a free box of cereal. Sure, he would have made four times what the cereal cost if he had actually shown up at work, but he was still happy because he got it for free!

Most online publications are free. You can pay $1.79 for TV Guide in the store, or you can read it for free on the Web—and the Web version can be especially customized for your tastes. For magazine publishers, this route makes a lot of sense, because the cover costs on a magazine generally go to pay for the printing and distribution. The real profit is made off advertising, even in print.

Heroic History

Blue Mountain: Billion-Dollar Hippies

Web site name: www.bluemountain.com

Founded: 1971 (Web site: 1996)

Service provided: Online greeting cards

Business model: Blue Mountain Arts is a lovely example of taking a successful-but-not-huge offline business and turning it into a huge online business. Blue Mountain, founded by artist/techie Dr. Stephen Schutz and poet Susan Polis Schutz, started life as a small publisher of posters, greeting cards, and poetry books. After decades of recognized success in those realms, they moved in 1996 to doing free online greeting cards, which are an amazing viral marketing medium. Let's say you head over to www.bluemountain.com and use it to send your Mom a free online greeting card. She gets emailed a link, and follows that link to view the card. While she's viewing the card (and presumably getting some pleasure from doing so), she is offered the chance to send similar cards to her friends, some of whom are then moved to send ones to their friends, and so on. It's an amazing way to capture eyeballs (as well as building an email list) and to create opportunities to advertise deliverable gift items such as flowers or candy. Blue Mountain grabbed 65% of the electronic greeting card market, and offers cards not only for major holidays but also for Daylight Savings Time, Accountant's Day, Kiss-and-Make-Up Day, and other uncommon celebrations.

Where the money came from: Blue Mountain had planned to issue an IPO, but chose to scrap those plans. Excite@Home purchased Blue Mountain Arts in October, 1999, to draw more viewers to their online portal. The deal was worth $780 million in cash and stock, plus another $270 million in stock to be issued contingent on Blue Mountain achieving certain performance goals. True to their roots, the Schulzes planned to use their proceeds to support world health, hunger relief, and peace.

There are things besides publication that can be offered for free over the Internet. Oh, you still can't download physical objects (Thank goodness! Otherwise, my diet would be ruined with downloadable, ad-sponsored donuts!), but there are a range of information and entertainment services that are capturing users. Here are just some examples of interesting and useful free online services available today:

➤ NetZero (www.netzero.com) offers the big-daddy of free Internet services: free Internet service. That's right, people can get access to the World Wide Web and email without paying an ISP. The users just have to give NetZero certain personal information and allow advertising to be piped to their screen.

➤ Instead of spending hundreds of dollars per year on a fax machine, supplies, and an extra phone line, users can head over to www.FaxWave.com (as seen in Figure 3.1) to sign up for a free fax number. FaxWave will forward an image of each fax received to your email—with advertising tacked on. (This service is very useful for travelers, who can check their faxes from anywhere via the Web.)

➤ Free software abounds on the Web, with sites such as www.Sonique.com and www.winamp.com distributing free copies of their own software, or sites such as www.download.com distributing other people's software.

Figure 3.1

FaxWave, free faxes for fax-free fiends!

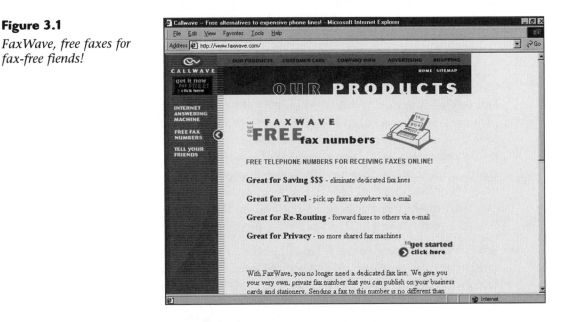

The trick to being comfortable with giving out something for free is accepting the fact that it's going to cost you something. However, as with many things it will cost you much less than the individual user would have paid for it. For example, if I want to send a fax from my home to my pal Rich Johnston in England, it would cost me several dollars in international long-distance charges. However, the folks at fax4free.com have worked it out in a much more intelligent manner. If I use their service to send the fax, they send it over the Internet to England (which costs them basically nothing), and then use a fax modem there to send it at a much smaller toll rate. Plus, they can send faxes for thousands of customers (each of whom would otherwise need their own fax line) with a few phone lines, and save money there.

Your Information Is Their Destination

The world used to be simpler. There wasn't a whole lot of information. If you needed some information, either it was in your almanac, or you went without. There just wasn't that much to keep track of.

Then Abner Doubleday went and invented baseball, and suddenly the world was filled with RBIs, ERAs, and track records of left-handed pitchers in away games at ball parks where the hotdogs were under seven inches long. Soon, there was more information than anyone could control.

People need to access all sorts of information, and don't always need the same information frequently enough to actually purchase the appropriate reference work. There are many popular Web sites built around information.

When considering whether offering a certain type of information will make an attractive Web site, consider the following:

➤ Is there a lot of information? If the information only fills a page, it won't draw a lot of repeat customers.

➤ Is it information that people need?

➤ Are people curious about the information? Information like this is a very good thing. People can become very absorbed in a site with interesting information, and spend literally hours surfing through it (particularly if the site offers a lot of links between related pieces of information).

➤ Does the information change frequently? Things that vary or get added to, such as stock values or sports statistics, encourage frequent visits to your site.

➤ Can the computer process the information in interesting and useful custom ways? For example, at MapQuest.com, they have street-map information for the entire United States. Not only can they show you any location you desire, they can plot a course for you between any two points, making their service much more useful than just a written map.

➤ Do you actually have a source for the information?

The answer doesn't have to be "yes" to all these questions. Believe it or not, you can actually build a site around information that you don't have. Sites such as www.longbox.com (comic book information), deja.com (product reviews and rankings), and epguides.com (TV episode guides) rely on their users to contribute the information.

Make Life Easier or Cheaper

As I noted before, people are cheap. Here's another carefully kept secret: People are also lazy. Why, these days they even use self-cleaning ovens! It's not like when I was a kid. Back then, when an oven got dirty, we just went and carved a new one out of solid rock. Ah, those were the days.

A good way to think of possible Internet services that might make life easier or cheaper is simply to keep track of what you do on a given day. I don't mean just the big things, like going to work or stopping at the CD store (although there certainly is potential in those things). I mean the little things. You tie your shoes. The Internet can't tie your shoes for you, and there probably wouldn't be that many visitors to a site that could teach you to tie your shoes, but if it gets you thinking about creating an online shoe store, even that note isn't wasted. Do you look up a number in the Yellow Pages? That's something that could be (and is!) done via the Web. Programming your VCR? Stopping at the market for milk? Remembering it's your cousin's birthday? There's potential in everything, depending on how you look at it.

Part of the trick is to remember that a service might be usable for other people even if you wouldn't choose to use it yourself. Me, I'd never buy shoes from a Web site, even if they were cheaper, because I prefer the comfort of trying them on at the local store. But if I had big ol' feet like my Dad, then normal shoe stores might not carry my size, and being able to go to www.monsterfeet.com might be handy. Or, if I lived out in rural Alaska like my Mom, I might be more than an hour's drive from a good selection of shoes, and the convenience of delivery might outweigh the downsides of Web ordering.

Do Business with Businesses

Don't focus only on ideas for people's leisure time or home life. While individual focused services are certainly the ones getting the most attention, there's much to be said for services aimed at businesses. Businesses tend to be more willing to pay money for services than individuals are.

Giving Them What They Can't Do Without a Computer

There's one thing that I can tell you about all computer users, and that's that they use computers. (At least, that seems likely to me, although I do hope to get a $13 million grant to study this question more thoroughly.) Sometimes the computer is used to do things that they would do anyway even without one (such as balance their checkbook, or send obscene notes to their congressperson). Often, however, the computer is used for doing something which had no real equivalent in the outside world, whether that's flying a simulated spaceship, creating a computer program, or trying to get a piece of bologna out of the floppy drive.

Keeping in mind that people are doing things that are specifically for the computer can lead to creating ways that can make their computer life easier or more functional. Some examples of these include

➤ **Off-site data storage** Look at www.StoragePoint.com, which lets you upload files for storage there. This is handy for those who want to check their files while on the road. It can be a great rescuer if some disaster destroys all the copies of your files that you have at home.

➤ **Software maintenance** For example, the product Oil Change manufactured by McAfee (www.mcafee.com) allows a user to use the Internet to maintain their software, making sure they have the latest updates, upgrades, and drivers.

➤ **Retailing** Even the major computer software-and-peripheral chain Egghead closed all their stores, focusing instead solely on selling products via egghead.com.

Picking a Specialty Market

Your Internet service doesn't have to be designed for everybody. Focusing on a particular category of user can make it easier to promote your site and to create a site of recognized value. Let's consider starting a general music Web site, with news, reviews, downloadable songs, and discussion areas. After all, everyone likes music, right? If you did that, you'd have to work hard to really distinguish yourself from the various other music-oriented sites that already exist, and you'd quite likely end up as a small player in a fairly large market. That's a very viable way to go about things, and there's a lot of potential there.

But consider, instead, focusing solely on jazz music. At www.jazzIQ.com, you have jazz files, jazz reviews, online chats with big-name jazz artists. You have some really jazz-knowledgeable people on your team to bring it all together. If there are no other big jazz sites out there, you've got a real magnet for the jazz buff. And the jazz buffs are fairly easy to reach through jazz magazines and radio advertising on jazz stations. After you have that going, and you've built a lot of know-how in your company, you've got a head start toward creating a second site just for the country music buff, and so on.

Consider also a site that helps people pick baby names. Sure, at any given time only a few percent of people are looking for baby names...but those people are about to need diapers, cribs, baby clothes, and child-proof pets, which makes them an audience that advertisers are eager to pay to reach.

Web Publishers Are Special People

People and companies with their own Web sites actually make a good specialty market. There are an awful lot of them these days, and they spend a lot of time on the Web. The Web technology is constantly advancing, so they really do need help to stay on top of things. Plus, a lot of the services that they need can be done quite well on the Web, because they mainly deal with moving information around.

Some examples of interesting Web sites aimed at folks who create Web sites are

➤ `WebDevelopersJournal.com` An online magazine of the latest tips, tricks, and advances in creating Web content.

➤ `NetStudio.com` An online program to help you design banners, headlines, and buttons for your Web site.

➤ `SpinFrenzy.com` An easy-to-use online Web design package for the neophyte designer.

➤ `www.LinkExchange.com` Offers free advertising-trade services for Web pages.

Everyone On the Internet Is Special

Even Internet users are a specialty market. This might sound a little odd, because after all 100% of the people on the Internet are Internet users. But, because they're Internet users, they have certain common needs that don't apply to people who don't use the Web. These users welcome things that help them use the Web more effectively. Examples of these are

➤ **Search engines and directories** The Web is huge, and without some sort of guide, you'll never find what you want. Sites such as `AskJeeves.com` and `www.Google.com` can help you find the information that you're looking for.

➤ **Free Web-based email services** Sites such as `www.Hotmail.com` are handy for a number of folks. Travelers use Web-based email to have an address they can check from any Web browser while they're on the road. People who don't have their own Internet access but use terminals at a school or at the library find them the only real way to get their own email address. Folks looking for a little privacy use them to have a second email address not connected to their real name, kind of like having an unlisted phone number.

➤ **Providers of software designed to run with your Internet connection** At `www.ICQ.com`, they offer a free piece of software that tells you if your friends are online, and then lets you communicate with them over the Internet. At `www.CallWave.com`, they offer a special answering machine product/service for people whose only phone line is tied up while they're on the Net; this service lets you listen to the messages while you're online.

Heroic History

Mirabilis: ICQ's No IOU

Web site name: www.ICQ.com

Founded: 1996

Service provided: Instant messaging software

Business model: Mirabilis Limited of Israel created *ICQ* (pronounced *I seek you*), a piece of software that runs chats over the Internet. With ICQ, you can see which of your friends/co-chatters are currently online and available for receiving messages. Of course, it only works if your friends also have the ICQ software, which means that existing ICQ users bring new users into the camp. There are now millions of ICQ users, and it is one of the most downloaded pieces of software on the Internet. For all that, however, there is no real income source yet in place, because the software is free. For the long term, though, there are clear possibilities for using the product to display advertising to the people who are using it. The software offered to date is also time-limited, requiring a fresh download of the new version with new features from time to time; this gives ICQ the option of starting to charge for the software, if they desire. Recent upgrades of ICQ have incorporated portal-like features, giving instant access to Web searches, calendars, and other such efforts, making it less a specialty product and more a simple all-in-one product for people of modest Internet needs.

Where the money came from: Mirabilis was purchased by online access provider America Online in a $287 million cash deal in June 1998. There were also contingencies for further payments of up to $120 million over the following three years, depending on continued growth. The new owners changed the company name to ICQ, Inc.

For Further Info

Instead of recommending specific Web sites to go looking for more information, I suggest all Web sites. That's right, look around at as many sites as you can, particularly ones that you find mentioned in magazines. See if they inspire you to come up with something similar, but aimed at a different market or somehow altogether better.

Memes for Youyous

To freshen your mind, check out the odd (and generally noncommercial) links at www.memepool.com.

Your friends, your spouse, and especially your kids are better resources for learning what people do than any book or any Web site can possibly be. Follow what they do, in as much detail as they'll let you.

The Least You Need to Know

➤ A good idea for an Internet service is one that makes life easier, cheaper, or more interesting.

➤ Offering for free something that people are used to paying for is the basis of many popular sites.

➤ Many good services are merely improved versions of services already available; however, the biggest successes are with those who do something new.

➤ Check your life and the lives of people you know to find things that could be done on the Web.

➤ Be willing to court a special audience, rather than aiming your Web site at everyone.

Chapter 4

Put Your World on the Web

> **In This Chapter**
>
> ➤ Moving your store onto the Web
>
> ➤ Offering your services via the Web
>
> ➤ Building off your respected name

If you're like most hard-working people, you already have a job. (Otherwise, you might be like me: not hard working, but *hardly* working!) It's quite possible that you already have your own business. It might be big, it might be small, but it's yours. That small business might be your key to a mountain of riches (although I've never actually seen a mountain that needed a key before).

And it doesn't even have to be a business. If you're someone who is obsessive about your hobby, that too can form the base for an attractive and lucrative Web site. (My favorite example of this is a man who goes by the name "Z Bone," who took his expensive and disreputable taste for Los Angeles strip clubs and turned it into an advertising-supported strip club review site, www.zbone.com. Things that might get other people arrested now get him a tax deduction!)

You Have an Upper Hand

e-Commerce has been discussed as a great equalizer, as though everyone who puts up a Web site has an equal chance to play with the big boys. There's certainly truth in that statement, but it does seem to take lightly the advantages that you have if you're taking an existing business to the Web. These include

➤ **Expertise**   This includes not only expertise in the product or service, but also expertise in the way that your industry works. If you already know the methods and pitfalls in dealing with suppliers or subcontractors, you've got an upper hand.

➤ **Relationships**   Remember when you just started in business, and the suppliers all treated you warily and the bank didn't want to extend you credit? Laugh with glee, because now they're treating your would-be new Web competitor with the same scorn that they used to treat you!

➤ **Reputation**   If you've been doing a good job up until now, the reputation you've earned with your existing customers will carry weight with your new online enterprise. (And if you've got a bad rep, then you can just pick a new name for the online version of your store!)

➤ **Merchandise and Equipment**   If you're keeping your offline store or service going, then you can use the same tools and store stock for both, which means that you're moving online cheaper than someone who is starting from scratch.

It Was Sears for Years, My Dears!

People's willingness to order items without directly seeing them is nothing new. Back when America was much more rural, no farmhouse was complete without the Sears Roebuck catalog. This thick book offered everything from slippers to horse buggies, offering the customer a far wider range of items than the local general store could offer.
The spread of the chain store and the advent of the automobile made standard shopping options a lot more reasonable, although the catalog didn't disappear altogether until 1993.

About the only disadvantage that you're likely to have in moving what you already do have to the online world is that you might be stuck in offline thinking. Your methods of doing business need to change when you move online, and you have to be willing to accept that some things should be done differently online. (This is when having a partner who is ignorant about your business but wise to the online world can be very handy.)

Taking Your Store Online

Just about anything that can be sold can be sold online. Pundits used to think that there were a lot of things that people wouldn't buy online, but with thriving sites offering everything from teddy bears to Chryslers, those pundits are now singing another tune. (Specifically, they're singing "The Wreck of the Edmund Fitzgerald," oddly enough.)

A basic online store is very much like a mail-order catalog. Most online stores specialize, allowing them to service a specific customer need with expertise. An online store has a lot of the advantages of a mail-order catalog. For example, let's say you're moving your store (Betty's Back Scratchers) onto the Web. The store is available to a customer at any time. You can offer a wider array of back scratchers because you aren't restricted by shelf space. Because the stock doesn't have to be easily reached and viewed by customers, you can use your space much more efficiently.

An online store also has many advantages over a print catalog. Donna McCustomer can pull up your Web site the moment that she has an urge for a back scratcher, and order while it is still fresh in her mind. This is better than having her call you and wait a week for the catalog to arrive, by which time she is no longer itching to make a purchase. It also means that you can update your catalog instantly, so when those new models with pictures of Buffy The Vampire Scratcher on them come out, you can offer them immediately without waiting until your next catalog update. Also, you can expand your offerings as far as you want, without worrying about the added cost of printing and shipping the larger catalog. (The cost of adding a Web page for an additional product is small indeed.)

Heroic History

Bibliofind: A Nook to Look for Books

Web site name: bibliofind.com

Founded: 1996

Service provided: Used book catalog

Business model: Michael and Helen Selzer were antiquarian book dealers who decided to build their business by coordinating the inventories of a number of used book dealers and offering them online. The consumer can use their site to search through a catalog that includes the contents of thousands of used and antiquarian bookstores. The orders are handled directly by the individual dealers, who pay Bibliofind a fee for the service. Because book fans and collectors are a chatty lot, Bibliofind managed to grow with relatively little marketing, relying instead on word of mouth. After a reader discovered that elusive books could be found in a matter of minutes, often with multiple copies at varying prices, Bibliofind became an indispensable site.

Where the money came from: Bibliofind was sold in early 1999 to e-Niche Incorporated, which already owned MusicFile, a site for those seeking out hard-to-find music. A name change turned e-Niche into Exchange.com, which was purchased by Amazon.com, the giant of Web-based new book sales.

Content That Breeds Discontentment

Don't just copy news and interviews from magazines or other Web sites. That's a lazy route to content, and a quick route to a copyright infringement suit.

More Than Just a Catalog

When you move a retail establishment online, you should provide more than just a catalog. After all, while a large portion of your business are likely to be *destination shoppers* (people who are specifically looking to make a purchase on a given day), if you only have a catalog you miss out on your chance at *impulse shoppers* (people who hadn't planned on buying anything, but happened to see something nifty for sale when they were at your site for some other reason).

What kind of material can bring customers to your site? Some sites have success with interesting articles and news items. You could have an interview with leading back-scratcher designer Itchy McCarver. You could have games, such as Bac-Man. You could have news on the back-scratching field. Anything that folks might hear about and go to your site to visit is worth it. It can even be something that isn't directly related to your product line, as long as it will draw the sort of audience who will be interested. (In fact, you should take great care that the content does not just look like more hype for the products you offer, because people will recognize it as a sales pitch and become disinterested in it.)

Chatting Up Customers

Putting up online message boards, where people can discuss your products and other related things with other customers, has a lot of potential. If the discussions catch on, you can expect to have customers returning daily, and viewing your site with the same sort of warmth as they view their favorite tavern.

Your best approach is to have something that not only gets Web surfers to your site once, but keeps them coming back. This means that you have to have something that gets updated frequently. People are, after all, forgetful. I knew this one guy who was so forgetful…I can't remember who he was or what he forgot, but boy, was it funny! Surfers who don't have a reason to visit your site at least once a week seem likely to forget to come at all. A news column, by its nature, needs frequent updates, making it a good option for regularly updated material. Be sure that you update the news frequently. If you find you can't keep up with the news, it might be best to remove the news entirely. There's little that can make a site look more like it has been abandoned than to have six-month-old news. That's not *news*, that's *olds*!

Interactivification

If the product you offer is custom-made for each customer, then you have another option to take the catalog concept one step farther. Let's say, for example, that you own Downhill Doggie Delivery, the leader in ski equipment for canines. One of the products you sell is custom ski masks for dogs, which are available in a range of colors and designs and can have the dog's name stitched on it in a variety of styles.

In a print catalog, you could just show a few examples of the masks. Online, however, you can have a program that lets the surfer select a mask design, a color, and type in their name and select a type style. The program will then show the user a picture of just what the mask will look like. (Of course, you aren't likely to have a lot of success with this product until we get more dogs that both ski the slopes and surf the Web!)

Putting Services Online

If you sell services rather than products, you might have to look at the Web a different way. Some services are a natural for moving online. Recruiting and researching, matchmaking and bookmaking; they've all been smoothly copied online.

Other services don't transfer so well. If you run a lawn-mowing service, it's hard to find a way that people can upload their lawn to you, so you can trim it and send it back. If you find a way to get it to work, then you're smarter than I am (which is an achievement roughly akin to being a better basketball player than Henry Kissinger).

The difference between services that adapt well online and ones that don't is that the ones that work are based mainly on the transfer of information. The Internet is basically a system for exchanging information. If what the user gives you is information, and you don't have to send him back anything but information, then you've got something that's a clear candidate for putting on the Web. Dating services are an example of that. My friend, Julie, told her dating service that she was looking for a serviceman who'd been stationed in the Persian Gulf—that's information. And the dating service responded with another piece of information—the name and phone number of a guy. He turned out to be a Persian man who worked at a Gulf service station, but it was close enough for Julie, and they lived happily ever after. There's no reason that same degree of confusion couldn't be achieved over the Web.

Services that require you to provide more than just information can still be good candidates for putting on the Web. Consider singing telegrams. A proper singing telegram needs to be sung in person (otherwise it's just a very strange phone call), and personal presence is not information. However, you can use the Web for people to tell you to whom they want a singing telegram sent and where and when to deliver it. Many people would find this simpler or preferable to trying to line up a singing telegram by phone, particularly if the recipient is in another city.

Of course, then you're left with the problem of how to deliver singing telegrams nationwide or worldwide. The answer to that is not to try to set up your own singing telegram service in every city, which would cost a bunch of money. Rather, you would make arrangements with existing singing-telegram services in all major areas, acting as an agent on commission for them. That would cost you no money up front, and would leave you in the business of taking in, processing, and sending out information.

The type of service that is truly hard to do well online is anything in which the client has to provide something besides information. Pet grooming, auto repair, and hat blocking really seem to have little use for the Internet, because people just can't upload their hat, their car, or their ocelot. (Of course, you might be the genius who sees a way around all this, in which case you are on your way to making billions.)

In a field where the user has to provide something besides information, about the best you can hope for is to use the Web for advertising and for arranging appointments. Those might be rather lackluster on the Web, because you'd have to put advertising effort in informing people about your Web site. That effort might better be directed to advertising your services, times, and location. Even buying ad space on other people's Web pages is likely to be of little use if your service is local, because Web pages get viewed by the world and you end up spending a lot of money advertising to people who are far away. You're better off advertising in strictly local media, such as newspaper, radio ads, and slogans painted on the sides of cows.

Information Sensation

When you're using information on the Web, it has to be information that can be read and transferred by a computer. It wasn't that long ago that that limited it to things that someone had typed in by hand, or information that the computer had derived from that hand-entered information. This is changing quickly. With the advent of scanners and now digital cameras, visual images can be turned into computer information. Sound cards turn music into computer information, and vice versa. Recently, folks have invented a way to store scents as computer information, transmitting, say, the information on the smell of school erasers to a peripheral that can actually create the indicated scent. Other folks are working on smart appliances that would be able to transmit over the Internet a list of food in your fridge or the temperature of your living room. As such, when you're thinking about what sort of information your Internet service could accept or present, keep your mind open to more than the usual possibilities.

You Can't Go Wrong with Rights

Depending on what sort of business you're in, you might have a lot of intellectual property. No, I don't mean an abandoned lot in the shape of Albert Einstein. Intellectual property includes patents, trademarks, and copyrights. This sort of property might be useless for a construction site, but it's often ideal for a Web site.

Trading on Your Trademarks

A *trademark* is a legally protected name or symbol that you use in selling product. Coca-Cola, Yugo, and Teenage Mutant Ninja Turtles are all examples of trademarks. If you have a trademark, then no one else is allowed to use that name on similar products. A trademark has to add something more than just simply describing the item; for example, you can't have a trademark on *neon-filled braces* but you can have a trademark on *Grin-Glow*.

Some people register their trademarks with the federal government, which gives them additional protection for their names. You can recognize when a registered trademark is being used because it has an ® after it, whereas an unregistered trademark usually has a ™ after it. You can also have a *service mark*, which is a close cousin of a trademark. It is a name or phrase used to identify services rather than products.

Why does the federal government deal with trademarks? Very simply, they want to be sure that folks can have exclusive rights in names and symbols in which they're investing effort to create customer recognition and goodwill.

Exclusive rights, *recognition*, and *goodwill*. All three are great foundations on which to build Web sites.

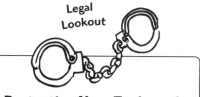

Legal Lookout

Protecting Your Trademark

The highly international aspect of the Internet leads to some confusion about protecting your trademark. In the United States, you own your trademark when you first use it, and you further protect your legal interest in the trademark when you successfully register your trademark with the United States government's Patent and Trademark Office. The U.S. is a *first to use* jurisdiction. However, in the United Kingdom, the first person to register the trademark wins the right of ownership. Be sure that you have dependable legal counsel to guide you through these tricky waters so that you can successfully protect your trademark on an international basis.

Let's say, for example, that you produce a brand of helium-filled bubble gum called *Hindenbubble*. You thought about having a retail Web site where you sell the gum, but nobody says "I feel like some gum! Let's order it off of the Web and we can be chewing it in under a week!" Besides, it would put you in competition with the retailers who carry your gum, and their goodwill is vital to your gum's success. So, there doesn't seem to be much point in having a Web site, right?

Patently Useless?

Patents are the intellectual property protection for inventions. Unlike other forms of intellectual property, existing patents aren't going to help you much online. You should keep patents on your mind, however, because if you come up with a way to make ordering from your Web site or looking through your catalog easier, you might be able to patent it. That patent could end up making you millions even if your e-business flops.

Suppose you took advantage of the fact that kids like your lighter-than-air gum and build a great general Web site for kids. You could have chat areas, games, contests, articles, and so on—all supported by advertising. Because kids already know the name of your gum and think well of it, you have an advantage over anyone else trying to set up a site for kids. Plus, you already have an easy way to promote your site to your gum fans; just put www.hindenbubble.com on every gum wrapper. Having a name that people already recognize and trust can be a great advantage in building a new business.

Compounding Your Copyright

Copyright is the intellectual property arena that covers most creative and informational endeavors. Stories, songs, movies, drawings, and other such things are protected by copyright. All these things would be considered content on a Web page. Exactly how you can exploit that content depends on what sort of content it is.

If you think about it, all those online magazines, downloadable software sources, music sites, and reference sites are just providing access to copyrighted material, and in many cases they're just reusing material that already exists. You might have sold all the copies you can of your collector's price guide to lunchboxes, because there are only so many people willing to shell out twenty bucks for such a book. The copyright to that book might seem pretty worthless. However, if you use the contents of the book to set up an online price guide, so that anyone who has a lunchbox that they're curious about can stop by and check out its value for free, then this has some value. When this casual visitor discovers that his old Space Bunny lunchbox is worth $800, he might want to buy a lunchbox display case from you, or a can of lunchbox polish, or simply to use your online classified ads to sell his lunchbox to the other lunchbox collectors that hang out at your site. Remember: The content you already have can be a starting point (but usually *just* a starting point) for a good Web site.

You can even charge directly for your content. Some magazines and newspapers have online archives from which you can pull up any article for a buck or two. Donna Shirley, the manager of the Mars Exploration Program (remember that little rover running around Mars? Wasn't that cool?!), wrote a book on managing creativity. When some traditional publishers showed little interest in it, she skipped all the middle-men and made a downloadable version available for a mere 12 bucks at www.donnashirley.com.

Name Value

If you're famous—and it doesn't have to be the sort of general fame that the Pope and Gary Coleman have; it can be simply respect within your own field—then your name could be the key to a successful Web site. Consider these two examples of well-known folk whose Web successes are based on trading on their respected names:

➤ Doctor C. Everett Koop was Surgeon General of the U.S. during the 1980s. In that role as the nation's top doc, he drew respect, admiration, and occasional giggles (smart man, goofy beard). He threw the value of his name and the value of his knowledge behind `drkoop.com`, a leading health-information site on the Web.

➤ Stan Lee is a comic book writer and editor who co-created Spider-Man, The Incredible Hulk, and The X-Men, among many other comic book properties. Now those properties would form a great basis for a Web site…but he doesn't own them, they belong to Marvel Comics. Based on his reputation among people who know comic books, and on his ability to create characters, `stanlee.net` was formed as the keystone to Stan Lee Media, Inc. Even before the new characters (whose adventures would be available for free on the Web) were revealed, the site received a lot of attention and the company gained a great deal of investment. Spider-Man might be able to walk up walls, but Stan Lee has shown his ability to walk all over Wall Street.

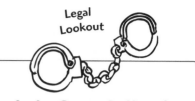

Legal Lookout

Is the Copyright Yours?

Some newspapers have gotten into trouble for selling articles online, only to discover later that they didn't actually have the online rights. In most cases, copyrights rest with the creator until otherwise specified. But, if you're a creator, don't be too sure that you've kept all the rights that you think you have. Whether you were the creator or the acquirer of the intellectual property, you should have a lawyer look over all the agreements to check just what rights you have.

Expand Your Offerings

Whatever the business is that you're moving online, don't just exactly copy your offline business. First off, it simply doesn't work. There are little touches that come from being able to walk into a store and hold an object you want to buy, or to talking directly to a knowledgeable human, which simply cannot be duplicated. That online tanning salon of yours just isn't going to be the same.

Secondly, if you stick with exactly what you're already doing, you are missing a lot of opportunity. The Internet lets you do a lot of things better. In most cases, it's more than enough to make up for the things that the Internet can't do at all.

Getting Away Scott-Free with Selling Stock-Free

An online retail site allows you to offer a lot more items without increasing your stock on hand. This is due to a simple fact: You can sell things you ain't got!

That sounds darned-near illegal, doesn't it? Well, it isn't. In fact, it's how almost all the biggest retail sites work. Amazon.com claims to offer more than a million different books. Do they actually have that many different books laying around? Nope. Oh, they have some of the big ones: *Dave Barry's Guide to Picking on Stephen King*, Stephen King's *The Ugly Death of an Evil Newspaper Columnist from Florida*, and, of course, *The Complete Idiot's Guide to MP3: Music on the Internet* (which you should, of course, buy, because Rod and I wrote it, and we like getting royalties).[1]

However, if someone orders a copy of *Horatio Space Bunny's Guide to Integral Calculus*, Amazon probably doesn't have it in its warehouse. Instead, Amazon contacts the publisher or the distributor, and orders the book from them. When Amazon gets it, it passed the book on to the customer.

Now, almost any bookstore can order any book in print for you. To the customer at a normal bookstore, however, the experience of buying a book off of the shelf is very different from (and far more satisfying than) ordering one that they will have to wait for and come in some other day to pick up. But the difference between ordering an in-stock book from Amazon and ordering a book that Amazon has to order is that the time waiting for the shipment to arrive will be slightly longer.

Working in a low-stock or stock-free situation means that you have a lot less money tied up in stock, and aren't taking the risk that the stock will not move and end up costing you. It also means that you aren't tying up a lot of valuable warehouse space. This is one of the biggest elements in allowing online businesses to sell at a discount, and that discount can be a major component in convincing a customer to buy from an online store rather than a brick-and-mortar retailer.

Taking Orders for Others

You might be able to expand your selection without even worrying about receiving and shipping the additional materials when ordered. For example, let's say you own Chris's Cacti, a popular cactus shop. You want your Web store, PointyThings.com, to carry cacti, roses, and barbed wire. You could go to the effort of hiring people who know how to order and handle those things, but that would involve a lot of overhead.

---

[1]*No, no, we're not really trying to convince you to buy our fine and affordable book about the Internet's biggest music craze. We just put that in there to remind you that, as entrepreneurs, you should always be looking for ways to promote your own projects and Web sites.*

Heroic History

1-800-FLOWERS: Hanging Up the Phone

Web site name: www.1800flowers.com

Founded: 1995

Service provided: Flower and gift delivery

Business model: Started as a phone-based flower delivery service, 1-800-FLOWERS was already an Internet-style business before it moved online. It was basically an order-taking service, giving folks a central location to call, and farming out the actual floral arranging and delivery to 1,500 flower shops nationwide. This model was very easy to move online, first onto AOL and CompuServe, and finally onto the Web in 1995. The Web gives it the same sort of national reach that the phone number did, plus offers the sort of visuals that let people make better choices of flowers. 1-800-FLOWERS handles the order, takes its cut, and pays the individual flower store.

Where the money came from: A private equity placement brought it a little more than $100 million in May 1999. Three months later, with the .com now attached to the name making it look like an Internet stock, the company's IPO brought it $117 million. The stock moves on the Nasdaq market under the ticker abbreviation FLWS. As of December 18, 1999, the company had a market capitalization of $766 million.

On the other hand, you could make a deal with Barb's Rose Shoppe and Rose's Barbed Wire Emporium. Whenever someone places an order through your site for some barbed wire or some roses, you just forward the order and the money, minus your commission. Not only does this give you the commission income, it also means that you will attract more customers. Visitors might come looking for roses or barbed wire, and then decide to buy a cactus as well.

Many of the larger e-commerce sites (and some of the smaller ones) offer *associates programs*. This means that they are set up to let your site act as a catalog, with their site and software actually taking the orders, and you getting a cut of each sale. (See Figure 4.1 for an example of such a site.) The bad news is that most of these programs don't give you any way to easily integrate selling the products you offer with selling the products these other shops offer; your customers will have to fill out two separate orders, and this is apt to confuse them.

Figure 4.1

My www.aaugh.com *site offers books, videos, and CDs based on the Peanuts comic strip. Actually, I sell nothing; Amazon.com handles the orders. Most items are not in stock, but the customers don't seem to care, as long as they get what they order.*

For Further Info

Following are a few handy resources for you if you're aiming to transfer your existing life to the Web:

➤ *Netrepreneur: The Dimensions of Transferring Your Business Model to the Internet* by Joe Lowery is published by the same fine folks who brought you this book.

➤ If you want a better understanding of your trademarks, the United States Patent and Trademark Office offers up a useful site at www.uspto.gov.

➤ The Library of Congress is in charge of copyright in the United States. Their site at www.loc.gov/copyright/ gives you a good start in understanding the advantages and methods of copyright.

The Least You Need to Know

➤ Your offline business and hobbies can serve as a good basis for a new online venture.

➤ Moving an offline business online enables you to transfer your expertise, your reputation, and your existing stock, equipment, and resources.

➤ Intellectual property that you already own can be of further value on the Web.

➤ Your online business should use your offline business as a starting point, not an end point.

➤ Doing retail on the Web means you can offer items without having them in stock.

Chapter 5

Eyeballs Versus Atoms: Your Economic Model

> ## In This Chapter
>
> ➤ Selling advertising
>
> ➤ Selling online or physical items
>
> ➤ Working with no profit in sight

A lot of people make a lot of money doing business on Wall Street. On any given day, there are people making no money or even losing money on Wall Street, but they're still doing business. If you were to head down to Wall Street and stand on the corner all day, smiling politely, you wouldn't be doing business, because you have no reason to expect that anyone will give you any money for what you're doing. You don't really have a business until you have some reason to expect people to give you money.

Economic Model Doesn't Mean Christie Brinkley, CPA

People in business throw around the term *economic model*, and it simply means a description of who will be paying your business, and what they'll be paying for. If, for example, you stood on that street corner with a sign that said "pay me a dollar and I'll sing the theme to *My Mother the Car*," then you have a business with an economic model. You're providing a service, which is available to a paying customer. It might not be the most profitable of businesses (you might actually make more money with a sign that reads "pay me a dollar or I'll sing the theme to *My Mother the Car*"), but at least you have some plan for income.

Do You Need an Economic Model?

One of the bizarre truths about the Internet is that you can end up making millions from creating a site or service that does not have an economic model. No visible source of income comes from it and yet you can come out with riches. I'm not kidding and I'm not crazy (well, maybe a little, but that has to do with a rocking-horse tragedy when I was a kid and has nothing to do with the matter here).

How? Simple. If you build a Web site or a service that is popular enough, somebody else will probably think of a way to make money from it. They might have a brilliant moneymaking scheme, or they might have the lamest idea you've ever heard. Believe it or not, that's not important. What is important is that they believe in their economic model enough to buy your Web site or service from you. This does happen. Often, the buyer is another Internet business that is looking to integrate what you offer with what they offer, to build something bigger.

If you end up going this route, you really do have an economic model. It's not an economic model for your site or service, though. It's a simple economic model for your larger business: selling off your site or service.

Advertising: Eyeballs for Sale

Most of the information and entertainment available on the Web, and some of the Internet services, rely on that old demon advertising for their income. The Internet user gets your site or service for free, but they aren't your customer. Your customer is the advertiser, who is paying to have access to the people viewing your site. The Internet user is actually your product. e-Business folks refer to having an ad-based site as *selling eyeballs*.

It might seem like a very odd way of doing business, not taking money from all these viewers you're attracting. However, advertising is what supports most TV, radio, and the bulk of the money for newspapers and magazines. Even movies generate money from advertising when a company pays to have the hero drinking their cola right before capturing the enemy headquarters. (This sort of unidentified advertising is called *product placement*.)

Heroic History

IMDb: Stumbling into Value

Web site name: IMDb.com

Founded: 1990

Service provided: An amazing movie reference guide, listing cast, crew, business information, and more about almost any movie you are likely to be interested in (and thousands of others beside).

Business model: IMDb (short for *Internet Movie Database*) is a great example of an Internet service that became valuable despite starting with no visible business model. Developed seemingly as a fan project in the days before e-commerce was significant, the site became one of the most linked-to on the Web. Other pages, when making passing mentions of a movie, would link to the IMDb info page on the film, or to IMDb's filmography of an actor. Once there, film fans would find themselves spending hours looking at listings for favorite films or obscure star appearances. IMDb started selling *eyeballs* to advertisers. Eventually, Amazon.com recognized the site's potential as a front-end for selling videos and other movie-related products. Now, when you bring up a film on IMDb, you also get links to Amazon.com for the videotape or DVD of the film, and any related books as well.

Where the money came from: The British-based IMDb was one of three foreign companies that Amazon.com bought out in April of 1998, shelling out a total of $55 million in cash and stock for all three.

Do You Have Valuable Eyeballs?

Not all advertising-supported sites are created equal. The more people that come to your site, the more people the advertising reaches, the more you can charge for advertising. Many people don't realize, however, that quantity of viewers is not the only thing that changes advertising cost.

Diversity is a wonderful thing in many ways, but it hurts in courting advertisers. To be able to charge the most for advertising, you need to be able to deliver users who are very similar in some way. If a skateboard company wants to advertise, they don't want to pay for an ad that appears in front of a million people, only 3% of whom are

Earballs

Internet advertising doesn't have to be visual. For example, amp3.com offers free digital music downloads, with a short ad at the start of each one.

Search and Target

A great example of targeted advertising on general sites is any Web index or search site. They sell advertising based on the words that the user searches for; for example, a pharmaceutical manufacturer can pay to have its advertisement appear on the results whenever someone searches for the word *asthma*. The manufacturer pays a large premium for that amount of precision.

skateboarders. They'll pay much more to advertise on a site that reaches 100,000 skateboard nuts, but nobody else.

Even folks who are selling products to general audiences like to be able to know what audience they're reaching and shape the ad to match. Flip around your TV dial and you're likely to find a lot of different ads for McDonalds. The ads on kiddie shows will be pushing their Happy Meal, while the ads on political talk shows will announce their new Grumpy Meal.

Not all select groups are equal, either. Sure, if you have a site for people who live in trailer homes, you might be able to run ads for trailer home accouterment dealers—but if you run a site for people who live in mansions, you're likely to sell your advertising for much more, because mansion-dwellers are a more lucrative market. If you have a site that reaches doctors, corporate PC buyers, gamblers, or any other group that controls a lot of spending, you are getting valuable eyeballs.

Having a general audience does not rule out being able to target audiences. If you can somehow identify who is likely to be using a page, you can show ads directed at them. If you're running HowToHaveFun.com, you might be attracting everyone from teenagers to geriatrics—but if you have a page that's updated every week with a new yo-yo trick, you can charge yo-yo manufacturers a premium to advertise there, as long as the yo-yo business is going well (it does have its ups and downs).

Measuring Eyeballs

To solicit or charge for advertising, you're going to need to know how much traffic your Web site is getting. There are traditionally four different standard measurements of Web traffic:

➤ *Hits* is a measurement of how many times Web browsers have requested files from your server. Web sites used to love to advertise how many hits they got, because it always sounded like a large number to anyone who thought that it meant visitors. However, when someone views a single Web page that has 14 button images on it, that counts as 15 hits. While the number of hits is easy to track, the inclusion of so many small graphics on typical modern Web pages makes the number not very meaningful.

➤ *Page-views* is a more meaningful statistic, tracking basically how many times different HTML page files (the primary files for Web pages) are downloaded.

➤ *Visitors* is a figure that shows how many different people visited your site. A Web site plants a little code (called a *cookie*) on each visitor's computer so that it can recognize them as they skip from page to page of the site, or if they go away and come back again (which means it's actually tracking how many different browsers visit the site, but that's close enough).

➤ *User-minutes* measures how much time people spent, in total, on your site. This is a particularly important measure if you have automatically updating ads, because it relates directly to the number of ad exposures the user gets.

Visitors and page-views are the two statistics that you'll be relying on in dealing with advertisers, as they'll let you know how many different people you're reaching and how often you're reaching them.

Naming Eyeballs

The more you know about your users, the better you'll be able to sell them to advertisers. Some sites require users to *register*, having them fill out a form with all sorts of personal and financial information before they can use the site or service for the first time. The system gives the user a password, and every time the user visits, he has to type his name and password to be identified. This way, for example, when I log on to SnackMania.com, it knows that I intend to purchase a new computer in the next six months and that my favorite form of gummi-snack is gummi-wildebeests.

Having registered users not only helps you build a demographic database, it also lets you target ads. The next time I log on to SnackMania, I can be presented with ads for new juicier gummi-wildebeests, or for tweezers designed for removing wildebeest-shaped snacks from my molars or from my new computer keyboard.

Registration does have some drawbacks, however. It puts a few extra steps between users and the content or service, and every additional step it takes merely encourages users to surf on to something else. Then, when they see you're collecting information on them, users who are concerned with privacy might well turn away, or simply give false information (more than a few Web sites will find Bart Simpson among their registered users).

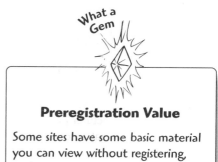

Preregistration Value

Some sites have some basic material you can view without registering, and only require that you register for more in-depth material. That way, users know that the site is a quality one before having to register.

If you ask users for an email address, they're likely to be concerned about ending up with an email box filled with junk advertising (and if you ask for their phone number, they'll expect to be stuck with calls asking them to change their long-distance provider).

Trusty TRUSTe

Many large Web sites that accept registration or customer information make use of TRUSTe, an organization that audits and certifies privacy practices. Surf over to www.TRUSTe.org to learn more.

If you do choose to go the registration route, have a *privacy statement* with clear explanations of what this information will be used for. Be sure you stick to what you promise.

Pay-Per-View

Ads are generally sold on a *per-view* basis. Advertisers are charged a small amount (we're talking pennies for general audience ads, more for targeted ads) every time their ad is downloaded from your system into a viewer's browser.

Advertisers paying on a per-view basis like to be sure that their ad is displayed *above the fold*, which means in the upper part of the page, so that the user will see the ad even if they never scroll down. After all, no one wants to pay for an ad that nobody sees.

Click-Thrus

Almost every ad on the Web is a link. Click the ad for Poodle Teasers, Incorporated, and you are taken to Poodleteaser.com. The ad is generally just an enticementto encourage you to click through to the site, which is often just a full-on advertising site for a single product. Because the advertiser really only benefits when someone clicks the ad, some advertisers want to pay only for users who click (called *click-thrus*).

Advertisers who pay in this manner pay a lot more per click-thru than they would pay per view. This isn't necessarily more profitable for the site carrying the ad, though, because only a few percent of the people who see a given ad will click it.

Adverse Advertising

Be picky about what sort of advertising you accept. While ads for porn and gambling sites are lucrative, they can also drive people away from an otherwise family–friendly Web site.

If you accept click-thru advertising, be sure that you get to see the ads first. After all, your income from click-thru advertising is very dependent on the quality of the ad.

Cut of the Kill

Pete's Pickle Place might offer you a different sort of ad deal. It won't pay when people see the ad, or even when they click the ad. Instead, Pete will pony up pesos only for the people who purchase pickle products. Again, you gain even more per user, but lose out because fewer users are clicking through. Now the amount you make is dependent not only on the quality of the ad but also the quality of the Web site and the reputation of Pete's pickling plant.

Advertising of this sort ranges from basic banner advertising to full affiliate programs (as described in the last chapter), where you are expected to list and push individual items and let the site handle the orders. One thing to realize is that, in many cases, the advertiser is hoping to pay you just for the first order from the customer, and then hope that the customer will keep returning directly to the store and ordering more without you being paid a cent.

Heroic History

Gamesville: Fun and Games and Money

Web site name: gamesville.com

Founded: 1996

Service provided: Online games

Business model: Gamesville offers an array of online games free to the user. They even offer prizes to game players. The site is advertising supported, with frequently updated ads showing while the user plays the game. Gamesville avoids the complications that other game sites present by offering games that are quick to load and which the user already knows. Games derived from black-jack, bingo, and trivia games aim at a mainstream audience, in contrast with the high-resolution, complex, arcade-oriented gaming that other sites use as a lure. With each new move or click, new ads are displayed. Playing some of the games feels a lot like gambling, although with other people's money. While that feeling is likely to keep people coming back and online for the same time, it is also likely to discourage players from clicking ads while games are in progress; it is the ads that appear between games that would seem the most lucrative to advertisers. Gamesville does have the proper excuse for getting user registrations; after all, they can't send you your share of the thousands of prizes distributed monthly if you aren't registered. This advantage has given them more than two million registered users.

Where the money came from: Lycos purchased Gamesville for $207 million in November 1999. Lycos noted that this purchase did not increase their visitor count by much, but would add substantially to their usage-minutes count.

Smashing Atoms: Selling Good Stuff

Another common Internet model is selling actual physical objects to your users in exchange for money. In this case, the person visiting your Web site or using your service is your customer (or potential customer). In a way, this seems a little low tech. Anything where you have to use the post office (or FedEx or UPS) to deliver seems a lot like old-fashioned business.

What a Gem

Information: The Internet's Most Valued Commodity?

Data about people, whether detailed information about certain large groups of humans or specific information about an individual, might be the basis for the most important Internet business model of the early twenty–first century. While many companies that gather customer data do so in a quiet manner, one company is very up–front about its practice and has even made *data mining* its central business scheme. Consider wishbox.com, an online *gift registry* where people can state what products they would like to get for holidays, birthdays, and other events. A loved one or friend of the wisher can access this information, find out what gifts a particular person wants, and then follow links to purchase them online. The importance of data gathering, as at least a portion of any business plan, cannot be discounted. (But you might find some discounts at wishbox.com.)

But old-fashioned businesses are not going away. Despite the advances in computer technology, we still can't download a dress, or a car, or a pumpkin pie. In a way, that's a good thing; otherwise, I would spend all day sitting around eating advertising-supported pies and surfing for a site that downloads magic weight-loss pills.

Some folks refer to retailing physical goods over the Internet as *selling atoms*, because there are actual physical objects being shipped.

Catalog Sites

A catalog Web site is the most straightforward and, in a way, the most honest sort of atom-selling site. The user going to the site expects to find things for sale; that's the reason to surf there.

There is an array of predesigned online catalog software available, which makes starting an online store seem easy. You still have to know a lot about retailing and promotion to really get started. See the preceding chapter for a better understanding of different methods of supporting an online store.

There is such a diversity of existing catalog sites that it might seem difficult to find a new niche. The truth is, you might not need a niche that no one else is occupying. There is room for more than one store in most categories—particularly if the existing retailers are under-promoted or carry a narrow range of stock.

Lifestyle Sales

Some sites might be eager to sell you something, but attract you first with useful information or entertainment. After they have your attention, they'll offer to sell you some item related to the topic at hand. You could, for example, set up www.exoticdinner.com, with free access to a large database of interesting and unusual recipes. When the user pulls up the recipe for Hummingbird A La Maurice, you can offer to sell them the hard-to-find frozen hummingbird steaks or the three pounds of garlic that the recipe requires.

After the customer begins to order the hummingbird meat, you can then bring them to a full catalog system, allowing them to order further items. (After all, the first item you order requires the most shipping costs; additional items ship more cheaply, making them an easier sell.) When you're doing lifestyle sales, you have to be certain that the content that brings the customer is fresh, vital, and exciting. If you can't drag in the potential shoppers and keep them on your site, your catalog isn't going to sell much.

Logo to Go

If you can create a site or service with a certain cachet that people want to associate themselves with, you can go into the business of selling items with your logo or brand on it. If people associate your product with class, or hipness, or cutting edge, they might want to associate themselves with that.

You're probably thinking that t-shirts and keychains are a lousy way to make a big profit (and they are, although they do have the advantage of also spreading the brand name), but sometimes you have to think bigger than that. Look at the competition between Microsoft and Netscape to give away Web browser software. One of the big reasons for doing this is to establish themselves as key, recognized names in the Internet business. This way, they have an edge when selling host software (the software that distributes Web pages).

Bits for Sale, Two Bits Apiece

The purest form of e-business is where you're getting paid directly by the user for the service, information, or access that you provide. With no third parties involved and no need to ship materials, you'll be working totally online and your dealings with your user are straightforward.

This is sometimes referred to as *selling bits*. *Bit* is computer jargon for the smallest possible unit of information.

Charge Per Access

One way to structure selling bits is to charge for each individual access. A good example of this is a site such as eMusic.com, which sells downloadable, compressed music files in the MP3 format. If you want to buy a They Might Be Giants album, for example, you give your credit card information, and eMusic will charge you $9.99. In return, it will give you a link that you can use to download the songs to your PC.

The per-access model is also used to sell computer programs, archived newspaper articles, and searches of specialized databases. It's a good model if you have downloadable files that the user can use repeatedly, or if you have a service that is of value even when the user is using it just once. (That is like the telephone 900 numbers—they have to offer you something that's worth paying several dollars a minute for.)

Subscription

The subscription model is good if you have a service that the user should want to use repeatedly, or a large body of regularly updated information that the user should want to access. Probably the most visible use of subscriptions on the Web are the porn sites, which charge a fixed monthly or annual rate to have access to all the materials on their site.

Cancel Concern

Some Web services with automatic-renewal clauses make it very difficult to cancel a subscription. These sites have no visible method of cancellation. Ultimately you have to email them and then they require you to supply all sorts of exact information about how you enrolled in the first place, under the guise of verifying your identity. These sites make money off people who can't figure out how to cancel, but it hurts their reputation. To get respect, either have your subscriptions not renew automatically or make cancellation a clear and simple procedure.

For an example of a business-oriented subscription service, check out `Quickteam.com`. It offers an online tool for project teams that need to coordinate schedules and communicate. By being on the Web, it makes sure that even your team members who are away from the office can access and interact with the rest of the team. For this, it charges $12.95 per member of your team per month. (To show a mix of economic models: It also has a less-powerful version of the tool that is ad-supported, and it is also willing to sell you its software to run off your own host.)

Subscriptions can either be *fixed term* or *automatically renewing*. If it's for a fixed term and the user tries to access the service after the subscription runs out, he finds he has to subscribe again. If it is automatically renewing, the user's credit card keeps getting charged each time the subscription runs out. The automatic renewing is more convenient, but some users find it off-putting. It's like ordering a hamburger, and having the waiter keep bringing you burgers and charging you for them because you never told him to stop—which explains how I got this particular waistline.

Access Sales Are Tough Sells

It's very hard to get individuals to pay for things on the Internet. It's not just that people are cheap (although that certainly is part of it). There are some very strong reasons behind their reluctance:

➤ **They're used to getting good stuff for free on the Internet.**   Because of all the ad-supported materials and services that are offered without charge on the Internet, people have become accustomed to not paying. You have to convince them that what you have to offer is substantially better than what they can get for free. This is a winnable fight. For example, people are willing to pay for cable TV when they're used to getting TV for free.

➤ **They don't get a physical object.**   It's always harder to convince people that something that doesn't provide a physical object is worth money, particularly when there is no visible human providing them with a service.

➤ **The purchase process is cumbersome.**   The entering of credit card information is a pain in the neck. When you're out shopping in the real world, you just dig out your wallet, swipe the card, and sign something. When you use a credit card online, you reach for your card and realize that you're still in your pajamas. So, you have to find your pants, get the wallet, dig out the card, carefully copy the huge string of numbers into the form on the Web site, type your address, verify the information, put in one additional form of contact in case there's a problem, and then twiddle your fingers while the computer accesses the credit card information.

➤ **Privacy is a problem.**   People are quite concerned about providing their credit card information online. This concern is largely unfounded; legitimate sites with proper security features have proven to be as safe as using your credit card in person. People are also wary of giving out their contact information, concerned that they'll wind up with piles of junk mail or suppertime phone calls offering them aluminum siding for their Volvo.

➤ **Price and value don't always match.**   To make credit card charging practical, charges really have to be a dollar at the very least. This is a rather high price for small items such as articles or individual songs.

Businesses are more likely than individuals to pay for online services. Purchasing decisions are less likely to be taken personally and privacy is not a concern. The service offered has to be important enough for someone to navigate the corporate purchase ordering system to get it, but with a company full of potential users, you can build substantial charges.

Micropayments

There are a number of plans being tested that would allow people to make *micropayments*, small payments too small for a credit card to handle. If an accepted micropayment system is established, you could charge a dime for reading an article, a quarter to download a song, a nickel to send a fax, and so on.

Some sites already have their own equivalent of micropayments at work. Auction site eBay, for example, accumulates the smaller day-to-day charges against the seller, actually processing the charges in larger, less-frequent credit card transactions.

Access Theft

A number of years ago, during a garbage collection strike in New York City, some folks came up with a rather novel method of getting rid of their garbage. They gift-wrapped their garbage, and left it in unlocked cars or on their window ledges. Sure enough, someone would steal it. The moral is that there will always be someone willing to steal anything that appears to have value. The bits you're offering for sale are no exception.

While there are various ways to gain free access to valuable materials (including using stolen credit card numbers), the most common method of theft from subscription services is probably password-sharing. Helga purchases a legitimate account, and then shares her password with her brother Buford. He shares the info with his bowling team, and then they share the information with fellow members of the International Association of Cat Scratchers. Soon, dozens of people are accessing Helga's account rather than paying for their own accounts. The more people using the account, the easier it is to detect this fraud. That is because it's hard to believe that Helga is simultaneously using her account from seven different computers.

Before *you* can detect it, there will be people getting free access. This is the Internet equivalent of shoplifting. As with shoplifting, you can't stop it entirely without doing things that drive away legitimate customers. It is a cost of doing business.

Mixing Models

Nothing says that you have to have just one source of income. Many sites freely mix advertising with atom-selling (as seen in Figure 5.1). Sometimes this comes in blatant ways with straightforward advertising. For example, consider MP3.com, which offers free downloadable music. It has standard banner advertising throughout its site. It also sells CDs by the same artists that you can download sample songs from.

Advertising can also be done in more subtle ways. If your band The Mummies and The Puppies wants to get more people downloading your music on MP3.com, you can bid for a place on the Payola list, which is marked (in small print) as a paid-for list.

When mixing models, however, you have to be careful about possibly offending your users. Amazon.com was the focus of negative attention when it was revealed that publishers were paying for having their books prominently recommended on the site. (This parallels the common brick-and-mortar business practice of selling key shelf space to suppliers looking to move more product.)

Similarly, if you have a subscription-based site, you should go easy on the advertising. If a user feels that advertising is slowing down the service that he paid for, or is making accessing that service awkward, he's going to be annoyed. It would be like having a movie at the theater stop in the middle for TV-style advertising. When someone pays for access, he wants to be treated as the customer, not the product.

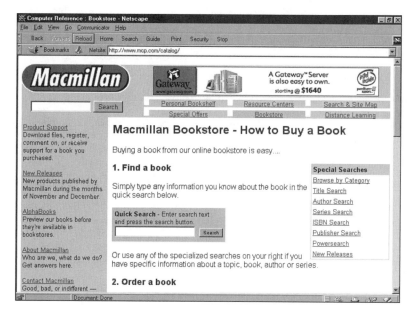

Figure 5.1

Nothing says you have to have only one source of income for a Web site. This publisher Web site has both online book ordering (selling atoms) and advertising (selling eyeballs).

Free Is Best

There are a lot of arguments for a lot of models on the Web, but generally speaking, keeping your service free for the typical consumer is probably the best route in making your millions. At this point, the big money being made on the Web is not from direct profit, but from selling all or part of a popular site or service. A free offering will build a bigger group of users, which not only makes the site more attractive to a buyer but increases the odds of finding potential investors among your customers. You can keep the site free by selling advertising, by some other back route to income, or simply by not seeking income. Just remember that if you don't keep it free, someone might come up with a similar-but-free site, undercutting you.

Free might not be possible if you're shipping atoms, but even then, low prices can be your most attractive lure.

The Least You Need to Know

➤ A business's *economic model* is the description of its business and where the income is expected to come from.

➤ Advertising-supported sites and services sell *eyeballs*, advertiser access to the site's users.

➤ Retail sites sell *atoms*, taking money for physical product that is delivered.

➤ You can charge the user directly for your online offerings, either on a pay-per-use basis or a subscription basis.

➤ You do not necessarily need an economic model for your offering. The value in your offering might be in its innovation or its large user base, which somebody else might develop a way to exploit.

Part 2
Ready, Set, Startup

A company is built from the ground up. Unless, of course, you're in the subway business, in which case you build from the ground down.

In this part of the book, you'll see the steps toward building your company. At the beginning, your company is nothing more than a group of people working together. Find the right people, and you should be able to move ahead with a good and attractive product. Find the wrong people, and you'll end up sitting around playing penny-a-point backgammon with your co-workers, which is not likely to make you millions unless you play for a really long time. You'll also learn about getting on someone else's team, registering your Web site address, and getting funding for the business. Follow this guide and you'll be able to build from the ground up without getting ground up!

Chapter 6

Building Your Team

In This Chapter

➤ Typical ways that Internet businesses get started

➤ Building teams for your own company

➤ What sort of employees you need to find

➤ Enticing high-quality employees to join your company when you have little operating capital

---

Following the Construction of a (Fictitious) e-Business

Sit back and relax, because I am going to tell you a story about a very small one-person business that grew up to become a multibillion-dollar corporate e-enterprize. This tale is fiction, certainly, but is based on various real-world models that I have studied. In any event, the particular e-company that stars in this story, and all the characters, are not real. They're totally invented, so please don't write them letters asking for work or surf the World Wide Web trying to find their site.

The story, like all good stories, has an ending. It is only one of many possible endings that this tale could have had. The story of your own Internet business also has many possible endings. Let's hope that you reach a happy ending to your own personal tale of Internet riches.

Our story begins in Lake Havasu City, Arizona. Have you ever been there? Interestingly enough, the London Bridge was moved there lock, stock, and, well, brick back in the late 1960s. It's still there, too, perched next to the lake itself. And this small desert town is where our little story begins.

Water, Water, Everywhere and All of It Tastes Terrible

Patty Sue Moore didn't have a lot in the world, but she did have a delightful fresh water spring located in the heart of a rather short mountain range located a few miles from Lake Havasu City. *Havasu*, as the locals called it, was stuck in the middle of the Mojave Desert, and the Colorado River ran next to it. A dam built in the 1930s created Lake Havasu, and a lot of the water from the lake was piped to a thirsty Los Angeles some 200 miles away.

Sending the water to Los Angeles was okay with Patty Sue. After all, she found the lake water to be pretty nasty tasting. She wondered if all the ski boats that skimmed the lake all summer long added small amounts of gasoline or other particulants. In any event, the lake water was simply not very good to drink.

Patty Sue had her own stock of fresh water. She had inherited a few acres of land up in the mountains and on that land was a spring. The water from the spring tasted heavenly. There was a small, rustic cabin near the spring and Patty Sue would usually spend her weekends staying at the cabin. She'd collect the delicious spring water in five-gallon jugs and on Sunday afternoons she would take a week's worth of water jugs home with her.

One day she realized that she'd been giving a lot of her water away to friends. Seeing a potential local market for her spring water, Patty Sue got a license to sell the stuff to the public. Soon *Patty Sue's Better Than Average Fresh Spring Water* was offered for purchase to the thirsty people of Lake Havasu City.

After a modest amount of proceeds from the sales started to roll in, she quit her day job to work full time on her water business. She was barely making a living, though, as the Big City Water companies 200 miles away in Phoenix, Arizona, were able to bottle and sell fresh water far cheaper than she could. Sure, their water was *processed* and not really spring water, but it was cheaper and tasted better than the lake water, so people bought the stuff. Usually the local Havasu people bought the competition's product instead of hers, because it was less expensive.

Patty Sue wasn't particularly sure what to do at this point, and was considering letting her business, well, dry up.

Taking a Dip into the Internet

Patty Sue's best friend, Emily Richardson, taught Internet-related classes at the local community college. Emily was pretty smart and knew a lot about setting up an e-commerce on the World Wide Web.

Emily suggested that the two of them team up and create an Internet business designed to sell the spring water on the Internet.

Many traditional businesses are finding that the Internet offers them a chance to reach a broader audience. Even local businesses are discovering that having a Web site can bring an ever-increasing number of clients to their doors. After all, even a simple home page acts as a 24-hour, seven-day-a-week, full-color online brochure of helpful advertising for current and potential clients!

They'd need some start-up money, so Emily mortgaged her condo and came up with about $30,000. They'd have to make that last as long as possible, so Emily agreed to try and run the business out of her home. They sat down at Emily's kitchen table and created a handwritten agreement. They'd be partners, 50-50, and they toasted themselves with some of Patty Sue's spring water.

It does take a certain amount of cash, or seed money, to launch a successful Internet e-business. But some of the Internet's most successful businesses were started from very modest beginnings.

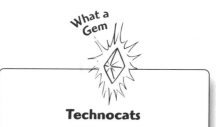

Technocats

Technocats, that is, Internet-savvy people, are often the central guiding figure of any start-up Internet company. As they are often quite informed about how the Internet works and how to lead a business along proven paths of success leading up to an IPO, perhaps they could also be termed Technocrats. Emily is, no doubt, well read on the history of various Internet business successes, something that is important for anyone who wants to lead a successful Internet business.

We Can't Give This Stuff Away!

Emily created a Web page for the Internet, and she paid a small fee for the Internet space. Although she wasn't an artist, she thought that she'd done a pretty good job with the graphics for the site. She'd scanned a photo of Patty Sue's mountain cabin and that photo was featured on the site's home page.

PattySuesBetterThanAverageFreshSpringWater.com would have been a fairly lengthy domain address for their Web site, so they decided to call the Internet business PattyWater.com. They raised the price of the water to include shipping and handling and waited for the sales to start rolling in. Sadly, the sales didn't start to roll in, they merely trickled in. People simply weren't buying the water in any large amounts. In fact, few visitors ever came to the Web site at all.

Sitting in Emily's kitchen one day, they talked about buying advertising for their Web site. Emily reasoned that advertising might increase the traffic to their home page.

But they just didn't have enough money to buy any meaningful amount of advertising. Other than buying ads somewhere, they couldn't think of any way to bring customers to their site. They were only presently averaging about 10 page views a day, which they both knew was just plain terrible.

Things looked bleak, and Emily exclaimed "We can't even give this stuff away!" After saying that, she sat still for a moment, put her hands to her mouth, and looked with wide eyes at her partner Patty. "Wait. Wait! Maybe we can give it away!" she shouted and turned to Patty with a big smile on her face.

People on the Internet like free stuff a lot more than they like to pay for stuff. Sure, some things such as books from Amazon.com must be paid for. But there are plenty of free services, information, music, short films, and more that you can enjoy without paying any sort of service fee. Why? Because a great free service on the Internet can attract a whole lot of eager users.

The *Multiple Threat* Person

In the early days of an Internet business, there is often room for a person who can successfully work a number of types of jobs, from taking care of shipping to answering the telephone. This is often a good way to gain entry to a start-up company while it is still in its infancy.

A New Business Model

Emily wrote a press release and sent copies of it to every Internet-related magazine that she could think of. A month later, they noticed that the daily number of visitors to their Web site had jumped all the way to a steady 20,000 a day.

Emily then quickly arranged to have some other companies place advertising on their Web page. One national chain of health food stores purchased a fairly amazing amount of banner space on the home page.

This resulted in some cash coming in to the company. That was grand, because they were going through a lot of water at this point. Although they charged a portion of the shipping costs to the customers, they were taking a pretty hefty loss on each bottle of water that they shipped. After all, the water was now being offered for free. The advertising helped a lot but they were still firmly in the red.

Patty Sue was overworked, bottling and lugging bottles of water from the spring seven days a week. So, she hired Manny, a thirtyish day laborer to help out with her efforts. Manny was a very energetic can-do sort of person, and was more than willing to take on all the many menial tasks that needed to be done around the spring.

Even somebody who has little more than muscles and an energetic personality has the chance of joining a startup early enough to become a founder. It all depends on the company's manpower needs when it is starting up.

Meanwhile, Emily had hired two 19-year-old college students who had been students in her Internet class. They were needed to create improvements for their home page and to keep the engineering aspects of their site running smoothly. Because they charged a bit for shipping, the engineers had to make sure that the credit card–related programming was secure and running smoothly.

Heroic History

eToys: Big Bucks Are Child's Play

Web site name: eToys.com

Founded: 1997

Service provided: Online toy retailer

Business model: The preeminent online toy retailer, eToys offers 100,000 different items for sale. Its economic model is the standard retail economic model: Sell item for more than it costs you to buy, and keep the difference. Word of eToys spread quickly, particularly with the help of a TV ad for credit cards, which focused on the eToys site as a place to use the card. Sales in the fiscal year ending March 31, 1998, were a mere $700,000; the following year, sales were $30 million. Marketing tricks used by eToys include allowing creations of wish lists of gifts for a given child, which can then be distributed via email to potential gift givers, with direct links to the products on the eToys site. They also offer customers the opportunity to set up a database of birthdays of the children they know, and eToys will send out reminders and gift suggestions several weeks in advance of each birthday.

Where the money came from: eToys proffered their initial public offering in May of 1999 at $20 per share. During 1999, the price reached as high as 86, but eToys faced some performance concerns during the crucial Christmas buying season. As of December 29, 1999, the stock was trading at 28 1/8, giving the company a market capitalization of $3.4 billion. The stock trades on the Nasdaq exchange under the symbol ETYS.

Everybody was taking a very modest salary, and the company's bank account was running dry very quickly. But their Web site was getting more and more popular everyday and the number of bottles that they were shipping was doubling every month.

As the demand for the free water increased, they decided to limit their customers to one free bottle of water each week, and offer additional water for sale. The day they announced that five thousand angry fans wrote nasty emails to their customer support department. Very few people bought any extra water. "People want free stuff and only free stuff, at least at our site," Emily remarked, somewhat sadly.

Eventually most Web sites that offer their services or products at no charge to their users must come up with a way to adjust their business model and make some money. Money from advertising on the Web site certainly helps to pay the bills but may not be enough to generate a profit.

What a Gem

The Needed Expert

Your Internet business might need the services of a real-world expert of some sort. Traditional areas of knowledge are often required even if the business is being performed strictly on the Internet. Whatever your business concept is, don't forget to consider hiring needed professionals from outside. They can often enrich your business by adding required experience. Every Internet business will probably have some sort of need for some non-Internet professionals.

Two More Helpers Show Up

Emily's Uncle Moe joined the team, for very little pay, as a general handy man. He worked seven days a week keeping the pump at the spring in tiptop condition. Meanwhile, Sydney Johnson, a former door-to-door water saleswoman, talked her way into a job. "I am first and foremost a closer and have some great ideas about how to sell water. I've been selling water all my life."

"You, of course, always have the right to say 'no.' Have I told you first and foremost that I am always a closer?" Sydney always spoke very quickly and seemed to know a lot more about water than anyone that Patty Sue and Emily had ever met. So they hired Sydney, for very little pay, although they weren't too awfully sure what she'd be doing for them because Sydney was a water salesperson and they were giving their water away.

But Sydney turned out to be a very valuable addition to the staff. Her background in water was rich and varied, and she helped to improve many aspects of their business, from bottling to shipping to quality control. They quickly decided that they were very lucky to have found the fast-talking Sydney.

Your startup will need both business experts and specialists in certain areas as it grows. Are you a marketing expert? If not, you'll need to hire some great ones. Are you an accountant? A lawyer? Any CEO must understand that he has to delegate a great deal of responsibilities and duties to his employees if the company is to be successful.

Enter Investment Capital

SuperAcme, Inc., an investment capital concern in New York City, had heard about their tiny company from a small story that ran in a national Internet magazine. They contacted Emily and Patty Sue, and arranged to come out and see their operation, which by this time had moved from Emily's condo to a small office in Lake Havasu City.

"You people are the first people on the Internet to give away spring water," remarked Mr. Elmo, the president of SuperAcme, Inc. "It is very good to be the first company on the Internet to do something. Here's a check for 10 million American dollars," he said, handing it to them. In return, SuperAcme was presented with a certain amount of ownership in the little spring water company.

Three Hundred Thousand Water Lovers a Day

Within a couple of months, more than a quarter of a million thirsty spring water fans were coming to their Web site every day. SuperAcme recommended to them that they hire a first-rate Internet businessperson to help run things. They agreed, and found one: Mrs. Mary McFain. They had heard about her during a lunch meeting with some people from SuperAcme. Emily and Patty Sue had learned that Mary had a great track record with another Internet company where she had successfully led the other company to a very well-received initial public offering on Wall Street.

Your start-up business will need all sorts of specialists and experts as it grows. Having just the right team of employees will be crucial for your success. However, as your business rapidly expands, you might find yourself redoing your employee organization charts every 90 days or so for the first year until you get things just the way you want them.

Business Gurus

Every successful Internet business needs an experienced Internet business expert. If required, the founders of a successful Internet company must be willing to step aside and turn over the reins to a more experienced business person after a company becomes successful. Don't let ego stand in the way of making your company highly competitive if you lack the required experience needed to act as the CEO or President of your company. It is far better to take a back seat after you've got the company off and running, rather than make leadership mistakes that could cost you your success.

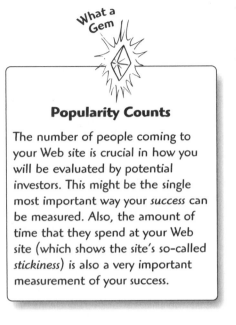

Popularity Counts

The number of people coming to your Web site is crucial in how you will be evaluated by potential investors. This might be the single most important way your *success* can be measured. Also, the amount of time that they spend at your Web site (which shows the site's so-called *stickiness*) is also a very important measurement of your success.

Mary came on board as President and Chief Operating Officer of the business and announced to Sydney and all the other employees "All of you people who were before me and the investment money are now founders." Quickly thereafter, Mary began to use some of the investment money from SuperAcme to ramp up the company by hiring new employees and buying needed supplies and bottling machinery. The spring itself got a much needed overhaul. "The water must flow!" exclaimed Mary as the new equipment was installed at the spring.

Emily took the senior position of President and Chief Executive Officer. Patty Sue was satisfied to label herself as Vice President of Water Quality and Production and she spent her days at the spring, reading a book while the water was bottled. Every hour or so she'd run a few tests on the water, but for the most part she took it pretty easy. After all, this was my whole idea from the beginning, she'd often think to herself.

Many more employees were hired. Patty Sue was given a staff of five very large people to take care of the bottling of the spring water. Writers were hired to write the text for the Web site. A Webmaster was hired to improve the overall appearance of the home page, and graphic artists were brought in to jazz up the appearance of the page as well as to design new labels for the spring water bottle that they shipped.

Shipping clerks, Human Resources experts, administrative assistants, and many various Vice Presidents were hired to round out the company's organizational chart. Security guards were hired to protect the spring around the clock.

The Great Employee Hiring Continues

Engineers were in short supply in Lake Havasu City, so the company executives decided to move the main headquarters to Malibu, California. The water production would still happen at the Havasu spring facility, of course, but all the nonproduction fulfillment departments of the company, from Web page design to engineering to marketing, would now be housed in a state-of-the-art facility located very near the Pacific Ocean. Most of the engineers liked to surf during their lunch break, anyway, and nobody wanted to stand in their way. Good engineers were difficult to find. To help ensure a steady supply of engineers, the company gave a $1,000 bonus to anyone who recruited a much-needed engineer.

Remember that stock options are not the same thing as cash. If the company fails, your options will be worth very little or nothing. Even a company that has a good Initial Public Offering can make some tragic mistakes and end up going broke.

Every day it seemed that at least five new employees were added to the company's roster. Only about three months after getting their investment capital, the business employed nearly 200 workers in various capacities.

Marketing experts working for the company were thinking hard all day to come up with new ways to try and make some money. "Let's put advertising on the water bottles," they cried, and Mary approved of this. Soon other companies were paying for ad space on their water bottles. Pattywater.com began to edge towards making their first quarterly profit.

Online advertising, as previously noted, can be a very important source of revenue to an Internet business. To survive in the long term, however, most e-businesses must have additional sources of income.

Stock Options

It is traditional to offer your employees a bit of the action by giving them stock options. The founders of a company usually gather the greater amount, but all your employees should get something in the way of stock options. This makes your employees feel like they have something more than a paycheck at stake and can lead to greater company loyalty. Also, very valuable employees will come to your company in the early days for very little salary and a substantial interest in stock options. This is crucial to starting a company when you are cash poor.

More Investment Capital

Fresh Water, Inc., the largest non-Internet water business in the United States, called up and offered $50 million of investment money to Emily and Mary. Accepting the offer, they sold off another chunk of the business to Fresh Water, Inc., but ended up with a lot more money in the bank, which they needed to take their company public. "Wall Street is where the real wealth is," remarked Mary.

During the months before the Initial Public Offering, news cameras were often at the Havasu spring and at the Malibu offices. The world was fascinated with the little company that gave water away, and all this publicity brought hundreds of thousands of new customers to their Web site. All the primary Internet magazines were printing stories about the business. They were becoming very well known in some very important business circles.

Hiring only the best Wall Street experts, the little company made a big splash during its Initial Public Offering. Emily and Mary flew all over the U.S. and Europe during a road show where they talked about the virtue of investing in Patty Sue's Better Than Average Fresh Spring Water, Inc.

Patty Sue was content to stay in Lake Havasu City and keep an eye on the facilities near the spring. They had used some of the investment money to tear down the little rustic shack and put up a first-class, five-bedroom executive abode where Patty Sue had a panoramic view of Lake Havasu and the desert beyond the town. Patty Sue enjoyed herself in air-conditioned comfort, sipping spring water and listening to music on her stereo as she passed the time between water tests.

The opening price of stock was set at $15 a share. By the close of the first day of trading, the stock was being sold at $30 a share. For the most part, there has been a steady climb in value in the shares of stock since then.

Even after a successful Initial Public Offering, a young company must still carefully evaluate their business model. Only companies that make a profit can hope to survive in the long run.

Hunting for a Better Business Model

Still, even after all this success, the company wasn't making a great deal of profit. There were some serious limitations in building a business around giving the only product away. Mary knew that she would have to come up with an improved business model or investors could lose faith in Pattywater.com.

The investors all wanted to know what the company's real business model would be. At executive meetings, Mary pointed out that Amazon.com hadn't made a profit after years of existence and their stock was still doing quite well. Yet, Mary could see the point of the complaints. A business should earn a good profit, Mary thought to herself.

She could see a couple of possibilities for changing their business plan so that they could make a substantial profit, but Emily and Patty Sue were burned out and wanted to retire early and move to Hawaii. "The water tastes pretty good there, you know," Emily said pointedly. Mary shrugged her shoulders and gave in. The company would be sold if a decent offer came along. "Any company should always be considered to be for sale at any time. It is simply a matter of price," Mary said to her partners.

Every Business Is Always for Sale

Fresh Water, Inc., was impressed with the fact that the little water company now had more than 10 million visitors a month coming to its Web page. So, they made an offer to Emily, Mary, and Patty Sue to purchase their controlling amount of shares from them.

After a variety of legal types carefully checked this out, the three ladies sold their interests in the company. Soon, most of the original employees were laid off. This was okay with them, however, because of a contract that they had with Patty Sue's Better Than Average Fresh Spring Water, Inc., that stated that their stock options would instantly vest if the company was ever sold and if they were ever laid off by the new owners. Yes, they were very happy, indeed.

Selling a company is just one of the many options that a company's owners might consider. Certainly, any successful startup will hear a lot of rumors and speculation about an impending sale, even when no such thing is impending! Some CEOs even step aside after a startup has been launched to allow a more experienced businessman to take the helm.

Sydney was asked by Fresh Water, Inc., to stay on. She begged them to lay her off so that her stocks would instantly vest, too, but the new president said "Sorry, Sydney, but we need somebody with your kind of drive around here." They did give her some additional stock options and a higher salary and made her Vice President of something or other.

Emily and Patty Sue were now billionaires. Mary had received nearly a billion dollars from the sale of her own stock in the company, and all the founders walked away with several million dollars.

In the beginning, a startup that looks very promising to business experts can sometimes attract top-flight business gurus as employees who will waive their normally huge salaries for oodles of stock options. You will need the best business gurus you can get to get your startup launched and on the road to success.

Fresh Water, Inc., made a few changes. They closed the Lake Havasu City spring down, and replaced the water with Los Angeles tap water that was purified through a *reverse osmosis process*. In time water was purified, bottled, and shipped from major distribution centers all over the United States. This cut costs and resulted in the company making a large profit. Pattywater.com no longer shipped water from the Lake Havasu City spring, which had been quickly shut down by Fresh Water, Inc.

> *What a Gem*
>
> ## The (Internet) World Offers Many Possibilities; Some of Them Are Not Good
>
> Internet companies are often purchased, both before and after they go public. Sometimes a company goes public via a *reverse merger* where they are absorbed by a previously existing public company. In any event, it is important that you have a written agreement that states that your stock options will instantly vest if your company is purchased, and if you are let go for anything other than being fired for *cause*. The definition of why you could be *terminated for cause* should be clearly explained in your contract and should include only those traditional activities such as being convicted of a felony, and other serious problems. Don't let *being fired for cause* be defined as anything coming close to simply being laid off. Consult with your attorney for more information about this important way to protect your stock options.

Heroic History

Akamai: Value in Speed

Web site name: www.Akamai.com

Founded: 1998

Service provided: Speeds up delivery of Web content

Business model: A common complaint with any given Web site is that it takes too long for pages to load. This isn't always the fault of the site itself; Internet data is passed from system to system, with plenty of possible bottlenecks along the way. When the site gets slow, the user visiting the site grows dissatisfied. Akamai (Hawaiian for *intelligent* or *clever*) has its own network of more than 1,000 servers linked to the Internet. It rents storage space on those computers to major Web sites. When a user requests a page with graphics, the graphics are sent from the nearest Akamai server, avoiding many potential bottlenecks. This causes a more-satisfying experience for the site user.

Where the money came from: Akamai had a spectacular IPO in October 1999. The stock was initially priced at $26 per share. By the end of the first trading day, it was selling for more than $145 per share, an increase of more than 450% in one day. This was the fourth highest one-day IPO growth on record. As of December 29, 1999, the stock was trading at 282 1/2 per share, giving the company a market capitalization of $25.8 billion. The stock trades on the Nasdaq market under the symbol AKAM.

Amazingly, most of the customers never even noticed the change in the water. The Web site stopped calling it *spring water* and now described the water as *Spring Time Water*. Investors kept buying its stock and the company's market value soared.

The Least You Need to Know

➤ Traditional businesses often can be successfully transplanted to the Internet.

➤ You will need both business experts and specialists as your company develops.

➤ You might want to step aside and allow a more-experienced person to take over the leadership of your company after it initially becomes successful.

➤ You will need Internet professionals, from engineers to e-commerce gurus, to help you operate your company. You might also require experienced workers from non-Internet backgrounds.

➤ In the early days, you should be able to trade stock options for high salaries and obtain needed top-flight employees.

Chapter 7

C'MON!!

Jumping on Someone's Team

In This Chapter

➤ Defining a founder and how to become one

➤ Types of jobs available in Internet companies

➤ Why engineers are so important to e-commerce

➤ How to learn about a hot Internet company before it's hot

The Wisdom of Joining Early: Founders and Other Lucky Ducks

Every multibillion-dollar e-business had to start somewhere. Sometimes the starting point can be very modest. Somewhere right now there might be a young Internet genius with that one-in-a-million Internet business concept. Virtually penniless, this visionary might not have much in the way of operating cash (yet) but is richly endowed with the right combination of moxy, brilliance, leadership, drive, and bad haircut to become the next Bill Gates. (Except that maybe he won't try to take over the entire world and learn the hard way that *monopoly* is more than a board game.)

In the early days of a startup, money might be short but that doesn't mean that a smart person shouldn't join the team. Those that do before the money comes raining down on the lucky e-company are usually deemed *founders* by the grateful originator of the company. If the company makes billions of dollars later on, the founders usually clean up pretty good. The earlier the founder joined the company, the better a stock deal he is usually awarded.

Wealth of Knowledge

Founders: Brave People Who Shared a Single Vision of Success

A *founder* is a person who believed in the future success of a company before there was any proof that the company would become successful. Founders are the workers who join a business when it is just starting out, has no venture capital, and is living primarily on hopes and dreams. Typically, founders work for very little money or no money at all, but instead are hoping to make it rich in stock options. Stock options are usually richly awarded to the founders of a successful company.

Exciting, isn't it? But who qualifies to be a founder—that is, what sort of help does a company need early on? There are several possibilities here. (This whole concept is so exciting that I bet you can't sit still. Take a deep breath and read on. It is going to get even more exciting.)

Finding Founders

Imagine one person with a great idea. A far-seeing Internet-savvy person who will, in due course, be hailed as the greatest Internet business star of the early twenty-first century. But, right now, he is just a guy working out of his living room. Maybe he needs a little money to keep going. Perhaps you have twenty or thirty thousand dollars that you can throw into his business account and some basic business experience that he could rely on. You might end up being a founder and the Vice President of Marketing, which doesn't sound so impressive when there are only four people in the company and its only asset is a semiworking coffee machine. But it will mean money and power after the company hits big.

All Internet businesses need engineers. No, not the railway type of engineers (although those cool hats those choo-choo engineers used to wear would be pretty dang neat to have around). Internet people call computer scientists *engineers* now. These engineers no longer keep slide rules in their pockets. Instead, they keep great, complicated links of computer codes in their heads. Such engineers are among the most popular early hires of Internet companies.

While engineering is a good bet for somebody who wants to get in on a company during its infancy, there are many other types of employees who might find themselves hired. It all depends on what the owner of the company thinks is important at the time. Maybe a telephone receptionist is what he needs. Or, maybe an all-purpose person who answers the phone, handles the mail, or runs and gets lunch. After all, if those engineers are so dang important, why not free up as much of their time as possible so they can keep squinting into their computers instead of running errands?

In short, if the CEO of the Little Company That Will Make It Big thinks that you have the right combination of energy and smarts, you might be able to talk him into giving you a job (and loads of stock options), especially if you will initially work for peanuts.

The Gung-Ho Office Worker

While special skills are often required to join highly successful Internet companies, the future CEO of WorldsBiggestInternetCo.com might simply need a low-paid-but-very-energetic office worker during his early days of bitter struggle. Answer the telephone and make a few millions as a founder! Sounds great, huh?

Cheap, but needed, labor can be very important to a start-up company during the early days. Of course, you will be taking a gamble regardless of whether you are an office worker or a highly skilled, but brave, engineer.

After all, the company might fail. I know one person who has worked for three different startups, each of which failed to hit the big time. (By the way, she is a gung-ho office worker.)

Such failures could very easily happen to you as well, especially if you are joining a brand new, impoverished, unproven Internet business.

But that is why founders can reap such big rewards. If you believe in a company before it has proven itself, why shouldn't you be richly rewarded when the company hits it big? That's the whole concept behind being a founder.

If you are clever, and lucky, you yourself might be one of a handful of people who can say "I was smart and knew how well this company was going to make it before almost anyone else did."

Wealth of Knowledge

Got a Special, But Non-Internet Business Background

Let's assume that you spent 20 years selling shoes. Nobody knows shoes like you know shoes. Should you come across a start-up company that is just now designing what could be the world's best Internet shoe shop, you might have found your pot of gold. Remember, despite all the high-tech workers that an Internet company needs, if the company's business model is based on some real-world thing, from books to soups to airplane parts, they will need a real-world expert. Maybe that's you.

Not a Founder, But Still Rich: Corporate Executives Wanted

After a company gets rolling and is very successful financially, you can still make it big if you come from an already successful background. Are you an already successful vice president of an established business who could use a few extra million dollars? After the Big Buzz hits the press about your company, it is often the Big Bees who can still come in and make a lot of honey.

Heroic History

Deja: Pennies for Your Thoughts

Web site name: Deja.com

Founded: May, 1995

Service provided: Web access to Usenet discussion groups and to user-based product evaluations.

Business model: By offering user-friendly access to Usenet, the original Deja service (www.dejanews.com) attracted many surfers. At that time, its model was strictly selling eyeballs to advertisers. The site underwent a significant change in May of 1999, when it switched its site location to Deja.com and made its central focus online product reviews. By encouraging surfers to cast their vote on the quality of products that they used, Deja hoped to create a destination which people considering purchasing a product would come to. The new economical model was based strongly around providing paid links to major online commerce sites for the items being reviewed.

Where the money came from: Deja.com, Inc., remains privately held. It is perceived as a company with value, due both to the popularity of the Web site and the value of its Usenet archives.

Finding a proven company that is already on the fast track to a hot Initial Public Offering might be a great idea. If you have an impressive corporate background, you could end up getting a job with a great salary and even more stock options than the founders themselves. It all depends on the company, your background, and your will to succeed.

Young Internet founders might have vision but lack solid business credentials. If that is the case, someone with a proven track record of corporate experience and leadership could find a very nice, and lucrative, position waiting for him. You'll need to make yourself known to the company that you target and offer your services.

Don't wait for a job listing to be posted in the classified portion of your newspaper. No, you will need to seek out such opportunities and nab them early. How early? Hopefully months before they go public.

Engineers: There Appears to Be a Shortage

As the Internet continues its explosive growth, computer engineers are getting harder and harder to come by. There are really a lot of jobs out there for engineers. But, if you are an engineer, are you going to take a solid, modestly paying job for an established Internet company? Or go for broke with an unproven start-up company?

That, of course, is up to you. Most of the engineers that I know who have become founders of successful e-businesses were young guys in college who dropped out to take a shot at the big time. (They figured they could go back to school after they made their millions and could afford to have a butler, maid, and cook share their dorm room.)

Because so many founders of Internet companies are engineers, let's spend some time learning what sort of engineers are in demand. I'll be mentioning some pretty technical engineering stuff, such as Perl, for example. If you are already an engineer, you will know what these terms mean.

If you aren't already an engineer, but want to become one, then a lot of this stuff won't make any sense to you. At least you'll have a background on what areas you will need to master if you want to become a computer engineer.

Database Programmers and Other Superstars

Very busy Internet sites usually require several gifted database programmers. You are usually required to write software that is used to maintain your company's Web site. Does this sound like your cup of tea? If so, you'd better be talented at using UNIX, HTML, Perl, MODPERL, SQL, and CGI.

Not intimidated yet? Then try this on for size: For bonus points you should know the full range of UNIX system-level programming, including shared memory implementations. Being a star with socket-based protocols wouldn't hurt either.

Wealth of Knowledge

The Internet, and Internet-Related Programming, Changes Quickly!

The required areas of expertise that you need to land that fantastic engineering job could quickly change! Be sure that you keep abreast of all the various modifications in the world of engineering. You must be on the cutting edge of technology at all times. So, subscribe to that certain magazine, or surf the Internet often so that you keep up with all the many changes coming to the realm of Internet gurus.

Database engineers who really want to shine should be able to speak fluent Perl/C, and have strong, genius-level backgrounds in Linux and Solaris. You should be able to design handle architecture and the diagnosis of very complex databases. Your company's database needs might grow like a weed, so you should be able to factor scalability into your designs and infrastructures.

A complete understanding of message queuing, database concurrency, transaction processing, and related subjects will help make you that database superstar that you want to be.

Engineering Managers, Web Programmers, and Other Cool Cats

Somebody out there has to oversee the design and use of software applications for successful Internet companies. That person is usually an engineering manager. I would suspect that, as an engineering manager, you would find yourself working with an engineering team of five to ten engineers as you work toward creating a really cool software application. (But, if you end up making a time machine, let me know. I have a couple of vacation ideas.)

You had better figure that you will need to have experience in programming via C and experience with relational databases. It would be great if you spoke fluent Perl, too. No doubt you will have to work well with fixed schedules and have experience in successfully getting projects completed within tight deadlines.

Maybe being a Web programmer is more your style? If so, you should be able to prove that you live and breathe UNIX, XML, SQL, and Perl. Knowing how to keep CGI and UNIX programming secure would be a major plus. If you land this type of job, be prepared to keep control over databases that capture oodles of information.

Protecting Against Hackers

Network and systems engineers are also in short supply right now. These guys are often in charge of making sure that host and network security is state of the art, as well as making sure that all the required clusters, databases, code, and computers are running smoothly.

You will probably need to be able to think like a system cracker thinks because, as they say, it takes a thief to catch a thief. Your background needs to include heavy UNIX kernel and system experience, a vast understanding of TCP/IP and routing, as well as a gifted level of smarts about Apache, SQL, Perl, and C. You should probably be the kind of person who likes to read about crackers a great deal.

Even More Engineers, Even More Engineering Positions

Usability engineers often are members of Web development teams. Experience required for this type of employment should include Java, Perl, or UNIX backgrounds plus massive experience with JavaScript, Web page/site design, and HTML.

The basic design of your company's Web page will be part of your job, and you will no doubt work closely with visual designers, Web artists, and engineers to be sure that your company's Web presence is top notch and on the cutting edge.

Expect to jump from one quickly paced project to another as a usability engineer. The Internet moves quickly and you will have to move even quicker to stay caught up.

UNIX systems programmers handle data warehousing, database concurrency, and data management. The very highest skills in Perl and C systems and applications will be required to land one of these jobs at most successful, commercial Web sites.

Plus, the UNIX systems programmers need a very strong skill set in (whew, hold tight) UNIX, IPC, TCP/IP stack, threading, scheduling, caching, IO, sockets, Perl, networking, and even more. And when I say UNIX, I mean Linux, Solaris, and FreeBSD, my friend. Oh, knowing XML, NFS, and SQL wouldn't hurt, either.

Keeping All Those Engineers in Line

Engineering departments also usually need project managers. Now, they are not engineers, precisely, but rather people who help coordinate the engineers' activities with workers from other parts of the company, and help to keep engineering projects on task.

Deadlines have to be met in the real world, and project managers keep a weather eye on deadlines. You will be expected to tell jokes whenever appropriate, keep smiling in the face of engineering setbacks, and be sure that the engineers remember to eat at least once a day. (Mainly, they seem to survive on Doritos dipped in Jolt.)

Expect to maintain a communication line between marketing and sales departments so that the engineers stay on the project designed and don't wander off to build a time machine. (If they do build a time machine, please give me a call. Always remember that I want a time machine.)

Someone Has to Make the Software

Mars might need women, but Internet companies need software engineers. How come? To help build all those fun Web sites that we all love to go to—like `Rodney's-Time-Travel-Vacation-to-Ancient-Greece.org`.

Wealth of Knowledge

Proven Experience Rules!

Your experience as an engineer is currently much more important than having a degree in a particular engineering field. Why? Because of the shortage of engineers, companies seem willing to snap up clever employees regardless of whether they have a university degree or not. This might change in the future, of course, but for the present don't let a lack of a degree keep you from shopping for a job. Many engineers continue to finish their formal studies part time while earning big dollars in the here and now. Others just retire after four years on the job and buy a hotel in Manhattan or something.

As a software engineer, you'd better have a proven track record building Web sites that include CGI scripts and such. What else do you need to know? How about Linux, Perl, SQL and mySQL? Access commands, databases and more should be something that your brain adores. Raw, unassisted HTML should also be one of your favorite things in the whole, wide world.

Oracles Are Present and We Are Nowhere Near Ancient Greece

Oracle database programmers are always welcome at most major Internet companies. If you want to label yourself an Oracle guru you will need to be a wiz-bang-star at PL/SQL, Perl with DBI, C/C++, and Java. Plus, they might make you wear some sort of robe and mumble incomprehensibly about the future.

Oracle data warehouse administrators work with large Oracle databases and need to know the latest versions of Oracle that operate on massive Sun platforms. RAID device configuration, backup and recovery plans, and Oracle instance and query tuning knowledge are musts. If this sounds easy, remember that you have to keep from tripping when you walk in that silly Oracle robe that they will make you wear.

Can You Draw Blinky? Walking the Design Path to Glory

Graphic artists are currently in demand, too. For the most part, your art brushes will be replaced with Photoshop; your easels will be replaced by Illustrator or Freehand. Because graphics can really cause speed issues on the Internet, you will have to know how to keep your image files lightweight.

You should be very experienced in HTML, as such knowledge is absolutely required regarding the construction of Web pages. Macromedia Flash is becoming more and more popular, so you should bone up on that, as well.

If you are very familiar with both computer graphics and HTML, you might be able to land a job as a Web developer. Here you'd not only be in charge of the graphics that make your Web site magical but, also, the integration of the graphics into the overall Web design. As an artist, you will be entitled to wear a beret, if you want.

Web operations people work in HTML, UNIX, and Perl to be sure that the whole Web site works smoothly and doesn't turn upside down in the middle of the night. I think this job also entitles you to wear a beret, but you should ask that up front at your job interview. I wouldn't want you to be disappointed.

The Internet World Requires People Other Than Engineers

If you aren't an engineer or an HTML wizard, will you starve to death while you look for work? Nope.

All businesses, particularly successful Internet businesses, require the traditional host of support people. Accountants must keep books, writers must write content, advertising guys have to think up advertising plans, and financial wizards must deal with money issues. Lawyers, of course, must torture people in some fashion or their hair falls out. The more successful the Internet business becomes, the more it will need to hire such typical corporate employees.

Large Internet companies need industrial engineers, sales superstars, human resource gurus, marketing geniuses, and even janitors. The right job, like the truth, is out there. I know you'll be able to find it.

All these jobs, except janitor, might be able to qualify you to join a company early enough to be deemed a founder. It all depends on what the owner of the company needs during the company's very early days. (If the company, however, is called JanitorialSupplies.com, then I might be wrong about that janitor remark.)

Be a People Person

Many startups are founded by folks who are techno-saavy but awkward around human beings. They often need someone who can deal with suppliers, customers, and investors without being confusing, off-putting, or shy. Sometimes they don't know they need someone like this, but if you present yourself, they could see the value to it. (It does help if you speak a little geek-speak, as you might have to translate at times.)

The Multiple Threat: Jack of All Trades, Will Trade for Stock Options

The multiple-threat sort of worker can be a tempting morsel for the starving CEO of a brand new Internet company. Are you pretty good at HTML and fairly good at Perl? Are you willing to learn? Do you mind doing about 20 different jobs a day, from opening boxes of computers and setting them up to writing a few lines of code?

Often startups are so poor that they are more than willing to allow somebody to, well, if not work for food, to at least work for very little. So, are you brave, slightly skilled, but a hard worker?

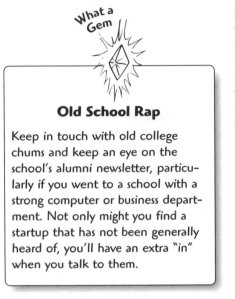

Old School Rap

Keep in touch with old college chums and keep an eye on the school's alumni newsletter, particularly if you went to a school with a strong computer or business department. Not only might you find a startup that has not been generally heard of, you'll have an extra "in" when you talk to them.

If so, you might become a very rich founder. As time goes by, and the company gets bigger and richer, you will find more experienced workers ending up getting the managerial, directorial, and vice-presidential positions. But that's okay, because you'll be sitting there at your desk smiling on the inside because you were an *early adopter* and are, well, richer than most small nations.

Finding an Internet Company While It Is Still Poor

Actually, finding a company that is poor is probably a very easy thing to do. Finding a company that is poor but will shortly be wealthy might be the tricky part!

Timing is everything, dear reader. When you read about a successful Internet company because the CEO is on the cover of *Time* Magazine as Man of the Year, well, it will be too late for you to become a founder. Oh, you might be able to still get a job if you qualify for an open position, but I doubt you'll get rich.

But, before the CEO was on the cover of *Time*, he probably got some major coverage in the prominent computer magazines. Oops! You'd probably be too late, then, as well.

The right answer here is to find the company when a few people are talking about it.

The early people who find jobs in the beginning days of a soon-to-be-successful Internet company won't find those jobs listed in the local want ads. You'll have to hunt them down yourself by keeping an eye on the Internet via magazines or by surfing the World Wide Web. Of course, if you are very lucky, one of your friends will have a tip for you. It wouldn't be a bad idea to build your list of friends who are hip to the Internet.

When You Hear About It, It's Not Necessarily Too Late

People are a little, well, uninformed sometimes. I've known certain founders of multibillion-dollar companies who have gone to cocktail parties after they've made a killing on Wall Street and were surprised at how many people hadn't heard of the company that they helped to start.

"You work for who? Never heard of it."

Heroic History

Monster: Employed for Employment

Web site name: Monster.com

Founded: 1994

Service provided: Job search and personnel search

Business model: Monster.com offers prospective job-seekers the chance to search through more than 100,000 available jobs, and to post their résumés in the résumé database. All this is free to the applicant. The prospective employers pay money to post their job listings and to advertise to the people whose résumés suggest they would be useful. To entice a larger number of job-seekers (who are, in this case, the product being sold), Monster offers career-oriented chat and expert job-hunting advice. This set-up is of particular interest to companies with high-tech needs, as high-tech job seekers are the most likely to be on the Web, and thus able to post their résumés. In addition, high-tech employees have a particularly high turnover rate (a rate that the presence of something like Monster.com can only add to). The site (which has been supported by a very effective TV ad campaign) is so eager to entice folks into seeking jobs that when a human resources employee goes online to find out about using Monster.com to fill personnel needs, they are also offered the chance to search for a human resources job with another company!

Where the money came from: Monster.com, as it currently exists, is actually a combination of two earlier sites: The Monster Board, and The Online Career Center. Both were purchased in 1995 by TMP Worldwide, a major advertising company with a strong base in yellow pages and classified ads.

Those uninformed people are a bit sad, aren't they? I know that you don't want to be like them. What you have to do is to keep a very close eye on the Internet. The best way to do this is to read the major Internet-related magazines. Don't concentrate on the major stories, but rather, the small news articles about minor businesses.

If you are lucky, you will encounter a news blurb about an Internet start-up company that has only three or four employees. Give the owner a call. If the company is local, go and have lunch with the guy. If you are very lucky, you might have discovered a company on the verge of a breakthrough. Maybe you can figure out a way to join the team.

The point is, when you read a small bit in a magazine or newspaper about an Internet company, you still might have time to join the team before they hit it big.

Remember that the founders of a successful company are the ones that join before the company's future is secure. Sure, finding the right company can be very difficult and can require a great deal of luck.

You have to become a detective of sorts, nosing for clues in every possible source in your effort to find just the right company to join if you want to try to be a founder. Or, you have to meet just the right visionary as he is just starting out.

After the company has made it rich, you won't be able to make the big bucks in stock options unless you have the special credentials that the company requires. Very special credentials, indeed.

You can learn a great deal about how to successfully launch an Internet e-business by reading the major business- and Internet-related magazines that are available. Figure 7.1 features LYCOshop where you can order your favorite magazines online.

Figure 7.1

LYCOShop: Where you can order your favorite magazines from the comfort of your own home, found at shop.lycos.com.

For Further Info

The following list includes some of the Internet-oriented magazines you should be reading to see where the new startups are coming from:

➤ *Red Herring* is a very business-oriented new technology magazine.

➤ *Upside* is a business technology publication concentrating on the leading and up-coming digital companies.

➤ *PC Computing* is a good magazine to learn about emerging technologies.

➤ *PC Magazine* is the primo resource spot to learn about things that interest computer professionals.

➤ *Yahoo! Internet Life* gives you a bird's eye view on what's happening on the Internet.

➤ *Web Guide* seeks out high-quality Web sites and tells you all about them.

➤ *e-Business Advisor* gives you the technical advice that you might need to make your online business a success.

➤ *Wired* is, according to them, "daring, compelling, innovative, courageous, and insightful." I think so, too. You'll find this magazine to be a powerful guide to e-businesses and more.

The Least You Need to Know

➤ Founders of Internet companies come from all types of backgrounds, but are mostly engineers.

➤ Gung-ho office workers and general support people can become founders.

➤ Corporate executives with impressive backgrounds can join a company after it has hit the big time and still do very well.

➤ Finding the right Internet start-up company will take research, detective work, and no small degree of luck.

Empowering Yourself

This is for all us normal people. We know that we really, really, want to get rich on the Internet, but would rather do it the easy way by jumping on someone else's team. Okay, so maybe we aren't true visionaries of e-commerce. We are pretty darn sure that we lack the ability to come up with a billion-dollar Internet biz idea all by ourselves. But, we highly suspect that we are smart enough to spot a great business idea when we see one.

So, what do we want? We want to work for the next Bill Gates and get rich doing it. That's right. That's what we want. But we also know that we want to get that special job just as the next Bill Gates is starting out. Let's assume that right this instant there is a brilliant visionary who is laboring away all by himself in his small garage. You want to be his first employee, right? Or maybe his fifth or sixth employee, but the point is you want to get on his team as early as possible.

However, it might be helpful if you had a way to evaluate the potential for success regarding someone else's vision of Internet wealth.

So, how do you accomplish this? Let's give it some thought.

Ruling Out Ideas

The Internet is your greatest resource for finding a starting point. Do you have any special interests in an area? This doesn't have to be something that you are currently working in. For example, maybe you are working a dull day job right now as a Superior Court Judge and giving nasty looks all day to innocent attorneys who are just trying to make an honest living. Really what you would much rather be doing is teaching people how to fly fish, for example.

So you surf around the Web and look at all the fly-fishing Web sites that you can find. Maybe you find a fantastic fly-fishing Web site that isn't doing very well financially but seems to show a great deal of promise.

You think about the fly-fishing Web site day and night for a while. Maybe this little site isn't doing very well right now but with a few changes it could be doing a lot better.

So what do you do? You start out by contacting the owner of the Web site. Drop him an email. Nearly every Web site has an email link so that you can contact the owner. So, you contact the guy behind the fly-fishing home page and you learn that his name is Gerry.

You end up spending quite a few hours trading emails for a while and go from that to calling one another on the phone.

"Friend," he says, "you have many fine ideas for my Web site, but I lack the capital to bring them about. Why don't we partner up?"

You think about it for a while, but then you go to your computer and try something. You type flyfishing.com just to see what you find. And what you find is a pretty cool fly-fishing Web site that already exists (and it does). Dang, you think, somebody already beat us to it.

Visionary ideas almost never concern something that somebody else is already doing. Be very wary of jumping on a team that is attempting to duplicate someone else's success.

Be hard on the ideas that others have. Try to look at any prospective business plan from all possible angles. You must carefully weigh how successful the business idea is before you put your money, talent, or efforts behind someone else's vision.

This is particularly true when you are joining a new, unproven business that has no operating capital. Of course, this is where *founders* come from. (Founders are people who start a startup from the very beginning.) Risk can equal fortune in the Internet. It can also equal disaster.

Is the Idea Truly New?

When you consider joining someone else just as he is creating his new Internet business, ask yourself this: "Is this business truly a fresh, new idea?"

You should always start out by going to the World Wide Web to conduct a search to see if any other businesses are out there on the Internet in the same *space*. That is, to see if anyone else is conducting the same or a similar type of business as the one that you are interested in developing.

If his business deals with *whatever,* see if there is already a *whatever.com*—because you really don't want to run a business called *whatever-me-too.com*, if you can help it.

If the Internet business idea isn't original, what then? Then you need to decide if there is a chance that significant improvements in the Web site can transform it into the number-one Web site in your space. Domain names carry great power, but good management can also lead to success even with a second-best domain name.

There is always room for a business that can enter a space and do a far better job than the previously existing competition. However,

What's an Internet Space?

When people talk about working in the same *space,* they aren't talking about outer space, but rather cyberspace. If you open a bookstore on the Internet, you would be operating in `Amazon.com`'s space. Space is just a way of describing a type of business on the Internet. If you are the first to create a type of Internet business, you will be the sole company in that space. If competitors begin to adopt your idea, you could state that *other companies are operating in my space.*

attacking a previously established competitor usually takes quite a bit of capital, lots of new ideas, and some serious intestinal fortitude. If you are going to act like a Viking and attempt to pillage a village of pre-established Internet businesses, you had better be ready to fight hard to establish your toehold.

Here's an eternal truth for you to consider. The Internet contains as much competition as any other area of business, maybe more. If you have a very successful Internet business, you might find yourself attacked on all sides by those who want to come into your space. Original, first-run, killer businesses on the Internet soon find themselves plagued by Johnny-come-lately competitors who want a piece of their space pie.

Honest competition is the American way of doing business. Whether you are trying to join an already successful business space on the Internet or create a new business space, competition with rival Internet companies will likely play a major (and sometimes distressing) part of your business life.

If you want experts to help you evaluate your Internet business idea, you might want to consider becoming involved with an incubator, which I'll discuss later in this chapter. First, let's take a look at how you can search for a job at a preexisting Internet company.

Searching the (Internet) Want Ads

In the old days, when you wanted to find a new job, you got the local newspaper and began to search the classified ads looking for a suitable help-wanted notice. Or, you might find yourself hiring a *head hunter*, an expert in finding people jobs. There are similar activities now happening on the Internet.

Let's take a look first at HotJobs.com. This Web site specializes in helping people find work at a variety of companies. They call themselves the experienced professional's job board.

Here you can search out information about new companies and obtain information about career fairs that might be coming soon to your town. At a career fair you will be able to meet representatives from numerous businesses that are looking to hire employees with certain backgrounds.

HotJobs.com enables you to search for jobs by location, job type, or company. It also gives you a personalized "My HotJobs" page which allows you to better control your job search. You'll find that this Web site makes it very easy for you to apply online for that new job that you would like to land. You can take a look at the HotJobs.com home page in Figure 8.1.

Figure 8.1

Search for work on the Internet at HotJobs.com*!*

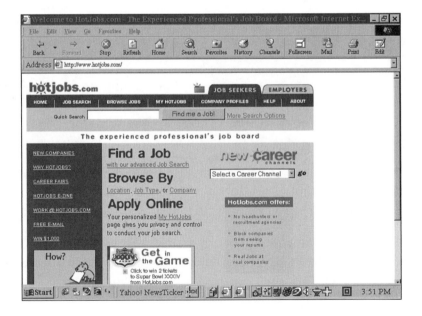

Heroic History

HotJobs: You Work, It Makes Money

Web site name: www.hotjobs.com

Founded: February 1997

Service provided: Job search

Business model: HotJobs tempts professionals and high-tech employees with its large library of lucrative available jobs from thousands of employers. Searching its database and applying for the jobs online costs a prospective employee nothing. HotJobs charges the employers membership fees for listing their jobs, a price which the employers are glad to pay because HotJobs not only gives them access to a steady stream of qualified candidates, it also allows them to list jobs much more quickly than traditional print advertising outlets. On-site ad sales (primarily to particularly eager employers), job fairs, consulting services, and licenses of a recruiting software package generate additional income.

Where the money came from: HotJobs went public on August 10, 1999, offering up three million shares in the company for eight bucks apiece. When it offered up another 3.6 million shares three months later, they were at a price of $30 each. As of January 19, 2000, the stock was trading at $34 5/8 per share, giving the business a market capitalization of just more than one billion dollars. The stock trades on the Nasdaq market under the symbol HOTJ.

JobSearch.com offers a similar service. In association with Headhunter.net, it boasts that it offers fresh jobs everyday. Specifically it offers listings of jobs in the Internet, as well as computer, engineering, sales, accounting, marketing, and other types of employment. This Web site offers both a listing of jobs, broken into categories, and a listing of résumés, also broken into like categories. You can get a glimpse of the JobSearch.com home page in Figure 8.2.

Just to be sure that this book stays on the cutting edge, we are going to tell you about a job-hunting Web site that is so new it isn't even up and running at the time this book is being written. However, you should find it ready to serve you by the time that this book is shipped to your friendly, neighborhood bookstore. InternetJobs.com is scheduled to open for business on February 1, 2000. It will offer careers for the new economy.

Figure 8.2

Both job hunters and companies looking to hire new help should check out JobSearch.com!

What's this *new economy* stuff? Well, Internet jobs, along with certain other high-tech jobs such as the telecommunications industry, are now being touted as making up a new economy. What's the *old economy*? Well, businesses such as traditional printers, steel mills, and taxi-cabs, I guess. These guys at InternetJobs.com must think that the new economy is where it's at for clever job hunters. Who are we to argue? We think that they are right! Figure 8.3 gives you an example of what InternetJobs.com's home page looks like.

Figure 8.3

A brand new place to find an Internet job!

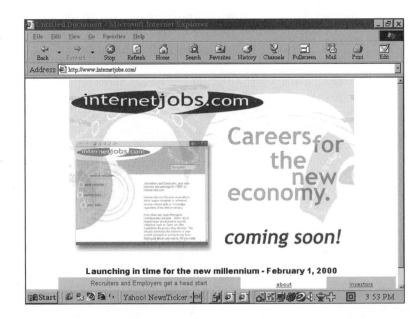

Incubators: No Room for Chickens

Do you think that you have a great idea for an Internet company? Want to get some expert advice? Good. Welcome to the world of Internet incubators.

In the pre-Internet use of the word, an incubator was a warming device that helped chicks survive and grow up to become chickens. In Internet-speak, an *incubator* is a company that helps baby Internet companies grow up to become successful, thriving businesses.

They don't help all baby Internet companies, of course, only the ones that show exceptional promise. And, they do exact some sort of price, usually a percentage of ownership in the infant Internet company. They might even want to purchase the company outright.

Let's take a close look at one particular Internet incubator called eCompanies.com.

According to information that it has posted on its Web site, eCompanies.com believes that despite the amazing growth the Internet has already achieved…only about 20% of its applications have been invented. This is nothing less than an industrial revolution, where powerful new brands and the companies behind them are being created in months instead of decades. And most of the companies that will exist 100 years from now have not even been invented yet. That's something I can't argue with. These are exciting times to be alive.

eCompanies.com believes that there are more good Internet ideas in existence than there are talented people who can execute those ideas. eCompanies.com hopes to solve that problem by putting the right people together with the right Internet business concepts.

Two guys by the name of Sky Dayton and Jake Winebaum created eCompanies.com. Sky had already founded EarthLink while at Disney, Inc., and Jake built and ran various Internet businesses such as Disney.com, ABCNews.com, and Go.com.

Sounds to me like a partnership made in heaven.

Nat Speaks

I Predict the Future Will Be Unpredictable

History is laden with good, responsible people who figure that technology has reached its limit. There have been patent officers who expect the patent office to close down due to lack of business, and early computer manufacturers who felt that the worldwide market for computers could be counted on one hand. There were even folks who thought there would be no more great applications for personal computers— before the Web was invented. People who tell you that we have nowhere to advance just have too little imagination. Count on advancement occurring, but don't count on anyone knowing exactly what that advancement will be. Seers of science have a poor track record. I mean, we're living in the year 2000, *where's my hovercar?!*

Jake and Sky's eCompanies.com exists to help launch Internet startups. Operating as an incubator, it provides services from a wide range of needed areas, such as finance, design, technology, and marketing. Jake and Sky's personal areas of expertise are augmented from blue-chip executives in each (needed) discipline, so entrepreneurs can tap not just Sky and Jake's expertise, but a whole team of Internet veterans who have done it before.(Take a look at Figure 8.4 to see an example of eCompanies.com's Web site.)

Figure 8.4

An incubator for suitable Internet startups!

Understanding Internet Speed

eCompanies.com provides the initial management team for suitable startups. Understanding the need to get a business up and running as soon as possible in the quickly moving world of the Internet, it strives to take no more than six months to get a business from concept to actively operating on the Internet.

It plans to help up to eight companies a year move through their incubator process. Afterwards, successful graduate companies might obtain financing from eCompanies Venture Group, the venture capital arm of eCompanies.com.

You can learn a lot more about business incubation at the Web site produced by the National Business Incubation Association. It's located at nbia.org. We've provided you with an example of the Web page in Figure 8.5.

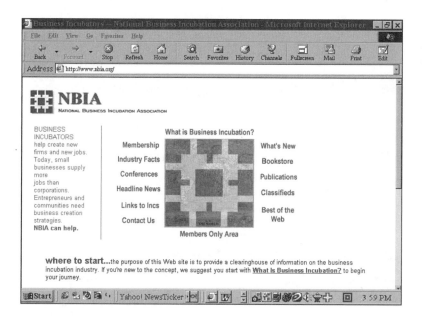

Figure 8.5

Learn a lot more about business incubators from the NBIA!

Doing Further Research on Your Own

There are various locations on the World Wide Web that exist to help you become successful in the Internet world of business. You might want to start researching the various elements of e-commerce that fascinate you. The idea here is for you to learn as much as you can so that you can find a start-up company or an already-established company to join! Or learn what you need to know to launch your own business!

Let's take a look at some of the resources that the Internet offers to further your studies:

➤ ClickZ.com touts itself as "The ultimate resource for doing business online." Here you will find many informative articles, commentary, and services. See Figure 8.6 for an example of its Web site.

➤ AllEC.com features information on business strategy, news, and resources.

➤ TheStandard.com is an online news magazine that covers Internet companies, personalities, and exciting new business models. (And, no, we aren't talking about Cindy Crawford.)

➤ WebMarketingToday.com centers on nearly every aspect of doing business on the Internet. Here you'll find thousands of links to needed e-commerce resources.

➤ Builder.com provides a rich resource of Internet business-related articles and links.

105

Figure 8.6

Expand your Internet business knowledge at ClickZ.com*!*

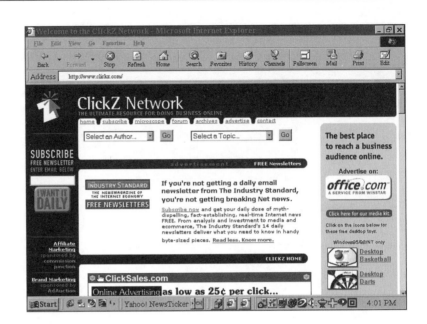

Approaching Businesses Directly

Most well-established Internet businesses have a link somewhere on their Web site that will provide you with a list of their job opportunities. If you want to work for a company with a proven track record, I encourage you to see what jobs are open and contact the company directly. You can usually fill out a job application right online!

If you are interested in a job with an unproven startup, you probably won't find a job listing on its Web page. The owner is no doubt so busy building his business that he hasn't started recruiting employees. For those companies you will have to email the company directly, telephone the owner of the Web site, or make an appointment to drop by and speak to the owner of the Internet business in person. Good luck!

Heroic History

eBay: A Cut of Others' Sales

Web site name: eBay.com

Founded: 1995

Service provided: eBay manages online auctions, allowing just about anyone to auction off just about anything.

Business model: People with things to sell use eBay's forms to post information about their items on the site. At this point, eBay charges them a listing fee, and offers the seller additional attention-getting listing services for a further fee. Over a set period of time (usually about a week), would-be bidders can find the item up for auction using any number of methods for searching through the huge number of auctions that are running on eBay at the time. Using the online software, they can place bids on any items, with eBay tracking how their maximum bid compares to other bidders for the item. After the auction is complete, both bidder and seller are sent contact information for one another, and eBay charges the seller a percentage of the sale price. The percentage is a sliding scale, reducing as the sale price increases. The site has a registered user base of more than five million buyers and sellers, and has hosted more than 50 million auctions. It has had a visible impact on the collectibles market. It has also expanded its brand to the newsstands via *eBay Magazine*.

Where the money came from: eBay is that rare gem among the big sites: It's actually making a direct net profit from its activities. It went public in September 1998, with a an IPO offered at $18 per share. In March of 1999, there was a three-for-one stock split. As of January 20, 2000, each split share of stock was worth $150 7/8, giving the company a market capitalization of $19.5 billion. The stock trades under the symbol EBAY on the Nasdaq market.

The Least You Need to Know

➤ You must carefully evaluate your Internet business idea before you start your own company.

➤ Internet business incubators exist to help evaluate and launch your business but the costs might be substantial.

➤ Job searches at existing Internet companies are fairly easy to accomplish via the Internet.

Chapter 9

Domain Is De Name

In This Chapter

➤ Pick a name for your Web site

➤ Purchase your name

➤ Protect your name

A *domain name* is your main address on the Internet. For example, I own gertler.com as a domain name. That means that when you go to gertler.com (or www.gertler.com or baldguy.gertler.com or any other address that ends with .gertler.com) on the Web, you're going to my Web site. It also means that all the email addresses that end with @gertler.com (such as uglyguy@gertler.com, baldguy@gertler.com, or incrediblehunkylovemachine@gertler.com) are under my control.

Picking a Name (But Not Any Name)

The domain name you choose for your Web site is very important. Your domain name is going to define your company in the mind of the people who use the site. A well-chosen name can be memorable, informative, and even intriguing. A poorly chosen name will be forgettable. If people forget the name of your Web site, they won't go there in the first place—and if they do happen to make it there once, odds are they won't be able to make their way back.

Very Topical Domain Names

A *topical domain name* is one that makes it very clear what the site offers. If you saw a bumper sticker for cdnow.com, or cheaptickets.com, or freedonuts.com, you would have a pretty good idea what that site has to offer. Better still, with something like cookbooks.com, people don't even need to know that there is such a site to find it. Some people will just try typing **cookbooks** into the URL field of their Web browser, and some browsers will take that to mean that the user wants to go to www.cookbooks.com.

The bad news is that if you're selling just about anything reasonably basic (or anything else that's a single word), somebody probably already owns the name. They aren't necessarily actually using the name to do business under. *Cybersquatters* are people who buy domain names hoping that someone else will want them later, and will pay them a huge markup to get the name. It is sad to have to pay that extra sum (after all, this cybersquatter didn't add any value to the name; all they did was hoard it for a while); however, sometimes it can be worth it. There's more information later in this chapter about finding out who owns a name and buying it from them.

Some people point to online music source mp3.com as a good example of a topical site name. *MP3* is the nickname of a popular format for downloadable music. The term might not mean a lot to you, but there were a lot of people looking for MP3 files, and by purchasing the right domain name, site president Michael Robertson had a bit of leverage that helped build a company worth billions from practically nothing in just a couple of years. (Because someone had already registered the mp3.com domain, Michael had to pay out a few extra bucks to buy the domain from the registree. He would later tell *Forbes* magazine "My wife said I was crazy paying $1,000 for two consonants and a number.")

Very Untopical Domain Names

Some sites take a very different direction to picking a name. For example, what does yahoo.com have to offer? Judging from the name, they'd sell chocolate drink (no, wait, that would be yoohoo.com; a *yahoo* is an ill-mannered person, and there are so many of those on the Internet that you could never restrict them just to one site). When yahoo.com started, it was an index to the Web, and the founders could have picked a generic name like webindex.com. When they started adding features to their site, however, this name would have been a poor fit. You wouldn't want to buy plane tickets from webindex.com or go there for free email service, any more than you'd want to buy donuts from Muffler City. Picking a name that doesn't tie you down to any one product or service lets you keep your options for growth wide-open.

The biggest online retailer is Amazon.com, which started as an online bookstore. It's never sold a single Amazon, neither the river nor the fierce female warriors who bear that name. But the lack of the term *books* in the title means that it has been able to expand unhindered into other products, including CDs, videos, and even services such as online auctions.

Heroic History

MP3.com: Big Money from Free Music

Web site name: MP3.com

Founded: 1996 as The Z Company; MP3.com site established November 1997.

Service provided: Downloadable and streaming music in the MP3 compression format.

Business model: MP3.com's primary income comes from onsite advertising. The site's main content is provided free by musicians who are generally seeking to expand their exposure or sales. More than 40,000 musical acts have posted hundreds of thousands of recordings on MP3.com. The site fleshes out this content with commentaries by the site founder (see Figure 9.1), discussion groups, and coverage of MP3-related products. MP3.com also generates income through sales of CDs by its artists. These CDs are made to order. The company has sought to take advantage of its recognizable brand name and its large user and artist database in other ventures, as seen by its purchase of concert ticketing site SeeUThere.com.

Where the money came from: The company received several infusions of venture capital before going public in 1999 with an initial public offering of 12.3 million shares offered at $28 apiece. As of December 30, 1999, the company had a total market capitalization of $2.2 billion. MP3.com trades under the symbol MPPP on the Nasdaq exchange.

Figure 9.1

Michael Robertson, the Main Man behind MP3.com Mania!

Having an untopical domain name can be harder at the start (you're going to need more than just a bumper sticker to tell people what your site does), but it does indeed have some long-term advantages. Even if you choose to go with a name that specified your product (allmycookbooks.com, for example), you might want to also get the rights to a similar, less-specific name (allmystuff.com) which you migrate to later on.

Making a Deposit in the Memory Banks

If people are interested in your site, word will spread. Your site will be mentioned in magazine articles, in people's conversations, on radio shows—all sorts of places where people are being exposed to your name without having that name right in front of them. It would be a shame if, when they sit down to their computer, they can't remember the name.

The best way to keep your site name memorable is to keep it short (no more than two words) and to make sure it builds an image in people's minds. If you and your two friends were to get together and name your site aliceandbobanddana.com, you'd miss a lot of your audience. Even if people heard of the site, they'd end up typing in aliceandbillanddonny.com or something else that is similar to your site name, but not exactly the same. However, if you named your site bigpeanut.com, people will remember it. When they hear the term, they'll think of a big peanut, and when they go to type the name, they'll remember that image of a big peanut and type it correctly. In fact, you could even use pictures of a huge peanut in your ads to help keep it in people's minds.

Spellling Is Important!

There are some things that are just tough to spell. If a person can't spell your Web site name, he won't be able to visit your site. If your Web site is for an online comic strip about a soldier named George, for example, you probably won't have any trouble if the site is PrivateGeorge.com or GeneralGeorge.com. Oh, there will always be some people who will misspell any word, but you'll lose fairly few readers that way. You will, however, lose a lot of potential readers if George happens to be a Colonel or a Lieutenant, two words that are far easier to misspell than to spell correctly.

In the interest of "spellability," you also want to avoid cutesy spellings. Dan's Kountry Kitchen might be a cute name for a restaurant, but people aren't going to remember that K-for-C trick when they go online (or, worse, they'll try to go to danskountrykitchen.kom!) My brother has a fine online car review site at hardrive.com, but every time I hear him explain that it's "Hard Drive but with one D," I flinch. He's lost a lot of effort in explaining the name and probably lost a fair number of visitors to the site.

Infringe in Haste, Be Sued at Leisure

There is actually a very quickly growing and messy body of law surrounding the use of trademarked names as part of domain names. Between written laws, case law, and the policies of the companies that handle the domain name business, you're best off trying to steer clear of any name that anyone else has trademarked. This is true even if the product you make doesn't compete with the trademarked product at all. Companies have a watchful eye out for anyone who includes their valuable trademarks in domain names, whether or not it's done for profit, and whether or not there is any real risk of confusion. Odds are that if you get the site dyspepsia.com, Pepsi probably won't sue you—but if they wanted to, they would actually have at least some legal ground.

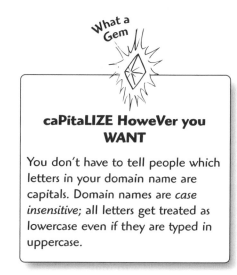

If you decide to go ahead with a name that might possibly cause an infringement issue, be sure that you have a trademark lawyer check your position carefully. More importantly, be sure that your lawyer is conversant specifically with the laws surrounding domain names. There are actually restrictions to domain names that aren't the same as restrictions on using the same name as a magazine title, for example.

Negative Associations

You should be careful about possibly picking a name that has negative connotations for some people. Terms which one person views as positive or strong might have strong negative overtones for others. Names which reference military or weaponry, historical figures, or religion are apt to rankle some of your would-be site visitors.

With the worldwide nature of the Web, you might be aiming for an international audience. With that in mind, you should consider steering clear of terms that have accidental meanings in other languages. The legendary example of this is the international marketing of the Chevrolet automobile called the *Nova*; in Spanish, *no va* means *doesn't go*. If you're planning on using the same site name worldwide, run it by a few people who are familiar with other languages and cultures.

You also have to watch out for words that run together badly. The folks at The Original Lumberman's Exchange probably didn't see any problem with getting lumbermansexchange.com as their Web address—but some members of the national media sure had fun pointing out that the name ends with *sex change*. If that's really the image they want to project to their customers, then the forestry business is quite different than I've always imagined it to be!

What a Gem

Offend If You Want To

There's nothing wrong with picking a name that polarizes people, if that's what you mean to do. If you're competing in a large field, picking a name that will turn off 25% of your potential customer base but will act as a magnet to another 20% is worth it—getting 20% in a crowded field is quite an achievement. My favorite example of this is the folks at Guaranteed Overnight Delivery. Their trucks have their initials, GOD, in big letters on the side. Their phone number is 1-800-DIAL-GOD. I'm sure this turns off some potential customers who find it sacrilegious, but it guarantees that an awful large portion of people who see their trucks will remember them and might think of them when they need something delivered quickly. Similarly, I'm sure that folks who aren't comfortable with gay people wouldn't be comfortable with a site named gay.com, but because that site is aimed at gay people, it really doesn't matter what everyone else thinks. There's no point in changing the name of it to the more discreet confirmedbachelor.com.

Gotta Be Dot-com!

The letters after the last *dot* in a domain name are called the *top-level domain*. There are many different top-level domains, such as .edu for educational institutions, .mil for military sites, and a whole bunch of different ones that are accorded to different countries (.ca for Canada, .gr for Greece, and so on). The companies that have the right to register U.S.-oriented domain names sell them from three different top-level domains:

➤ .com is for commercial sites.

➤ .org is for nonprofit organizations.

➤ .net is for providers of online service.

These are really just guidelines; the people who handle the domain name registry don't actually check to see whether your site matches the description of the top-level domain it's under. Don't waste a lot of time thinking about which of these you want; the answer is you want .com no matter what sort of site you have.

Why? Because people recognize it and even expect it on a Web site. While there are plenty of .org and .net sites out there, the sites that most people deal with most of the time are all .com sites. If you tell them your site is bigpeanut.org, by the time they get home they're going to think it's bigpeanut.com anyway, and whoever owns that site will get the visitor that actually wanted to visit your site.

Better still, when people hear the term *dot-com*, they automatically know that it's a Web address. This is even true for people who aren't Web users. In the early days of the Web, many sites promoted themselves with a www. at the front of their domain name just to make it easier for people to recognize it as a Web address. Some even went so far as to read off the whole precise URL in their ads ("Just take your browser to *ach-tee-tee-pee-colon-slash-slash-doubleyou-doubleyou-doubleyou-dot-big-peanut-dot-com*"), but these days neither the Web browser nor the user needs that full descriptor.

You Don't Have a Hit If You Can't Make It Fit!

The section before the `.com` can't just be whatever you want. It's got to fit the following rules:

➤ It can't be more than 63 characters long. Sorry, but your dreams of owning `the-absolute-and-uncontested-greatest-site-in-the-whole-unbelievably-wide-world.com` will not become reality.

➤ The characters all have to be letters, numbers, or dashes. You can't use spaces or any other punctuation. So `big-peanut.com` is fine, but not `big peanut.com`, or `big-peanut+more.com`.

➤ The first and last characters cannot be dashes. So `minus-sign.com` is fine, but not `-sign.com` or `minus-.com`.

You really wouldn't want it to be longer than 63 characters anyway. That's an awful lot to expect a user to type without making a mistake!

Naming Consultants (No, Joe Nameth Isn't One)

If you don't have a blatantly great name for your site, and if you have the bucks to spare, you can hire a professional naming consultant to come up with the name for your site. A *naming consultant* specializes in coming up with names for products and services. They consider all the factors described previously, as well as a number of others. Many naming consultants also do logo development.

How much will a naming consultant cost? It depends largely on how much attention to detail you want. A good consultant can offer anything from the results of a simple brainstorming session to complex international investigation of the effect of the name with consumer research. The more rigorously you want your name checked, the more it will cost you.

Wealth of Knowledge

Naming Central

To find a directory of Web sites for naming consultants, surf on over to `http://dir.yahoo.com/Business_and_Economy/Companies/Marketing/Naming/`.

Getting the Name

Now that you know what name you want, it's time to actually get ownership of that name. Getting ownership is fairly cheap if no one has previously registered the name; the basic registration cost is $70 for the first two years, with a charge of $35 per year after that. If someone has already registered the name, however, you're going to have to contact him or her and negotiate the transfer.

Is It Available?

The first step is to find out whether anyone has already registered the name. To do this, surf over to Qwho.com. As you'll see in Figure 9.2, this site is designed to help you look up the owners of domain names.

Figure 9.2

Qwho is qwhat you qwant to use to find out qwho owns a qweb domain.

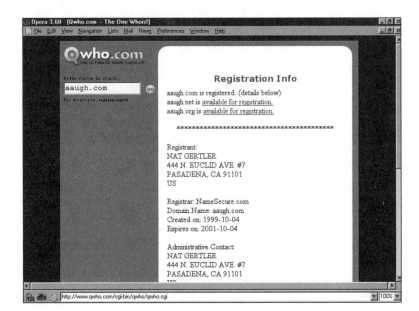

Type the domain name you're interested in, including the `.com` extension, into the lookup field and then click **Go**. If that domain is still available for registration, Qwho will tell you so. If someone owns that domain, Qwho will tell you who that person is.

Registration Station

Assuming that no one has already registered the name, pounce on it quickly! The process you'll use to register depends on what computer is going to *serve* (distribute) your Web pages.

➤ If you already have your own Web server set up in your offices, surf over to a Web registrar site to register your domain. (I recommend `namesecure.com` if you're registering a .com, .org, or .net site. For international extensions, try `networksolutions.com`.) You're going to need to have two *IP* (Internet Protocol) addresses for your server. Your Internet set-up geek should know them; they're just two strings of numbers.

➤ If you're renting space on the Web server of an Internet service provider (ISP), contact them. They will be able to take care of registration for you.

➤ If you don't have a Web server set up yet, or don't know what you'll be doing, you will want to *reserve* or *park* your domain. Reserving means that you own the domain name, but it's not pointed to any server yet. You can park your domain through namesecure.com. Parking means that you registered your domain, but it points to a single blank or simple Web page, which might display just the domain name and owner. Many ISPs will register and park your domain name for you, charging you only the registration cost. They do this hoping that when you actually do get your Web site set up, you'll rent Web server space from them. Some of the sites you can go to for this include www.midwestinternet.com, websolo.com, and coastline.com.

Save Your Fingers

Remember, you don't have to type in all the Web addresses in this book. Just surf over to www.MillionsOnTheInternet.com where you'll find links for all the sites discussed in the book.

"Someone's Taken My Name!"

If Qwho tells you that someone already owns the domain name you want, it's not time to panic! Take three easy, slow breaths. Feel better? Okay, now it's time to panic.

No, even that's not true. Even if someone else has already registered the name, the odds are good that they'll be willing to sell you the name. You'll just have to pay a bit more for it.

Print out the page of Qwho information. Included in this information is the name and phone number of the administrative contact for the site. Don't call this person yet—first, you want to know what they're doing with the domain name. Type the domain name into your Web browser's address field and see what comes up. You're likely to find one of the following things:

➤ **Nothing comes up** Your browser tells you that it could not find that Web page. This might mean that their server is not working at the moment, or it might be a domain that they only use for email, not for the Web. Odds are, however, that they aren't really using the domain name. The domain name was registered either because they might want to use it in the future, or they're hoarding it hoping that someone will want to buy it from them.

➤ **A page appears that advertises a domain parking service** This indicates that they've parked their domain name and aren't using it. Again, they registered the domain either for later use or with hopes of selling it.

➤ **The Web page advertises domain names that they have for sale**
You've found yourself a Web name hoarder. The name is available, but it might cost you.

➤ **A Web site appears, and it looks like it hasn't been updated in a year**
This is actually the best possible scenario. Someone owns the name, ran a Web site for a while, and then gave up on it. The owner might be willing to part with the name for around the same cost that he paid to register it, because it isn't worth anything to him at the moment. Of course, there is the risk that this user has already built a negative reputation around the site name, but the odds are that he failed because he didn't bother to build any reputation whatsoever.

➤ **A Web site appears, and it looks like it's a regularly updated, big-hit site**   This is the worst thing that can happen. It might still be possible to buy the site name, but you'll likely have to buy out the entire site to get it. You're probably better off finding a different name for your site.

Cheapskate Name Purchasing Tricks

Don't just call up and offer to pay the domain owner whatever he wants, unless all those piles of money are just cluttering up your living room. With a little careful work, you can save a lot of money.

If the name isn't actively being used, check the Qwho information. There will be an Expires On date. Domain name licenses have to be renewed two years after the initial registration and once a year after that. If someone was just hoarding the name, or had been using it and stopped, there is a good chance that they won't renew. If the expiration date is within the next month, you could just wait to see if they choose to renew it. If they don't, then you can register it yourself.

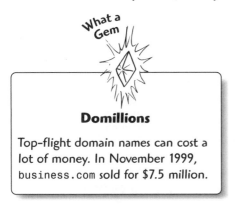

Domillions

Top-flight domain names can cost a lot of money. In November 1999, business.com sold for $7.5 million.

Barring that, if you want the name you're going to have to buy it. If you found a site advertising that those domains are for sale, that site will have the proper contact information there. Otherwise, use the Administrative Contact information from Qwho.

Domain name hoarders frequently don't have fixed, advertised prices. They want to get as much from the name as someone is willing to give them. Because of that, it's in your best interest to act not very interested. There are many times in starting up your Web site that you will want to act like your business is bigger than it is, but this is not one of those times. If the person who owns the domain thinks that this name is a key part of your plan to build a billion-dollar business, they're going to think nothing of asking you to pay $100,000 for the name. On the other hand, if they think you're just someone who is idly considering owning a few domain names for possible later use or resale, they might be willing to settle for a few hundred dollars of quick profit.

The first key to this is to represent yourself as an individual, not as a business. Maintain this throughout the deal; say "I'm interested in buying this domain name," not "we're interested." When the deal is done, have the domain name transferred over to you personally; after the seller is no longer involved, you can transfer it to your corporate identity. Don't ever give them a phone number that will reach a receptionist; use your personal phone number instead. (If you don't understand why you're doing this, imagine that you have a used car for sale, and a guy in jeans and a T-shirt asks you what your price is. You'd probably quote him a reasonable price with a little negotiating room. Now imagine that the same guy was wearing a three-piece suit, said that he worked for CBS, and that this was just the car they needed to build their new TV series around. Wouldn't you start thinking "Boy, I bet I could get more than a couple thou for this!"? I know I would. When trying to cut a deal for a domain name, which has no real fixed value, it's best to act like that jeans'n'T-shirt guy.)

If you can find out the names of some other domains owned by the same hoarder, do. (A true hoarder will likely have more than a hundred domains.) Pick two other names not related to the one that you actually want, and ask the prices for all three. This will make you look more like you're just a general dabbler, rather than someone with specific big-money plans.

After you get quoted a price, feel free to haggle it downward. Remember that this name didn't cost the hoarder more than $100. The hoarder is stuck with a bunch of names that no one is interested in that he's trying to make up for, in addition to making a profit. However, if you act willing to walk away from it and get a name elsewhere, you should be able to bring the price down significantly.

Before you even start haggling, however, you should decide how much that domain name is really worth to you. Have some specific financial figure in mind. If you can't haggle the asking price down to what you want to pay, walk away. There are always other domain names.

Nat Speaks

Guilt-Free Guile

Don't think twice about building a false impression in the mind of a domain hoarder. These people are bottom-feeders. They are trying to make profits not by improving anything or building anything, but merely by standing in-between you and the domain name that you want. (On the other hand, people who honestly intended to use that domain name deserve nice treatment!)

Pay Your Bill

Don't make the mistake of the obviously understaffed company that forgot to pay the renewal bill for passport.com. Not only were the site's basic functions unavailable, but the domain name was also being used for some of the functions of a free email system. This left some people unable to access their email, a horrible situation for a service that requires reliability. If some online good Samaritan hadn't paid the bill for this company, the site might have been down even longer. And what was this tiny company that could make such a huge mistake? Microsoft. You're never too big to make basic errors.

Checkmark Your Trademark

To quickly search the U.S. federal trademark database to avoid obvious conflicts with the trademarks of others, visit www.uspto.gov/tmdb on the Web...but be aware that a strong knowledge of trademark law is needed to really interpret the results.

Maintain Your Name!

If you registered your own domain name, it will be two years before you'll get a renewal notice. After that, you'll get billed for $35 each year for each domain name.

If you purchased a domain name, however, you have to be on your toes. Be sure that the name is properly transferred (the seller should contact InterNIC, which maintains the central registry, and have your name and address put in as the owner and for the administrative contact for the site), and then be prepared to renew the site much sooner. Remember, all the time the previous owner had that domain name, the initial two-year period was ticking away.

Protecting the Name

After you own the name, you have to protect it, like a jungle traveler must protect his stash of donuts from all the fierce donut-eating creatures that lurk in the bushes. If you're a success, there will be people looking to profit from your name in ways that could hurt your business. A little diligence up front might save you a lot of metaphorical donuts later on.

TMing It: Transcendental Trademarking

A *trademark* is a legally protected name that you can use to identify your business or brand. A proper legal trademark can keep other people from using your name (or blatant variations of your name) to do similar business.

Trademark law is a whole special branch of law filled with special concerns and loopholes. You can find a lawyer who can steer you through the trademarking process in the Yellow Pages under **Attorneys: Patent, Trademark, and Copyright Law**.

Coping with Missspelings

People are terrible typists and spellers. I mean, they're relatively good compared to most other members of the animal kingdom, but they still make a lot of mistakes. If they make a mistake while typing in your domain name, at best they end up nowhere. At worst, however, they end up at the site of your competitor, who has registered a common misspelling of your site name and directed it to their site. This is not good.

You should cover yourself by finding likely misspellings of your domain name and registering them as well. For a good example of this, consider the popular bookstore chain Barnes And Noble. If you try to look them up in the phone book, you won't have much trouble, even if you think of *Barnes* as being *Barns*, or of *Noble* as being *Nobel*, as in the famed Nobel Prize. When they put up the Web site, they knew people might misspell barnesandnoble.com. They were smart, and they also grabbed up the domains barnesandnobel.com and barnsandnoble.com, so if someone misspelled either name, they'd still get to the right site. (However, they didn't count on people misspelling both names; someone else snatched up barnsandnobel.com.) To make things easy on people who don't like typing that much, they also picked up bn.com.

How can you find out what spelling errors are likely? Easy. Call some friends on the phone, tell them the name of your site, and ask them to spell the name for you. If more than two people misspell it the same way, then you have a likely spelling error.

A spelling error occurs when someone simply doesn't know how something is spelled. A *typo* is when you know how something is spelled, but the wrong spelling rolls off your fingers (like when you mean to type **I report to the VP of Engineering** and accidentally type **I report to ol' weasel-nose**.)

Some of the most common styles of typos are

- ➤ Transposing (switching the order of) letters that are typed with different hands, such as typing **usper** instead of **super**.
- ➤ Accidentally taking a double letter (like the **l** in **silly**) and typing it either once (**sily**) or three times (**sillly**).
- ➤ Dropping a dot when typing in the URL. (You can cover some of the problems caused by this error by registering domains like wwwbigpeanut.com and, for some browsers, bigpeanutcom.com.)
- ➤ Dropping a letter that's at the far left or right side of the keyboard, such as **euipment** or **equiment** for the word **equipment**.

Again, the easiest way to predict these errors is to count on the incompetence of your friends. Ask them each to type your domain name 20 times without making any corrections, and see what they come up with!

Heroic History

Amazon: Earth's Largest Example

Web site name: Amazon.com

Founded: 1995 by Jeff Bezos

Service provided: Originally established as an online bookstore, Amazon has expanded to include a range of retail businesses, as well as providing access for other online retailers.

Business model: Amazon makes most of its income selling physical product. It is able to offer more than a million different books, most of which are not actually in stock but are ordered from the publisher (or from a used book source) when the customer places an order. Amazon also gains product sales through affiliate programs, allowing people to set up their own sites that essentially act as catalogs for Amazon; Amazon pays the affiliate a cut for all orders made through their catalog. Income also comes from charging for handling order information for other retailers (zStores) and through processing online auctions. It has also bought out or created a number of other online sites, such as imdb.com (The Internet Movie Database, a great reference site for film buffs) and PlanetAll.com (online address book and calendar service). It has significant investments in drugstore.com, Gear.com (sporting goods), HomeGrocer.com, and Pets.com.

Where the money came from: The company went public in May of 1997, releasing three million shares at an offering price of $18 each. The shares have split several times over the years. Each one of those original shares would be worth $948 as of December 30, 1999. The total market capitalization on that date was more than $26 billion. Amazon trades under the symbol AMZN on the Nasdaq exchange.

Connecting All the Dots

Another way to keep your options open and protect yourself from people exploiting your name is to register your name in different top-level domains. If you bought everyonelovesbeets.com, perhaps you should also grab onto everyonelovesbeets.net and everyonelovesbeets.org.

If your Web site has international possibilities, you should keep an eye on the world-wide market. Don't find yourself in the same position as Amazon.com, who found out that a Greek online bookstore registered amazon.gr (.gr being the top-level domain for Greece). Although Amazon.com was able to use the law to wrest away this challenge to their trademark, an ounce of prevention is worth a pound of cure. The folks at idNames.com can (for a fee) research the availability of your name at the various top-level domains throughout the world, and help you register in the countries that you feel are important. After all, the whole world loves beets!

For Further Info

There is a lot of information out there on domain names, trademarks, and naming in general. Here are just a few handy online publications to get you started (remember, you can find links to all of these at www.MillionsOnTheInternet.com).

➤ Some basic questions about domain names and registration are answered at www.networksolutions.com/help/general/general.html.

➤ The U.S. government has a sizable set of online publications at www.uspto.gov/web/menu/tm.html to inform you about trademarks.

➤ For specific information on trademarks as applied to domain names, see www.uspto.gov/web/offices/tac/notices/guide299.htm.

➤ A set of simple practical cautions about trademarks can be found at www.nameit.com/question.htm.

➤ Some naming companies have very interesting sites, which discuss naming theories and have interesting examples. Check out www.nametrade.com and www.metaphorname.com.

The Least You Need to Know

➤ Your domain name is the name of your site. Examples of domain names are yahoo.com and earthlink.net.

➤ Good domain names are memorable and easy to spell.

➤ If nobody else has registered or reserved the domain name you want, the name will cost you $35 per year, with two years paid up front.

➤ If someone else has obtained the name that you want, you'll have to find out who owns it (use Qwho.com) and negotiate with them.

➤ Protect your domain name by trademarking it and by registering likely variations on the name.

Chapter 10

The Venture Adventure

Venture Capital

What is venture capital? (Those of you who know are already salivating like Pavlov's slobbering dog at the mere sound of those two magical words.) *Venture capital* is when somebody gives you money to develop your company in exchange for an investment in your company.

Typically, you will need venture capital because you have no way to borrow enough money for your business through normal channels, such as from your friendly neighborhood Savings and Loan. In fact, if you go down to your favorite bank with your hand held out, you'll probably hear the words "high risk" a lot. Internet startups are often described as being high-risk investments. Success, remember, is never guaranteed for any Internet startup.

Yet, appropriate Internet startups do receive venture capital from investors. Commonly, the person or corporation who invests in your startup will receive stock in your corporation. But getting an actual loan from a venture capitalist isn't totally out of the picture.

In these days of *incubators* (companies that mix guidance with venture capital), you will find that venture capitalists might try to reduce their possible risk by having someone of their choice on your management team. Having a proven management team is one of the crucial elements of success for any company and is something that a venture capitalist will be very concerned about.

Do you have a startup that you intend to take public in a year or so? If so, and your startup looks promising to potential investors, you might have a suitable company to obtain significant venture capital.

P/E Isn't About Gym Clothes

A *price-earning ratio* is often referred to as a *P/E*. If you had a sudden dread of some mean coach making you duck-walk across the gym floor carrying a fat person on your back, don't panic! This is actually a way that you can calculate the value of a corporation. For example, if a company had a P/E of 10 and annual earnings of $100,000, it would have a credible value of one million dollars. Take the number of outstanding shares of stock and divide that number by the plausible value of the company and you'll come up with a probable value for the shares of stock. Easy! How is the P/E ratio established? Investment analysts determine it based on the market, how other companies similar to yours are doing, and other factors. Not all experts may agree on a P/E ratio for a particular company.

Getting the Latest News on Venture Capital

A very good starting point for up-to-date news about venture capital is at SiliconValley.com. This handy Web site is produced by the good folks at the *San Jose Mercury News*. Another highly entertaining Web site that carries some very enjoyable articles about the Internet, IPOs, and venture capital is Salon.com. I suggest that you visit both these sites often to keep abreast of all the current news and opinion regarding venture capital. Take a look at Figure 10.1 to see what Salon.com's home page looks like.

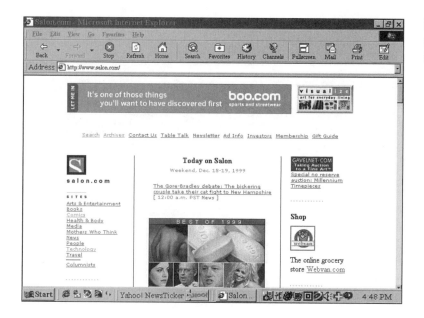

Figure 10.1

`Salon.com` *brings you the best in high-tech news!*

Money from Angels

You might have a parent with some cash on hand or maybe a rich aunt or uncle. Money from friends or relatives is, after all, money. During the early days of your startup, you might find someone close to you who is willing to invest a tidy sum in your startup. These types of investors, even certain individuals who you don't know personally but who have some money to loan to lucky and deserving companies, are often called *Angels*. That's an old Broadway term, and originally it meant a person who funded a Broadway show. Recently, it has taken on a different, but similar, meaning as it relates to start-up venture capital.

If that happens, you should take the effort to see an attorney and come up with some detailed, written agreement regarding precisely what your relative or friend is going to get as consideration for his money. Is it a bit of equity in your company, such as stock? Will he have any role in management? Or, is this merely a loan with a certain amount of interest, a schedule of payments, and other terms and conditions?

Whatever your agreement is, you should clearly document it in writing so that there are no hard feelings or misunderstandings later. After all, this might be your mother that we are talking about and you only have one mother.

`SiliconValley.com`'s Web site is another great place for Internet business news. Take a look at Figure 10.2 for more information.

Figure 10.2

SiliconValley.com *is another great place for online news about the Internet and high-tech companies.*

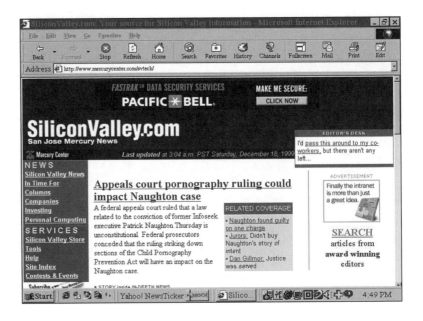

Adventure Capitalists

Some private parties like to find hot little startups in which to invest. Their primary business might be investing part of their own fortune in others who appear to have an exciting e-business that needs an infusion of cash.

These people are *adventure capitalists*. Although the risks are high for adventure capitalists, the possible rewards are also high. They don't necessarily have as much money to invest as a major investment company but sometimes they will pony up a million dollars, sometimes much less.

During the very early days of your startup, you might find that the major investment capital firms aren't interested in your company. But a private investor might give you enough to build your company up to the level where you can succeed in obtaining the interest of one of the really big players.

As always, be sure that your attorney puts in writing each and every aspect of your agreement with an adventure capitalist. Be sure that you get all the money at once. If your business doesn't speed to success as quickly as your investor feels that it should, subsequent agreed-to payments might be difficult to obtain. When dealing with any private party, you can only spend the money that has actually been given to you. Promises, even promises in writing, are not money.

Heroic History

Salon: Sex, Politics, and Culture

Web site name: www.salon.com

Founded: 1995

Service provided: Online magazine

Business model: Salon is perhaps the most visible online magazine. Its content, updated at least daily, covers a wide range of general-interest topics, with strong focus on politics, health, culture, and sexuality. The largest burst of attention the site received was over its controversial revelation of the extramarital affair of House Judiciary Committee Chairman Henry Hyde. However, it has also built respect on the basis of calm and thoughtful commentary on such topics as the Littleton shootings, while other media outlets were dealing more in hysteria and inaccuracy. Salon has multiple economic models. It sells advertising and it helps e-commerce partners sell products. It sells service in multiple ways; one is through memberships, which are much like public TV memberships, giving the members the exact same access as nonmembers, but with a few logo-bearing items as gifts. It also bought out and operates The Well, one of the oldest and most-respected online communities, which charges for access. Salon also provides contents to other sites such as CNN.com. With the cable TV giant Cablevision having bought into Salon, there are plans for Salon to begin producing material for television.

Where the money came from: Salon went public on June 22, 1999, with shares trading for $10 apiece. As of January 20, 2000, the stock was trading at 9 1/16, giving the company a market capitalization of $103 million. The company trades on the Nasdaq exchange under the symbol SALN. Naturally, stock prices can vary a great deal from day to day, so please consult your favorite online stock quotation service for the latest quotes. I like to use the one found at www.motleyfool.com.

AdVenture Capital Register

The AdVenture Capital site (adventurecapital.com) claims that through its merchant banking correspondence relationship it can make direct investments up to 10 million dollars. However, it also does something that is very interesting. It claims to send out to about 10,000 venture capital firms, individual investors, and other subscribers, its *AdVenture Capital Register.* This is a traditional, printed document, which is either mailed to subscribers or sold on newsstands. For $99 you can buy a listing in this monthly periodical. See Figure 10.3 to find out what its home page looks like.

Figure 10.3

AdVenture Capital Register *is a* Journal of Entrepreneurial Financing. *See it at* adventurecapital.com *to learn more about its advertising services.*

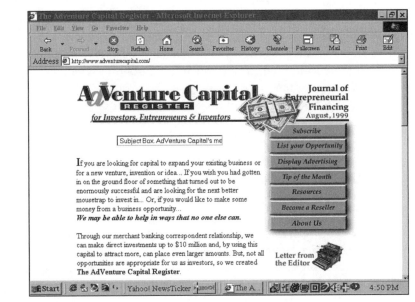

Business Development Agencies

Some governmental agencies exist for the purpose of lending money to needy and deserving businesses that exist in their cities. This is particularly true when a company serves a purpose that the agency deems is a necessary service to the city. If you are interested in finding out more about *community business development agencies* (and they might have a different title in your home town), call your local City Council, Mayor's Office, Board of Supervisors, or County and City general information telephone numbers.

Money from Corporations

Some large companies make rather substantial investments in start-up companies. This is especially true if a particular large corporation can forecast a valid partnership between the start-up and themselves if the startup makes the big time.

If you are creating new technology that a particular company could benefit from or building out a space on the Internet that the company could directly profit from, you might be able to interest that company in funding you. It will expect a high rate of return from its investment, but if it believes in your startup, that means that it has carefully considered all aspects of your company and it feels that it is making the right decision in funding you. That's a very good sign.

If a major company invests in your company, other potential investors will get very excited about that. Nothing speaks as clearly about how well your startup is doing than when some huge company hands a few million dollars over to you.

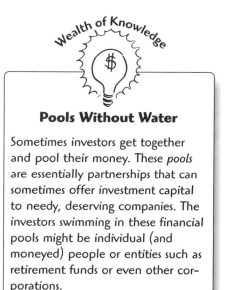

Wealth of Knowledge

Pools Without Water

Sometimes investors get together and pool their money. These *pools* are essentially partnerships that can sometimes offer investment capital to needy, deserving companies. The investors swimming in these financial pools might be individual (and moneyed) people or entities such as retirement funds or even other corporations.

How Much Will You Have to Give Up in Exchange for Investment Capital?

It would be nice if there was an easy answer to this question. But there isn't. I could make up an easy answer but it wouldn't be accurate and that would make us both feel badly.

When investors consider how much stock in your company to request in exchange for their investment, they first attempt to *price* your company. They determine how long it will be before you could reasonably be expected to go public because that is where they think the big money is. They also will try to figure out what your company's value will be at that time.

They will think hard about how much money your company will need to make it to your IPO. What if your company fails? They will ponder long and hard about how likely a failure might be. If your company *does* fail, they will try to predict how much of their money they could get back, if any.

This is their money, after all, and we can't blame them for trying to figure out how risky your company is before they sink a few million genuine American dollars into it.

Investors also consider how the stock market is doing and how companies similar to yours are doing. If there seems to be some science mixed in with some guesswork as you consider all this, you're right. But the guesswork is educated guesswork, we guess.

Return on Investment

Venture capital doesn't come cheap. Venture capitalists can demand as much as a 50% return of their investment compounded annually if they invest while you are still a startup. It could even be higher. The sooner you pay off your venture capitalist, the better it will be for you. Each year that goes by in which your venture capitalist hasn't yet *exited* (had his debt completely paid off) will result in making the investment money that your company received a lot more expensive!

Doing Your Own Valuation

Because evaluations can be very complex, your best bet is to hire your own expert before you conclude negotiations for venture capital. For example, you might be offered a great deal of money but be dismayed by the fact that the investors want 50% of your stock in return. You'll sit down at the table and carefully study all their facts, figures, and educated guesses and maybe it will all seem very impressive.

But your own evaluator might chew over the same data and advise you that his conclusions are that giving the venture capitalists 10% of your company's stock is much more reasonable. This might be the single most important negotiation that your company ever enters into and you'll need the services of a good lawyer and an established pricing analyst or you'll run the serious risk of giving away too much of your company. Don't let all those millions of dollars that they are offering you put stars into your eyes!

Having more than one offer to evaluate might make your negotiations run a bit easier, of course.

Small Business Investment Companies

The United States government wants you to have money. Well, maybe they do, especially at tax time. In any event, Uncle Sam has created agencies that might invest in your company. These agencies or firms are the Small Business Investment Companies. (Let's all give these guys a big round of applause!) Some of their money comes from private investors, and some of it comes from the federal government.

How does this work? The Small Business Investment Company collects money from private or corporate investors, which is then matched or even doubled (or more!) by Uncle Sam. Then, the money is given to worthy startups.

This arrangement might have the attributes of a traditional loan rather than other types of venture capital. You might have to make payments on this investment money much earlier than you would like.

The federal government's Small Business Administration will give you a free copy of the very exciting *Directory of Operating Small Business Investment Companies*. You can call the SBA Answer Desk at 800-827-5722. Are you too shy to call? Feel like sending them a fax, instead? Then dial 202-205-7064. Or write a letter (remember them? And aren't those stamps cute?) to

U.S. Small Business Administration, S.W., Washington, D.C. 20416

National Association of Small Business Investment Companies

The NASBIC considers itself to be the voice of the *Small Business Investment Company (SBIC)* industry before Congress and the administration. It has some pretty exciting information on its Web site. Here's a quote that will make you sit up and pay attention. (Stop slouching. I can see you with my secret nano-camera embedded in page 99.)

"To date, SBICs have disbursed more than $13 billion to more than 78,000 small businesses. The concerns they have financed have far out-performed all national averages as measured by increases in assets, sales, profits, and new employment. Thousands of profitable business owners can relate how much they have benefited from the dollars and management counseling made available to them by SBICs for over 35 years."

Check out its Web site at www.nasbic.org and you'll find a lot of exciting stuff like that to read. Figure 10.4 will give you a sneak preview of the Web page.

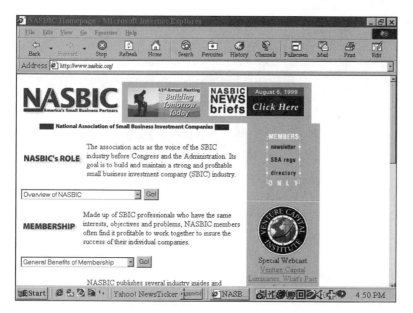

Figure 10.4

See the voice of small business investment companies at www.nasbic.org.

Folks Who Might Have Money for You

Members of NASBIC include the following:

➤ **Wasatch Venture Fund**   Located at wasatchvc.com.

➤ **First Capital Group**   Located at firstcapitalgroup.com.

➤ **San Diego Regional Technology Alliance**   Located at sdrta.org/sdrta/home/home.html.

➤ **Seacoast Capital**   Located at seacoastcapital.com/intro.html.

The National Venture Capital Association

The NVCA is another group that you should know about. Its Web site, located at nvca.com, is chock full of a lot of information about venture capital and the people who hand it out.

The U.S. government's Small Business Administration itself can be found online at sbaonline.sba.gov. Meanwhile, its very exciting Small Business Investment Company–related site is found at. sba.gov/INV/. Any reasonable person could get absolutely giddy while reading some of the stuff that it has on that Web site. Check out this exciting quote taken from its mission statement:

"Congress created the Small Business Investment Company (SBIC) Program in 1958 to fill the gap between the availability of venture capital and the needs of small businesses in start-up and growth situations. SBICs, licensed and regulated by the SBA, are privately owned and managed investment firms that use their own capital, plus funds borrowed at favorable rates with an SBA guarantee, to make venture capital investments in small businesses."

The National Venture Capital Association home page is shown in Figure 10.5.

Figure 10.5

Learn tons of stuff about venture capital firms at the National Venture Capital Association home page, cleverly located at www.nvca.com.

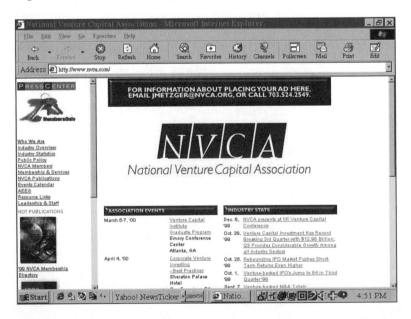

Show Me the Money!

By now you are probably very interested in finding out just who these investment capitalists actually are. No need to frown. You'll find a pretty big list located at `nasbic.org/links.html`. Hurry on over there and start hunting for venture capital companies!

Some of the companies listed will be companies that are willing to consider funding startups, others will not be. Carefully check out each company and contact the ones that you think might be interested in your company.

Garage.com

As the story goes, the very successful company Hewlett-Packard got started in a garage. Deep in what would later be called the *Silicon Valley,* an area in Palo Alto, California, a Stanford University professor encouraged his students to create their own high-tech companies in their own home town, instead of joining high-falutin' companies out on the East Coast. (And this was way back in 1938, which explained why he really didn't use the term *high tech,* but rather, *electronics companies,* or so the story goes.

David Packard and William R. Hewlett listened well to their professor's advice. In 1938 they started their company in a small garage. They got their first big break a couple of years later when they sold some cool electronic equipment to Walt Disney (Hey! That Walt guy is all through this book!), which Disney used to help make his movie *Fantasia.*

Garage.com (as shown in Figure 10.6) has adopted this story for its own use, specifically in the naming of its company. What doesn't good old Garage.com do? Well, it doesn't sell new and improved automatic garage-door openers. (Although I could use a new one. My own garage-door opener accidentally put my 10-speed bike into the hospital yesterday.)

Garage.com helps entrepreneurs and investors build great high-technology companies. They screen startups to find seed-level companies with the greatest potential. So, essentially, Garage.com is very much like an incubator, but it does not itself invest in a startup.

Garage.com essentially puts the best startups with the best possible investors, or so it seems. Its Web site is loaded with tons of information about how it goes about its business. If Garage.com accepts your company, you can then proudly call yourself a member company. Most of its member companies are seeking between one to four million dollars in start-up capital. According to Garage.com, this is an amount far lower than most venture capital firms are looking to invest.

So, you should perhaps consider an amount of between one and four million dollars as being seed money. That is, start-up money that allows you to grow your company to the point where a venture capital company might be interested in offering a much larger investment to you.

Figure 10.6

Got a garage? Got a start-up company hiding in it? Or maybe you don't have a garage but need start-up capital to get one? You might be able to find venture capital at www.garage.com.

Indeed, Garage.com says "It is rare for a company to need only seed capital. We'll help entrepreneurs launch and grow their companies, preparing them for additional financing from VCs and corporations."

Check out its Web site and see if it meets with your approval. Meanwhile, we'll take an even farther look into venture capital in Chapter 17, "Please Sir, Can I Have Some More Moolah?"

Heroic History

FreeMarkets: Bid Low, Sell Big

Web site name: FreeMarkets.com

Founded: 1995

Service provided: Business-to-business auctions

Business model: FreeMarkets runs an auction Web site with a very different target than the well-known sites such as eBay or Yahoo! Auctions. FreeMarkets is aimed at businesses that need materials or services. The needed item is put up for auction with a maximum bid. Because the needs of a company buying thousands of dollars worth of material can be very precise and require more sorts of control than someone buying a used Hummel figurine, the FreeMarket auctions are heavily customizable. Various approved suppliers try to bid lower than all the other bids, looking for a price that will make them the cheapest and yet still bring them a worthwhile profit. The auctioning business gets its needs filled cheaply, while suppliers can easily find customers without spending big bucks on promotion and advertising. FreeMarket makes its money from membership fees (businesses are more comfortable paying fees than are individuals), performance incentives, and commissions from the sales.

Where the money came from: FreeMarket has run at times as an actually profitable operation. In 1998 alone, it auctioned off nearly a billion dollars worth of items, enabling it to bill $7.8 million and get a profit of $234,000. As it's sought expansion, its sales have grown but its expenses have grown more quickly. At least one estimate predicts that it will auction *more than* $100 billion per year by 2005, so there is vast potential for profit. As such, it should come as no surprise that its IPO was an impressive one. The originally announced expected share price was in the $14–$16 range. By the time the offering came, it had upped the price to $48 per share. When the stock actually hit the open market, the price skyrocketed to $280 by the end of the first day of trading (December 10, 1999). By January 20, 2000, the price had calmed slightly, to $244 5/16, for a market capitalization of $8.3 billion. The stock trades on the Nasdaq exchange under the symbol FMKT.

The Least You Need to Know

➤ Venture capital can be very expensive and you need to carefully negotiate your best possible deal.

➤ You will probably benefit from professional help regarding the evaluation of your company before you accept venture capital.

➤ The U.S. government's Small Business Administration can be a valuable resource for you.

➤ Shop very carefully for venture capital and don't merely accept the first offer you receive until you have had a chance to fully investigate all aspects of the venture capital offer.

Part 3
Building the Business

Now you've gotten in on the ground floor of a business. It's time to make sure that the ground floor is not all that exists! Time to get the Web site working! Without that, you're just a small group of workers with a really cool unused domain name.

The bad news is there are a lot of decisions that need to be made. Who will put your site together? Will they work for you, or just contract out? Is there a cheaper way? Where have all the good donuts gone? In this part of the book, we'll help you find answers to at least some of these questions.

Getting It Working

In This Chapter

➤ How to launch a startup from your home

➤ Learn the best way to obtain help designing your Web site

➤ How to avoid getting ripped off

From the Living Room to the Board Room

It is quite possible for someone to launch a successful Internet e-business from his living room. Short of cash, but rich with drive and concepts, a very hard-working person can start a business from a very modest beginning. Whether the business is launched from a living room or a garage, I can tell you one thing: It has been accomplished.

It is also a very, very difficult thing to achieve. It takes a very unusual person to accomplish this sort of amazing achievement. You have to be incredibly focused on your ultimate goal and be willing to make many personal sacrifices along the way. It isn't easy.

Why start from your living room, garage, attic, or whatever? Because you might not have enough money to have an office. You might want to put what money you do have in equipment and services necessary to start your startup.

The Total Control Method

Call me a control freak but I like to have as much control over my life as I possibly can. I bet you feel the same way. I don't like the idea of *outsourcing*, that is, hiring independent contractors or freelancers to help me start a business. I would much rather delegate work that I can't or don't want to do to a trusted partner or employee. I can always yell at my partner or fire the employee if they screw up. If you yell at a freelancer, they simply don't return to the job until they cool off.

Let's assume that you have come up with what you believe is a very hot idea for an Internet business. You've already secured your domain name and created a business plan. Now you have to launch the site.

You'll need to use an Internet service to help you set up your business on the Internet. (We'll discuss such services a bit later in this chapter.) Although you will need an Internet service to help you to some extent, if you are wise you will try to do as much as you can on your own.

To get started on the right foot, somebody in your small company—either you, a partner, or an employee—needs to be an expert at Web design and Web site management. If you have such resources at hand, then you need a way to get your business on the Internet itself.

Web Site Hosting

You are going to need to find a place to set up your own servers and obtain connectivity to the Internet. You need a business that will provide you with the services that you need yet allows you the freedom to do as much of the work on your site as you can handle. The more you handle, the more direct control you have over when and how the work is done.

One company that is very reliable is AT&T's CERFnet. CERFnet offers a wide variety of Internet connectivity options as well as Web site management services, if you are so inclined to use them. Any serious e-business requires a reliable Internet connection, and CERFnet supplies that via a world class Internet *backbone*, or direct connection to the Internet.

Your transmission speed and access method to the Internet are two things that you have to discuss with CERFnet, or any other similar service provider that you might select to use.

You'll want to start out with the most inexpensive services you can obtain, as long as they fill your particular needs, and upgrade later as your own individual requirements dictate.

Small Business Hosting on CERFnet

It doesn't take a fortune to launch a business on CERFnet when you use its Small Business Hosting Services. For as little as $25, you can get 25MB of data storage, six email accounts, and 1,000MB of data transfer for your business. But, lemme tell ya, that's a very small business, indeed.

For $125 a month you can get 100MB of data storage and 5,000MB of data transfer—still a pretty small operation. But, maybe that's all you need to get started. As your business swells, you can upgrade your service on CERFnet. That's what advertising or seed money is for, after all. It takes money to make money, right?

CERFnet even provides you with software to create and design your Web page, helps you with domain name registration, and gives you 24-hour technical support. You'll find CERFnet at www.cerf.net. (See Figure 11.1 to take a gander at its Web site.)

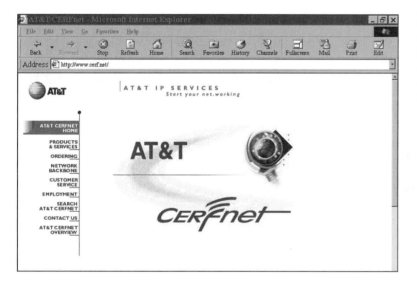

Figure 11.1

CERFnet will cheerfully help you set up your own Internet Web site. Find them at www.cerf.net*!*

Even More About CERFnet

The really cool thing about CERFnet is that CERFnet is not a fly-by-night business. It has been around for a long time and is dedicated to helping you set up a successful e-business. It won't run your business for you but it will give you the tools that you need to get up and running.

Its Small Business Hosting Center, according to information posted on its Web site, "...gives you hints and tips on running your Web site, step by step instructions on complex tasks, as well as account and billing management." That sounds pretty cool to me.

You are able to have complete access to your Web site usage log files. It updates these records every 24 hours. You can either view these logs with your Internet browser or download them to your own computer for later analysis. This way you can easily judge how well your Web site is doing.

Better than that, CERFnet will smoothly transition your Web business to new capabilities as your business grows. When you need increased bandwidth, CERFnet is ready to give you what you need.

The most popular MIME types, such as Apple QuickTime, Apple QuickTime VR, Macromedia Flash, and Macromedia Director, are supported by CERFnet. You can use your own CGI scripts and programs, but they do not troubleshoot these scripts unless you have obtained them from the CGI library that CERFnet provides you via its Business Center. Popular scripting languages, such as Perl, C, and UNIX SH, are also supported.

You can also easily switch your existing Web site to CERFnet if you want. CERFnet makes it very easy to sign up by providing you with an online registration form.

But All I Have Is a Good Idea for a Web Business and Almost No Knowledge About the Internet

Then you might find yourself to be great prey for a fly-by-night organization. There are many businesses that exist who are looking for people like you. Do you have a few thousand dollars in the bank? Want to set up an e-business but don't know the first thing about how to go about doing it? I think you should hide under the bed before the bad people find you.

There are scads of people who will gladly help you set up a Web business. They will tell you how great your business idea sounds and, for a fee, will provide you with connectivity to the Internet, help you get a domain name, and provide you with a designed Web site.

But you might find that you are paying a lot more for far less than CERFnet can provide. Why get a lot less in the way of services, options, and experience when you can go first class for a decent fee?

Worse than that, using the services of a less-than-stellar Web hosting company might result in you ending up with a partially completed e-business that will make no money for you and go nowhere.

Dreams are wonderful things. But some people prey on dreamers. The world is full of people who know that others dream of creating a successful Internet business but who lack the full range of expertise and education needed to do so on their own. These bottom-feeders call dreamers *suckers*.

Let's take a look at a real-life story.

Heroic History

Fatbrain: Books Holdable and Otherwise

Web site name: www.fatbrain.com

Founded: June 1995

Service provided: Online bookstore

Business model: Fatbrain began life in the most trite and wonderful tradition of innovators: in the garage of one of its co-founders. At that time, it was called CBooks Express, and it focused on selling technical books. However, it went about it in an unusual way. Instead of running its own Web site for people to order from, it arranged with various tech-heavy companies to set up in-house technical online bookstores on the corporate intranets. This was good for the companies, because it meant that their engineers weren't taking several hours in the middle of the day to go hunt down and pick up a needed book. CBooks specialized in rapid delivery, so that projects weren't tied up while waiting for books. CBooks glommed onto a chain of retail bookstores (Computer Literacy Bookshops) in 1997, giving it Silicon Valley retail fronts in Sunnyvale and San Jose. It finally went out onto the Web in 1998. By keeping the focus on carrying computer books for computer professionals, the site could provide particularly helpful recommendations. It set itself up as a provider to businesses, helping various high-tech companies set up their own internal book-ordering systems. In 1999, CBooks changed its name to the more catchy Fatbrain. That year the company also moved into downloadable books, called *eMatter*. Fatbrain offers eMatter authors a far larger royalty rate than physical book publishers ever could, attracting more than 5,000 authors of everything from computer manuals to poetry.

Where the money came from: Fatbrain (then known as Computer Literacy, Inc.) went public November 1998, with an offering of shares at $10 apiece. The stock rose as high as 42 1/4 per share before settling down. As of February 7, 2000, the stock was trading at 23, giving the company a market capitalization of $263 million. Fatbrain trades on the Nasdaq market under the symbol FATB.

Like I Said, a Real-Life Story

A friend of mine is a pretty good artist. He had the idea that he would create a killer Web site that would make him rich. The trouble is, he knew very little about how to go about setting up an e-business. Scripts? CGI? It was all a blur to him.

So he took out a copy of the Yellow Pages and scanned the ads relating to small business Web site hosting. He found an ad that looked pretty good and called the number. That's when he should have put down the phone and gone to hide under the bed, but I wasn't there to tell him that.

In the Wrong Incubator You Might Get Plucked

In Chapter 8, "Empowering Yourself," you learned about *incubators,* companies that help other companies get started. True incubators are wonderful things, as they can give you expert help regarding engineering, marketing, and even help you obtain venture capital. But be wary! Not all incubators are the same. If your company really has value, an incubator should help you for a percentage of ownership in your company. After all, a venture capitalist gives you *money* in exchange for a piece of your company, so why shouldn't an incubator exchange advice and professional assistance in the same manner? If someone professes to own an incubation company but wants to charge you a flat fee or hourly rate for his help, you should ask him, "If you believe in my company, why aren't you willing to share in the risk?"

The owner of the very impressively named Web site hosting business was more than pleased to drive over to my friend's house to discuss things. Of course, my friend didn't know at that time that the man didn't have an office. When the Internet professional (as I'll call him for want of a better or more accurate description) showed up, they sat down and discussed what my friend wanted.

"I am an artist and I want to set up an art gallery on the Internet. I need to have a cool Web site that will show off small images of the art. The small pictures will entice the viewers to pay to see larger images that they can download. That way I'll make some money."

The Internet professional smiled and said, "Hey, no problem. You'll need a site that looks cool and I can get that designed for you. You'll also need to have a credit card service and I can set that up for you. We can get the site hosted and get you up and running in a couple of weeks." My friend asked for a couple of days to think things over and the Internet Pro smiled and said, "Sure, just call me when you are ready to get things going." Before he left, the Internet Pro quoted one flat fee for his services, which would include the Web design needed to get the business up and running.

The Internet professional was really just a middleman. He went out and hired a Web designer who was unemployed and looking for full-time work. In the meantime he was willing to take odd jobs designing Web pages. The Internet professional couldn't design a Web page if his life depended on it.

My friend paid twice as much as he should have for the Web designing services. Oh, he didn't pay that money to the Web designer. He paid it to the middleman. The middleman had negotiated a much lower price and pocketed the difference.

There were hosting fees and other service charges that the Internet pro passed on to my friend. The middleman merely set up various accounts needed to obtain an Internet connection and Web page hosting. In turn these accounts were billed to my friend's credit card. The middleman made sure to tack on a lot of extra charges and never showed my friend any invoices or bills.

Worse than that, the Internet professional didn't stick to the original quoted fee. I need another thousand dollars for this and another thousand dollars for that the Internet professional would intone, and my friend would cough up the money.

My friend should have figured out that his Internet professional was a fly-by-night kind of guy. Why? Because when my friend had been instructed to drop off all payments for the Internet pro at a dental office where his wife worked, my friend was informed that his wife would make sure that the payments reached him. That was when my friend first figured out that the Internet pro didn't have any sort of business office.

The Web designer that the Internet Pro hired was an honest sort of person and did a very good job designing the Web page. If my friend had independently met the designer and created a partnership they both might have been better off.

The original idea that my friend had for his e-business did have some merit. The first day that the Web page was on the line he had 3,000 users show up to check out the Web site. None of them paid to see the larger images, though, so he made no money. If he had started on the right foot with a decent Internet service provider, this sad tale might have turned out quite differently.

The poorly conceived business plan wasn't the fault of the Internet professional or the Web designer, of course. But my friend quickly understood that his business model was flawed, so he decided to shift gears and come up with another.

"Okay, I'll give the art away for free," he thought. "They can look at all the big versions of the art at no charge. I'll try and make some money from advertising instead." Of course, this meant that the money he spent setting up a credit card account on his Web site had been wasted, but he wanted to do his best to make his infant e-business a success.

My friend surfed the Internet and found some sites that offered payment if you put ads that they provided on your own Web site. The payment would be based on how many *click-thrus* happened, that is, how many times users clicked on the ads and followed the links to the advertiser's home page.

He tried to reach the Internet professional on the telephone because he needed some help changing the design of his Web page, but he couldn't reach him. The middleman had never given him the telephone number or even the name of the man who actually did the design work on the page. After all, the last thing he wanted was for the client and the designer to have a chance to compare notes and learn the full facts of what had happened.

My friend dropped by the dentist's office where the wife of the man worked but she wasn't any help. "Just call him and leave a message and I'm sure he'll get back to you," she remarked with a smile. But the Internet pro never returned his call.

So, my friend tried to set up the click-thru ads on his site but couldn't figure out how to do it. If he'd had partners who were experienced at Internet advertising and Web design, he might have been able to build his business up to something that could have been successful.

In the end, my friend simply abandoned his Web site and forgot about the thousands of dollars that he had thrown away.

If you don't know how to do a task that you need to have done for your business, you are far better off having a partner or an employee who does know how to do the task rather than hiring a freelancer to do it for you. Or, hire only somebody from a reputable business such as CERFnet.

It is perfectly okay to be the idea man for your business. But if you aren't going to be the person who understands how to launch a business on the Internet, you had better either hire or partner up with someone who does.

What If I Hire Real Internet Professionals as Freelancers?

Certainly, there are many very experienced Web designers and programmers that you can hire to work for you on a part-time or freelance basis. You won't necessarily find them in the Yellow Pages, but might be able to find them via a location such as www.hotjobs.com.

You will find your needs for building and expanding your Web business to come in spurts. You could hire people as you require them. I think, however, the better way is to expand your employee list with full-timers, as your investment money comes in. You can start your business with the help of a couple of experienced and trustworthy partners and then add employees as you need and can afford them.

One of the troubles with freelancers is that you usually have to pay them at least one-half of their fee in advance. What if they don't do the work? You could fire them, but what about the money that you have already paid them? At least with an employee you can fire them if they don't get their job done promptly and efficiently. Dealing with independent contractors can be a very big pain in the behind. If you do hire independent contractors, try to hire only the most experienced and trustworthy ones that you can find. Ask to speak to past clients or otherwise check their references before you hire them. Make sure that all the elements of your agreement are put into writing.

Heroic History

Beenz, Beenz, the Monetary Fruit

Web site name: www.beenz.com

Founded: December 1998

Service provided: Internet currency for incentive purposes

Business model: Green Stamps (for those too young or raised in the wrong place to recall) were a once-common form of incentive at grocery stores. For each purchase you made, the store would give you some number of these stamps, which you could paste into booklets. Fill enough booklets, and you could exchange them for merchandise from the Green Stamp catalog. On the Internet we now have *beenz*, their cyberspace equivalent (which involves a lot less licking and sticking, thank goodness.) Web sites purchase beenz from beenz.com, which they can dole out as a reward for visiting a site, making purchases, answering surveys, or whatever else the site wants to encourage. Each user's stockpile of beenz is tracked by beenz.com. When a user has accumulated sufficient beenz, he can spend them for products and services at any of a number of beenz-accepting merchants. The folks at beenz.com then pay the merchant actual dollars (or whatever the local currency is; beenz can, after all, be used internationally) for the redeemed beenz. The site makes its profit on the price difference between what it sells the beenz for and what it pays for the redeemed beenz. It also makes some profit from beenz that are earned but never spent. There are hundreds of thousands of registered users earning beenz, and major sites such as MP3.com and Motley Fool (www.fool.com) offer beenz. Your beenz can be used to buy CDs, DVDs, candy, magazine subscriptions, gift certificates, or even donated to charity.

Where the money came from: As of February 7, 2000, beenz.com Inc. was still a privately held corporation. It had received three rounds of venture funding, totaling $34.5 million.

You probably need to start with a team that includes a visionary or idea man, a Web designer and programmer, and an advertising salesman. More programmers and advertising people will be needed as you expand. If you aren't making any money from online advertising or see the capability to do so in the near future, your Web site is probably going to have financial trouble. If enough people are using your Web site, you should be able to sell some advertising space.

Legal Lookout

Who Owns the Work?

The difference between using employee programmers and freelance programmers can be very important when it comes to ownership. Let's say Debbie, an employee, comes up with a new program that automatically puts the customer's name in rotating 3D on your Web page. Because Debbie was doing this as part of her work for you, this program is considered *work for hire,* and you own that program. If another site wants that program for its own Web site, you can license it to that site. If Debbie was a freelancer, however, you might not have that option. The law often considers that freelancers own their creations, and all you get is the right to use it for your own site. Debbie would be the one making the licensing money, and her licensing out that program may cost your site its uniqueness. This problem can be avoided through carefully written contracts. That's something you should talk to your intellectual property lawyer about.

If at least some investment capital fails to materialize within a year of your launching your business, you probably will have to seriously consider moving on to another e-business entirely. Of course, that is a purely arbitrary time period. It is up to you to set such goals and schedules. In any event, remember that failure happens to the best of us and most of the really successful people in the world have had at least one major failure happen to them before they finally had a success. You must know when to cut your losses and move on to another idea.

Ownership Issues

Be sure that when you establish your business on the Internet that you have a written agreement with your Internet hosting service that clearly states that *you own the e-business and the domain address and that they have no financial interest in either.* I'd hate to see some fly-by-night Internet middleman claim that he got you started and was your partner all along if your business ends up being a multimillion-dollar hit on the World Wide Web.

Some Final Comments

If you are going to start your own business on the Internet you probably need it to be a full-time activity for you. In truth, it will be much more than full time. I'd say you will probably find yourself working at least 60 hours a week.

If you only want to create a bit of extra business for yourself, there are far easier ways to go about it than trying to create your own Internet start-up company.

I have a friend who makes about two thousand dollars a month in his spare time selling stuff on eBay, the famed Internet auction site. (See them at `www.ebay.com` if you want to check them out.) He spends his Saturdays scouring garage sales for cool stuff to sell and his evenings running his auctions on eBay. He didn't try to start his own Internet company. Instead he merely used the services provided by a preexisting e-business.

There are many other Internet sites where an enterprising person can make an honest dollar, if that is what you are really interested in.

Is a bit of extra income all that you really want? If it is, then starting a startup probably isn't what you want to do. If you want a decent full-time income, perhaps you need to find a job at a preexisting, well-established Internet company.

If you want to be rich, well, you can roll the dice of fortune and try to get hired by a plucky startup early enough to become a founder and grab a few million dollars worth of stock options. Remembering, of course, that the company might very well fold before your options are worth more than the paper that they are printed on.

Or, if you want to be filthy, stinking rich, then maybe launching an Internet startup is precisely what you should be doing. If your business plan is incredible, if you have the right partners, some financial backing, and don't step on any landmines as you build your business, then you might not fail.

The more you shoot for, the greater the risk. Remember that always and keep it close to your heart.

The Least You Need to Know

➤ Try to do as much as you can within your own company rather than outsourcing to third parties.

➤ You will have to use an Internet service provider to some extent, so try to use the most experienced one that you can find.

➤ Carefully evaluate your goals and risks before you launch your own start-up company. You might find yourself far happier with a much more modest involvement in e-commerce than if you started your own company.

Cheapskate Shortcuts

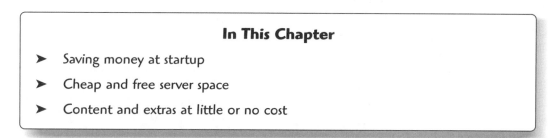

In This Chapter

➤ Saving money at startup

➤ Cheap and free server space

➤ Content and extras at little or no cost

You probably aren't a millionaire yet. After all, you bought this book because you wanted to become a millionaire, and (as good as this book may be) I doubt you achieved your first million before reaching Chapter 12. As such, you may not have all the money you need to get your Web site rolling in an ideal manner. In this chapter, you'll see some tricks for spending a few hundred or even a few thousand dollars less to get your site started.

Shortcuts Are for Startup

Many of the tricks listed here are intended for the new Web site that's starting small. In this world, nothing is truly free and little is reasonably cheap. Some of the tricks seen here will limit how much traffic and content your site can reliably handle. It's like telling your friends how to avoid the traffic on the way to your house by using the shortcut down Shrewsberry Avenue; it works fine when you only have two or three visitors, but when you have a hundred thousands visitors a day, you'll simply cause a traffic jam on Shrewsberry, riling the visitors and the local inhabitants.

Other tricks involve adding ads in various places on your site or service. At best, this is giving away ad space that's worth money. At worst, it makes your site look less than professional.

Don't Serve Yourself

Many startups assume that if you're in e-business, the business has to actually be in your office. They figure that you need to have the actual host (the computer that spits out files over the Internet) sitting there at your feet, convenient for resting your coffee mug on or for spilling coffee into when you're mad.

The expenses of having your server on-site are high. Not only do you need the computer itself (which will run you a few thousand dollars), you need someone to run and maintain the server, and you need a high-speed Internet connection running into your offices. These things can cost you thousands of dollars per month, money that you'd rather be spending on advertising, legal costs, or buying the fancy two-ply toilet paper instead of the cheaper mono-ply.

Making a Web Space Deal

The most straightforward way to get your files out there is simply to rent space on someone else's server. There are plenty of companies offering host services for a monthly fee. This saves you from a lot of expenses (although it does leave you worrying about how quickly things will get fixed when—not if—something goes wrong). Pick up any computing-related magazine these days and you'll see plenty of ads for Web host services in the back, at prices ranging from $9 per month on up. Everybody is offering a different bundle for that money. Here's some of what to look for:

➤ **How much file space do you get?**   This figure, listed in *megabytes* (millions of bytes), lets you know how big a Web site you can run from their host. This space will not only have to hold the files and images that you'll be sending out, but also any programs and data that it takes for your site to run.

➤ **How much traffic are you allowed?**   Host services generally limit how much data you can send and receive over their lines. After all, they have to pay for the high-speed connections that your data will use. This is measured in *gigabytes* (billions of bytes). That may sound huge, but if your site has a thousand visitors a day, and each visitor views 10 typical Web pages, then you're using more than 10 gigabytes a month. If your site is offering streaming audio, video, or downloadable files, that figure increases many fold.

➤ **Can you run CGI scripts on their host?**   If you're doing anything more than just putting out standard files on your site, you'll need the capability to run programs on the host, including *CGI scripts* (the simplest form of programming for Web interactivity). This includes interactivity, customizing features, taking registrations, and so on. This just steers you away from the cheapest deals.

➤ **Can you point your domain to their host?** Some cheap host services offer you a location on their own domain, and require an additional payment if you want to use your own. You really do want your own domain.

➤ **What is their uptime percentage?** Every computer in existence has to go offline sometime for maintenance, or due to a power failure, or because Fluffy Whiskerkins got her tongue stuck in the floppy drive. (Cats are the cause of many problems and are apt to bring about the fall of civilization. But they're cute, so we forgive them.) Many companies offer a guaranteed *uptime percentage* (how much of the time your site is available), and it's almost always more than 99%. First, realize that 99% is not that good; it means that your site could be down for seven hours over the course of the month, and you can lose a lot of new visitors in the course of seven hours. Second, realize that a guarantee generally does you little good. It means that if the site is down for more than the advertised percentage, you get some reduction of what you have to pay that month. That's a small reward for having your site unavailable. When inquiring about host services, instead of asking what uptime they guarantee, ask them what their actual uptime track record has been for the previous few months.

➤ **What server extensions do they offer?** If you're going to be putting out streaming audio or video, or using the special services supported by the Web design program FrontPage by Microsoft, you will need a host that has those *extensions* (programs built in to the server function).

➤ **Do they offer e-commerce services?** If you're running a retail site, you'll need e-commerce software of some sort to

Demand Your Domain

Many hosting services will offer to register your domain name for you. Be sure that it gets registered in your name, not in theirs. That way, they can't hold your domain name hostage, and you won't have as much trouble if they go out of business.

Don't Fall for the Mall at All!

From time to time, you might get email looking for merchants for an "online mall." They'll try to convince you how much traffic you'll get by being in the same online area with other folks. These are appeals designed to fool folks who don't have a sense of how cyberspace works, that online shops don't get foot traffic for being "next to" other shops. Although there are legitimate efforts to try to create communities of shops, just about anyone who contacts you through unsolicited email is just preying on hopes and ignorance.

manage your catalog, to allow customers to fill up their virtual shopping carts with items, and to take credit card orders for them. Most hosting companies offer some form of e-commerce software, generally as part of their somewhat-more-expensive packages or for an additional monthly charge.

In the long run, you're going to want your own server, because you don't want the traffic on other people's sites slowing yours. Even then, you might not have to get the server set up in your office; many site-hosting services provide and maintain a server in their office, freeing you from both the need to get a high-speed line and from major maintenance worries. (You'll probably have a bank of servers to keep up with the demand, and a whole bank of cats trying to stick their tongues in the floppy drives.)

Real Cheap: Free Web Space

If you're the sort of cheapskate who tips waitresses with cereal coupons and who refuses to join a CD club because a penny is too much to pay for eight CDs, then I've got a suggestion for you: Use free Web space.

There are basically two types of free Web space to be had for nonretailers, and each comes with a strong limitation. The first type is not so much free as it is Web space that you already have. Just about every Internet account out there comes with some free Web space. Your *ISP* (Internet service provider) probably offers you several megabytes of space to set up your own site. The big limitation here is that if your Web site starts generating a lot of traffic, your ISP will probably shut your site down with little warning. After all, putting that traffic out over their high-speed lines costs them money.

The other sort of free Web space is advertising-supported space. If you go to a site such as geocities.yahoo.com or www.tripod.com, you'll find that they offer you free Web space. What's the catch? They get to put ads on your Web pages—and lately, they've been using advanced technology to put more and more ads on your pages. The good news is that they won't cut you off if your site gets a lot of visits, because the more visitors you get, the more ads they get to show. (In fact, Tripod is even offering to pay admittedly miniscule amounts to sites that get enough visitors!)

If you're using either form of free Web space, you won't be able to register for a domain name and have it point directly to the Web server. Your ISP doesn't want that because it means you expect a lot of traffic, and the ad-supported sites just don't need the extra hassle it creates. You can, however, still get your domain name to work. To do this, you will need to sign up with a *URL redirection service*. It'll let you point your domain name to its servers, and every time a request for a page from your domain comes along, it will forward the request to point to your free Web space. This is like announcing that you have a store in Beverly Hills, when all you have there is a tele-porter that instantly takes the shopper to your location in beautiful downtown Burbank.

The bad news is that URL redirection service will cost you. The good news is that it doesn't cost much; for about $25, it will not only redirect requests for your Web site, but also will direct any mail that comes to `whatever@yourURL.com` to whichever mail address you normally use. Surf to `www.namesecure.com` to find out more.

Free Stores with Free Storage

If you're setting up an online retail shop without a lot of added features, then the cheapskate deep down in your heart is about to be made very happy. You see, there are several sites that will let you set up stores on the Web, for free. They provide the Web space, they provide the software, and you take it from there.

Sounds like there should be a catch to that, right? Well, there are some catches, but they're pretty small. You might be required to allow them to put advertising on your site, or you might have to let them sell you your *merchant account* (the account that lets you charge people's credit cards). And you might be limited to a fairly small store; if you intend to offer endless thousands of items in your store, this isn't the route for you. This is more for folks who are starting small, carrying maybe 100 items.

Generally, these sites are hoping to sell you additional services down the line. If you want those services, great, but if you don't want 'em, you don't have to pay for 'em! The sites all try to make their store-building software as easy to use as possible, because they know that not everyone putting up a store will have Web design experience.

To learn the details about getting a free store set up, surf to:

➤ `www.freemerchant.com`

➤ `www.eCongo.com`

➤ `www.Bigstep.com`

Sub-Domains Are No Sub-Stitute

Your free Web space provider might offer to let you use a *subdomain*, a URL address based on their domain address. For example, your online radish sales business might be reachable at `radishes.WhateverTheirDomainIs.com`. Because you want to move from this free Web space eventually, and you don't want to have to change your URL at that time (which would lose you customers), this just won't do.

Don't Be a Merchant No-Account

Don't try to just use your existing merchant account for doing business on the Web. You need a special merchant account that lets you take credit card orders without getting a signature.

If free is a little too cheap for you, and you like the control that actually comes with paying someone, here are a few sites that also let you set up online stores, but for a monthly fee:

➤ www.iCat.com

➤ store.yahoo.com

➤ www.VirtualSpin.com

Heroic History

Tripod: Free Web Space Fills Wallets

Web site name: www.tripod.com

Founded: 1992

Service provided: Free home page space

Business model: Tripod is primarily recognized as a provider of free Web space, which is supported by advertising. Not content to just let its users create lackluster pages, Tripod has created several schemes to encourage site creators to create more interesting pages (which would thus generate more views and more advertising revenue). Tripod organizes the Web pages into themed groups (called *pods*), and has professional content and chat for each pod that serves to spur on their content providers. (Pods also provide Tripod with the capability to offer theme-focused advertising opportunities.) Tripod also encourages page creation by offering creators of popular sites a portion of the ad revenue their page generates. In addition, it offers easy-to-use Web page creation tools, providing people who might find standard Web tools too complicated with an easy chance to find a home on the Web. Via affiliate deals with various major retail sites, Tripod encourages its users to create links to CDNow.com, BarnesandNoble.com, and others. These affiliate links generate profit for both the Web page creator and Tripod itself.

Where the money came from: In February of 1998, Tripod was sold to Lycos, a leading Web portal site. The payment was in stock then valued at approximately $58 million.

Off-the-Shelf Solutions

One of the key secrets to saving money is not to reinvent the wheel. After all, you'd expend a lot of money on research and development, and what would you end up with? A wheel. Although if you could get a patent on it, that might be worth it.

If you're creating a new and innovative Web service, you're going to need some custom software created. That doesn't mean that you can't flesh out your site with a lot of features taken from existing products.

Bulletin Board Software

For making a user feel involved with your site, nothing beats having an online bulletin board. Oh, okay, that's not true. Actually hiring the person to be part of your site would beat that, but hiring all your customers is a good way to go broke quickly.

A *bulletin board* creates online discussions by letting users post messages to start conversations, or add messages to existing conversations. This is different from a *chat room* because chat room conversations consist of people who are all online at the same time, exchanging messages that quickly disappear. The users of a bulletin board can add to a conversation at any time, and the messages stick around.

Bulletin board software is out there. You don't have to invent it. One of the more popular pieces of software is the Ultimate Bulletin Board (shown in Figure 12.1). It offers a free version of the software (which is pretty lame, actually) and a nicely robust version that will cost you less than $100 per year to use—at least in software cost. (Any bulletin board software requires someone's time maintaining the boards. After all, there is always some bozo using your salad-lovers bulletin board to tell

Trouble Finding Software?

Find a site that already does what you want, and ask the Web administrator where he got the software. (It might be software he designed himself, which you could license from him!)

Chat Rooms Are Lame on New Sites

The reason I'm pushing bulletin boards rather than chat rooms is that chat rooms work poorly on new sites. If you don't have a lot of people visiting the site yet, then there isn't anyone in the chat room. If someone heads into the chat room to talk and finds that there is no one there, it becomes obvious that your site is not attracting people. That person is not likely to return to your chat. This is a vicious cycle. Some sites break the cycle, but it's hard. With a bulletin board, you can always make sure that the site looks busy by posting some messages yourself (under false names if need be).

the world that Deth Metal R00lz! When, of course, everyone knows DethMetal sux, and TechnOPOlka R00lz.)

Surf to `www.ultimatebb.com` for more details and pricing information on this system.

Issues of Riot Control

One of the main problems with offering bulletin boards is that you will have to decide how much you will control the activities that take place on the boards. Censorship is a very sensitive issue among many Internet surfers. However, perhaps you will not want to see people coming to your site and slandering your business or posting pornography. *Spamming*, that is, the multiple posting of meaningless messages by troublemakers, is also a common problem. Another nasty difficulty is that you will encounter some pretty inflammatory comments on your bulletin board. People who hide behind the safety of a false name rarely are fearful of crossing normal social boundaries as they post their remarks. You will encounter all sorts of foul language and even racist commentary designed to goad your bulletin board users. When, if at all, do you act to squelch such arguments, fights, and harmful postings? Ultimately, all these issues boil down to a business decision that you have to make. You will be weighing free speech interests against keeping law and order on your boards and your desire to keep your own bulletin board from being used as a tool against you by your enemies.

Auction Software

A lot of retail sites like to hold auctions. Not only does it sell material, but it creates a sense that users have to return frequently to a site to be sure they don't miss something good being auctioned off. There are certainly existing auction software packages for a range of needs available from such sites as:

➤ `www.AuctionBroker.com`

➤ `www.moai.com`

➤ `www.beyondsolutions.com`

Think twice before setting up your own auction pages, however. It might be much wiser to simply use the existing services of a major auction site such as eBay. Your auction will be exposed to many more people, and might lure some of those people to your site. For the auction portion of you own site, just put up a page with links to your eBay auctions.

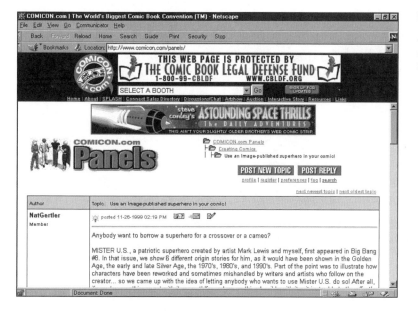

Figure 12.1

Bulletin: Having a bulletin board means fewer bored users.

Free and Cheap Content

If you want to keep people coming back to your site, you're going to have to provide material to keep the interested. Now, you could go out and hire a passel of writers, artists, musicians, and programmers to create material just for your site, but you really don't need to that. (But you should hire writers. And pay them a lot. I mean, pay *me* a lot! Otherwise, I'll have to return to my old career as a door-to-door salesman selling doorbells.)

There are plenty of existing sources for news, commentary, images, software, and other types of content. And even when there aren't good sources for these things, with a little imagination you can probably find some way to get people to create content just for you with little to offer but the chance to air their material in public.

Consider the revered newspaper, long a fixture of American homes and birdcages. Sure, your typical local newspaper does have a base of reporters covering local news, but an awful lot of the paper is filled with other things. If you look at the national and world news, you're likely to see the words *Associated Press* (or just *AP*) with the story. The Associated Press is a cooperative of more than a thousand newspapers that offer news stories to all sorts of news outlets, for a price far less than trying to cover those stories directly. "Dear Abby," everything on the comics page, some of the editorial columnists, and much of the entertainment news are *syndicated*, distributed on an on-going basis for a fairly small cost per day. Some of the news of what's happening

161

in the corporate and technical worlds is basically press releases sent out for free by the companies involved (although a larger paper will at least rewrite it some to edit out some of the more boastful claims). Serialized portions of novels are given to newspapers free to promote the books they are from. And readers who just want to spread the information provide the letters to the editor and wedding announcements.

Looking at all that, it becomes clear that newspapers are cheapskates. And if you're a cheapskate too, there's no reason you can't swipe some of their methods for your own use.

Heroic History

NetZero: The Ultimate Web Freebie

Web site name: www.NetZero.net

Founded: October 1998

Service provided: Free Internet access

Business model: NetZero is the epitome of the give-it-to-them-free sensibility. At a time when typical Internet Service Providers were charging about $20 per month for unlimited access, NetZero decided to undercut that price by a full twenty bucks. Using special NetZero software, its user base can access the Internet through phone numbers, which are local for much of the U.S. population. The software also opens up a little window in front of the Web browser, and this window displays a stream of regularly updated ads. NetZero also appends advertising to the email that its users send. It is the advertising that pays for the service (at least theoretically; as with many Internet startups, NetZero operates at a loss). NetZero has more than a million regular users and delivers more than a billion ad impressions per month. Because the user has to register with NetZero, and because NetZero can track what pages a user surfs, the company can gather precise demographic information. Thus they offer tightly targeted advertising. (They even offer threat of competition to build advertising, allowing companies to buy the advertising that displays when the user visits their own site, thus blocking out advertising from competitors.)

Where the money came from: NetZero went public in September of 1999, with an IPO priced at $16 per share. As of January 6, 2000, the stock was hovering around the $28 1/2 mark, giving the company a market capitalization around $3 billion. NetZero trades on the Nasdaq exchange under the symbol NZRO.

Syndicated Content

Not only can you use the same general tricks that newspapers use, you can use some of the very same sources. For example, if you want to buy your news from the Associated Press, surf to www.ap.org/is/ to find out how. If advice columns, editorials, TV listings, specialty columns, or comic strips are your bag, check out any of the following syndicate sites:

➤ **www.unitedmedia.com/info/ufs.html**   The site for United Features Syndicate, which offers popular comic strips such as *Peanuts* and *Dilbert*, and columns from the likes of Alan Dershowitz and Cokie Roberts.

➤ **www.creators.com/featurewire/**   The online syndication services of The Creator's Syndicate, which represents such properties as *B.C.* and *Rugrats* comics, and columnists such as Ann Landers and Ollie North.

➤ **www.tms.tribune.com**   The home of Tribune Media Services, which has become very Web-centric with its capability to offer you TV and movie listings, and weather matched to specific areas. Don't mess with these folks; they've got Dick Tracy on their side!

Not all material syndicated on the Web is merely a copy of what's available in papers. At www.iSyndicate.com you'll find material from hundreds of different sources available for use, with prices going all the way down to "free."

There are also a fair number of folks who are self-syndicating their own original material, targeted specifically at the Web audience. For example, Bill Holbrook (creator of the popular newspaper strips *Safe Havens* and *On The Fastrack*) has another comic strip that is syndicated solely online. *Kevin And Kell* features the adventures of an unlikely married couple: a rabbit who runs a Web site and a wolf who works in the offices of Herd Thinners, Inc. Head to www.kevinandkell.com for examples of this strip. Or check out the Hard Drive auto reviews at www.hardrive.com (as seen in Figure 12.2).

Press Releases

If you want to be able to include the latest news and announcements in a business or technical field you've got it easy. Businesses are already doing your work, writing your articles for you and sending them out as press releases! Of course, their writing tends to be a bit self-serving, focusing on the good side of their latest products and services and playing down the bad side. If you're selling stuff on your Web site, however, that might be just the sort of enthusiasm-building material that you need. Head to businesswire.com and use its search tools to look through the hundreds of new press releases and photos submitted every day. (Business Wire doesn't charge you anything; it makes its money charging the companies that release these press releases.)

Figure 12.2

Pickup reviews get picked up! The Hard Drive auto reviews at www.hardrive.com *get syndicated to such sites as* pickuptruck.com.

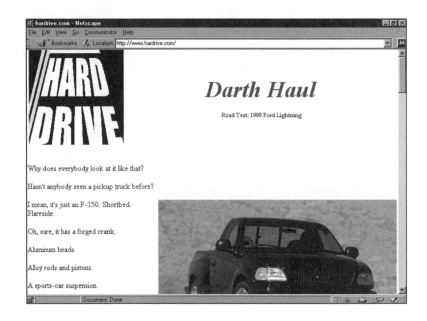

I'll Let You Provide Me with Content

You can often get people to provide you with free content by offering little more than the opportunity for that content to be seen. Not everyone writing, drawing, and creating is doing it for the money, and even those that are will sometimes be more than willing to give away free samples to build an audience.

Consider the free Web space sites such as Geocities or Tripod. These companies act like they are giving something to the people who put the Web sites up, when actually they're getting free content. If the only things that these sites contained were paid advertisements, almost no one would go there. By allowing people to use their Web space, they get content that attracts readers. Better than that, the people who are giving them this free content often go around promoting this content, and thus drawing more Web surfers to these sites.

It doesn't have to be standard Web pages to do that, either. MP3.com has built its business on musicians who want to give their music away. They give the songs to the site, and the site gives the songs (and some ads) to the Web visitors. Sure, some of the musicians are trying to make money from MP3.com's CD-release deals, but most of them just want to be heard.

Online chat and bulletin boards are nothing but your visitors providing content for you. Those are things that, if you get them going, will have your existing users spreading the word to their friends and recruiting more users for you.

Now let's say you're selling radishes over the Web, and you need to find some content for www.Radishes-YumYum.com. One day you're surfing the Web site of the National Ostrich Ranchers Coop (www.EatTheBigBird.com), and you find that they have a huge database of gourmet ostrich recipes. Amazingly enough, about half the recipes include radishes! How much do you think you'll have to pay them to include those recipes on your site? I'll bet you can get them for free. A lot of Web administrators are willing to share content with other sites (at least ones that aren't direct competition), as long as after the content is used it provides a link back to the original site.

Free Software

One type of content that doesn't have a direct parallel in newspapers is computer software. That doesn't mean that you can't find a source of it for free. In fact, there are a lot of sites out there that are nothing but software files distributed for free. This sort of software falls into three categories:

➤ *Freeware* is program software that people have created for their own purposes or just for the fun of creating it. They distribute these programs with no expectations of making money from them.

➤ *Shareware* is program software that people are encouraged to distribute for free. The user gets to use the program for free for a while, to try it out. After the trial period is over, the user is honor-bound to pay for it if they want to continue using it. (Don't laugh! Relying on people's honor has made millions for some shareware producers. Sure, the software gets used by some people who don't pay for it—but the producer has no packaging and distribution costs, and can generally get away with little marketing cost.)

➤ *Demos* are versions of software products that have some of their features disabled, such as a word processor that won't handle the letter *E*, or a tic-tac-toe game that only lets you have two moves. Companies distribute these for free, hoping that people will try them, like them, and decide to purchase the uncrippled version of the same software.

Where do you find these files? Go to any major download site (such as www.downloads.com) and use the search engines to find files related to the topic of your site. Download the ones that sound interesting and then check the documentation; most include a clear notice giving everyone permission to distribute the files, so long as you aren't charging money for them. *Violà*, you've found your free content.

Little Niceties

There is a wide variety of little add-ons and services offered to folks who run Web sites. And of course, they're offered out of the goodness of the creators' hearts. I would never stoop so low as to suggest that these service providers are offering you a service either to get access to you (to advertise to you or to tempt you into paying services) or to go through you to get to your users.

For example, the kind-hearted cuddly folks at Microsoft now own the Link Exchange (`www.LinkExchange.com`). In addition to their ad-swapping services (which we cover elsewhere), at their site you'll find such free services as:

➤ *Fastcounter* gives you traffic reports on your site. (This is a feature you'll get automatically and in better form if you're actually paying for Web space most places.)

➤ *Listbot* manages an email list of your customers, helping you do mass-mailings for people who signed up for your newsletter. (This is supported through ads tacked on to the bottom of your email, but after you get bigger, you can switch over to its for-pay service, which doesn't include the ads.)

➤ *SiteInspector* evaluates your Web site for browser compatibility, speed, and other attributes.

If you're one of those folks who is not too keen on Microsoft, you can get similar services from Netscape at `websitegarage.netscape.com`.

For Further Info

There are a couple of interesting Web sites aimed at the e-commerce user. Sometimes you'll find advice that will help you cut corners, saving time and money. Other times, the valuable thing will be the ads aimed at the commercial site, which may offer you just what you need. These are aimed more at folks doing retail sites, but there are gems for everyone. Check out:

➤ `www.ecommercetimes.com`

➤ `www.sellitontheweb.com`

As with all the other URLs in this book, you can find links to these addresses at `www.MillionsOnTheInternet.com`.

The Least You Need to Know

➤ You can keep the cost of starting up low by using preexisting software, services, and content.

➤ Many cheap start-up steps are things you should abandon after your site gets growing.

➤ Host space can be rented, and free space is even available with strings attached.

➤ Free retail sites can be set up at a number of sites.

➤ You can use syndicated content and even encourage your users to provide you with free content.

Part 4

Growing the Business

Okay, so you have a Web site. Now you're getting millions of Web visitors every day, all eager to take advantage of the very vital and enjoyable services your site provides. Right?

Ah, if only it were that easy, we wouldn't have to write this section of the book. We could have spent the weeks engaged in our favorite hobby—sucking jelly out of jelly donuts. You see, you won't get those millions of visitors unless they've heard of your site and have a reason to visit it. You have to spread the word out to get the visitors in. Once you have visitors, you'll want to find ways to turn their presence into money. And with money, you can buy jelly donuts!

Chapter 13

Getting Famous

In This Chapter

➤ Getting press coverage on your Web site

➤ Running both online and traditional advertising for your e-business

➤ Starting an affiliate program to drive customers to your e-business

Millions of People Doing Your Advertising for You

The best way for your Internet business to become famous is to have a few million people tell a few million other people how cool it is. *Viral marketing* is where a lot of people are talking positively about your business, resulting in millions of dollars of free advertising for you. "Hey, have you heard about this great Web site? Let me tell you all about it because it is really cool!" That's viral marketing in action.

There isn't anything better than viral marketing for the purpose of bringing millions of people to your Web site. All it takes is for you to open a Web site that is so incredibly useful (and probably free, as well) that every user that comes to it tells 10 other potential users about how cool the site is. As people tell lots of other people about your great Web site, the number of folk coming to your Web site geometrically expands. When you are the lucky recipient of a positive viral marketing campaign, you could find the number of users coming to your Web business doubling every few weeks, as you excitedly watch the number of daily users jump from tens of thousands to hundreds of thousands.

As far fetched as it might sound, this sort of incredible viral publicity has benefited some Web sites. It is the sort of thing that all Web businesses dream, of course. But, unfortunately, getting the people of the world to do your advertising for you isn't something that you can force.

It happens in those rare occurrences when your Web site is so compellingly cool that people simply can't stop telling other people about it. How do you accomplish that? Be the first to start to offer something on the Internet that is truly brand new and fantastically useful or exciting. Or, be the first to jump on a new trend or fad, whatever that might be.

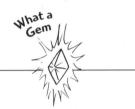

Encouraging Viruses

If you want people to spread the word about your service, it doesn't hurt to suggest that they do that. Some Web sites offer a *tell a friend* link on each page; the user clicks it and then fills out a simple form, and the URL for that page is mailed to the user's friend, with the user's recommendation to come visiting. (A user is more likely to do this if they're assured that their friend's email address will not be stored for future mass-mailings.)

Easier said than done, perhaps, but certainly some Web businesses have done just this.

Press Coverage

In the best of circumstances, thousands of people are talking about your new business and telling thousands of other people how cool it is. As the buzz about your business spreads it doesn't usually take too long for the press to pick up on it.

After all, if thousands of people are telling thousands of other people about your business, eventually some reporter is going to hear about it. After he checks your Web site out, if he is impressed, you might see a small article in a newspaper or magazine show up one day. Then a lot of the people who read that article will check out your business and in turn tell a lot more people about it.

The trouble is, there is never any way to predict or control viral marketing. People will either talk about your business or they won't. So, businesses will often attempt to jump-start things by trying to get the press's attention on their own, rather than sitting around and waiting for users to do their work for them.

Press coverage is cool because it is free. But, the members of the press aren't stupid and they will only print articles about businesses that they feel are newsworthy. Or worse, they might print an article that is more or less unfavorable.

If you feel that your business is newsworthy then you should attempt to contact the press. Local newspapers, Internet, and business magazines are a good start. You can do this by sending out a press release.

Press Releases

A press release is nothing more than a written announcement that discusses something exciting and (hopefully) newsworthy about your business. Typically it will have contact information so that any member of the press can easily reach you in case they have any questions.

You can find a lot of free information about how to write an effective press release at Press-Release-Writing.com, an online press-release service shown in Figure 13.1. It is located on the Web at `www.press-release-writing.com` and you will find this Web site to be very helpful. Its brief, but to the point, *10 Essential Tips to Insure Your Press Release Makes the News* should be mandatory reading for anyone interested in writing effective press releases. You'll also discover a sample press release, some formatting suggestions, a press release template, and more. It also offers a paid service that will send your press release to thousands of recipients, if you want.

In addition, many of the larger Internet service providers, such as EarthLink, have their own magazines that feature hot new sites. You might find that they will also be willing to provide you with free links to your own site from theirs if they think yours is worthy.

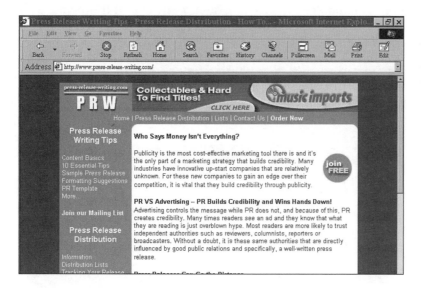

Figure 13.1

Learn how to write a press release at `www.press-release-writing.com`.

Press Release Services

There are many companies on the Internet that offer various press release services. e-Releases (seen in Figure 13.2) states that it will submit your press release to 10,000 journalists for a fee of $249. (Please note, any and all prices for services or products are subject to change after this book was written.)

Moreover, it will even *write* your press release for you for an additional $249. Or, give you a $100 discount if you have them both write and submit your press release. If you have no experience with press releases then you might find this type of service to be something that you are interested in. You will find e-Releases at www. e-releases.com.

Don't waste your time and money sending out press releases that aren't newsworthy. If you paint your building a new color or put in new carpeting, well, that probably isn't newsworthy. However, if you have created a killer new application for the Web that will change mankind for the better, well now, that would be *newsworthy*.

There are also various press associations in many states that might be able to provide you with press release services for a nominal fee. The best way to find them is to do a search with your favorite Internet search engine.

For example, I typed **Oklahoma Press Association** into my Yahoo! search engine and came up with www.okpress.com, which is the Web address for the Oklahoma Press Association. Give it a try! (You also can go to www.ncpress.com/pressassn.html and review its list of links of various press associations. This might not be a complete list, so don't forget to do a search for one in your state if it doesn't appear on the list.)

While I was visiting the Oklahoma Press Association site I noticed that it provides a *statewide press release program*. Contact your own state's press association and see if it has its own press release service.

Figure 13.2

For a fee, you can send your press release to thousands of people via www.e-releases.com.

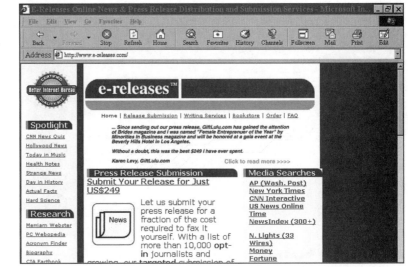

Your Media Person

As your company grows you will want to hire your own press officer. Ideally, this person should be very experienced at writing and issuing press releases. He should also be able to coach you regarding television, radio, and press interviews so that you will know how to handle yourself in such circumstances.

Your media person will be very important to you if your company becomes successful. You might learn that in the early days of your company's success you seem to be the darling of the media, and that there are a lot of reporters saying some very nice things about you and your company. However, success seems to create a certain amount of negativism over time, and you might find yourself having to deal with certain unreasonable expectations of the press.

The press can even set, through their favorable articles, unreasonable goals that you cannot possibly reach, and then castigate you later when you fail to reach those goals. Success brings its own special problems and your media officer is a crucial person who will help you through any rough times that the media might put your through.

Advertising Online

You might want to spend some money buying ad space on another Web site. This can be a good way to send some traffic to your own business, particularly if you appropriately select the Web site where you intend to purchase online advertising.

For example, if you are starting a new Web business that is going to compete with a preexisting Web business, you might be able to buy advertising space on your competitor's Web site. That might seem odd but I've seen it happen often. It might seem short sighted for a competitor to accept advertising from you but if he needs some cash he might be glad to accept yours even though the ads might send some of his own hard-earned users to your Web site. All you can do is ask and see what happens.

Nat Speaks

Be an Expert

One way to get your service mentioned in a positive light is to get yourself treated as an expert on a topic. I run Aaugh.com, a site that sells books and videos of the *Peanuts* comic strip. When *Peanuts* creator Charles Schulz announced his retirement, I used several methods (including posting on a *Peanuts*-related newsgroup) to present my phone number and let the media know that I was available for comment. During this situation, I was contacted by folks ranging from online auction news sites to *Newsweek* magazine. Not all used my quotes, but those that did ran my URL, letting people know what I offered and where it could be had. That's good free advertising.

Most Web sites will have a link to their advertising salespeople so that you can easily contact them and learn their rates and rules regarding what advertising content they will accept.

Otherwise, you want to advertise on a Web site that will have users who might be particularly interested in the services that you offer. For example, if you are running a Web site that sells used Volkswagen parts, you might want to advertise on a Web site that hosts a Volkswagen owners club.

Be careful how you design your advertising. Most people aren't terribly interested in Web advertising and have trained their eyes to ignore ads. While you don't want to be deceptive in how you design your ads, you do want your ads to be successful. To that end, you must design your ads so that they offer helpful information to potential users so that they will become interested in visiting your site. Just as you must target your audience, you must also design your ads so that they will interest your audience rather than turn them off.

Ad Exchange Systems

Some Web sites swap ad space on their own pages for ads on your Web site. The obvious benefit here is that you will obtain relatively free Web advertising. The downside is that you might not be able to as effectively target your audience.

Also, you will be giving up ad space on your own pages. In the beginning of your business giving up such Web space won't be such a problem but, as time goes on, if your business is successful, every single space that you can sell to your own advertisers will be very important to you.

You can contact the Web sites of your own selection to see if they will consider an ad exchange with you.

Using Usenet

The Internet has many public discussion areas collectively referred to as the *Usenet* or *newsgroups.* Internet users from all over the world post messages regarding a wide variety of topics on the Usenet.

The Lycos Message Boards

Lycos maintains its own independent online community, which it calls the Lycos Message Boards. It covers many topics and might be a good place for you to (gently) introduce your Web site to interested people. Don't spam! Stay on topic! Be nice! Follow any and all posted rules! You will find the message boards at http://boards.lycos.com.

You can use the Usenet to your own purposes, if you are careful and obey the rules. Proceed to www.lycos.com/computers/internet/newsgroups.html to learn a great deal more about the Usenet newsgroups.

The newsgroups are listed by their own individual topics. You will discover newsgroups that deal with cars, toys, health issues, pets, computer games, careers, movies, and thousands of other topics. *Do not post messages in newsgroups that do not fit in with that newsgroup's topic.* For example, if you post a message about your online dating service on a newsgroup that deals with surviving skin cancer, you are going to upset a lot of people. Stay on topic! (Check out Figure 13.3 for a sneak preview of the Lycos newsgroup Web site.)

LinkExchange: Eyeballs Everywhere

Web site name: www.LinkExchange.com

Founded: 1996

Service provided: Various support services for Web site owners, most notably its Banner Network, which distributes ads among various Web sites.

Business model: LinkExchange grew to prominence selling eyeballs on other people's sites. Membership in the Banner Network is free. Members add some simple HTML code to put a banner from the Banner Network library. For every two times that somebody views your page (and thus views the banner), your banner is displayed once on someone else's page. This means that half of the ads that LinkExchange displays are free ones. The other half, they can sell. While the perceived value of banner advertising on Web pages has slipped, the company has expanded to other revenue sources. LinkExchange also provides a number of services that allow it to distribute legitimate and requested email messages, both to Web site owners and visitors, and can append paid ads to those emails. As such, LinkExchange depends not so much on getting eyeballs at its own site as providing free services to sites that then generate eyeballs for it.

Where the money came from: LinkExchange grabbed a round of venture capital from Sequoia Capital in May of 1997. Software giant Microsoft then bought out the company in November of 1998, for an undisclosed (but undoubtedly lucrative) amount.

Your postings should not be written in an overly commercial manner, either. Don't talk about the *fantastic, incredible, unbelievable bargains* that your Web site is currently offering. Instead, post a gentle message about your services and give the Web address to your Web site.

Here's a good example. If your Web site offers used Volkswagen parts, then you might want to post a message in the newsgroup that deals with Volkswagen auto repair. "We have some really nice, hard-to-find, affordable used parts for 1971 VW Beetles on our Web site at www.NiceParts4Ureally.com. Thanks for checking us out."

Figure 13.3

Lycos will help you learn about newsgroups and the Usenet at www.Lycos.com/ computers/internet/ newsgroups.html.

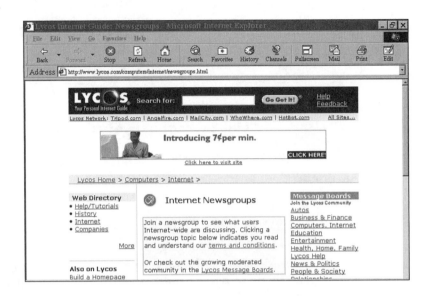

Don't *spam,* that is, post a whole bunch of repetitive messages on any one newsgroup or the same message to a bunch of newsgroups only tangentially related to what you offer. That will cause a lot of bad feelings. If you are polite and low key, you should be able to use newsgroups to reach thousands of potential users in an effective manner. Internet citizens really hate spam and some of them will figure out a way to reach out and touch you in a way that you will not like if you spam newsgroups.

It would be a good idea to read the newsgroups for a while before you post any commercial messages just so that you can get a good feel for what is tolerated by the Usenet community. Many newsgroups have their own *frequently asked questions* (FAQs) list, which fills you in on what's considered acceptable on that newsgroup when it comes to commercial messages. On some it's fine, on others it's the wrong thing to do.

And while we are talking about spam, please refrain from sending mass, unsolicited emails to strangers. Sending out messages to people who are expecting them is one thing, but sending them out to people who are not is considered poor form and shouldn't be done. This isn't just a matter of politeness, it's a matter of effective business. Most people strongly dislike unsolicited commercial email, and the handful of positive responses you may get from it aren't worth the negative image that you will give your site. Spam email is usually used to promote snake-oil medication and get-rich-quick pyramid schemes. You don't want your service lumped in with that lot.

Using Other Businesses' Bulletin Boards

Amazingly enough, many online businesses don't mind if you post messages about your own business on their online bulletin boards. This can be true even about your own competitors.

Simply find a worthy Web site that maintains a bulletin board and then carefully read any posted rules or guidelines that it has about bulletin board use. Be sure that you follow each and every rule and regulation.

Be sure that your postings are not libelous in any way and are gently written. Don't say things like: "This Web site sucks so why not come over to a decent Web site where we do things correctly and not like the idiots that run this Web site."

Be nice instead. Post some helpful information about your own Web site, complete with a link to your Web page, and let it go at that. Don't slam the competition on their bulletin board. Make sure that you post your messages in areas where they won't offend anyone. In other words, if you are selling used car parts, don't post your messages on a bulletin board that is discussing women's undergarments. (But if you know about such a bulletin board, please let me know.)

Don't spam your competition's boards by posting repetitive messages. Remember the Golden Rule and "Do unto others as you would have them do unto you." When in doubt, be nice. Wouldn't the world be a finer place if we would all just remember that?

Bribe Your Way to Success with an Affiliate Program

An *affiliate program* is a system where you pay money to people who send you business. Amazon.com established one of the first major online affiliate programs by offering a percentage of each sale sent to them from a registered, affiliate Web site. This allowed people to establish their own online bookstore and make some money. It also sent huge numbers of new customers to Amazon.com.

Amazon.com's *Associate Program* (as they call it) can be studied by going to www. amazon.com/exec/obidos/subst/associates/join/associates.html. (Whew, that is a long address, isn't it? Remember, you can surf over to www.MillionsOnTheInternet.com to find links to all these addresses and save yourself the typing.) For more on setting up your own affiliate program, see Chapter 14, "You Scratch My Link, I'll Scratch Yours." (See Figure 13.4 for a preview of Amazon.com's Web page concerning its affiliate program.)

Figure 13.4

Learn about a well-operated affiliate program at Amazon.com.

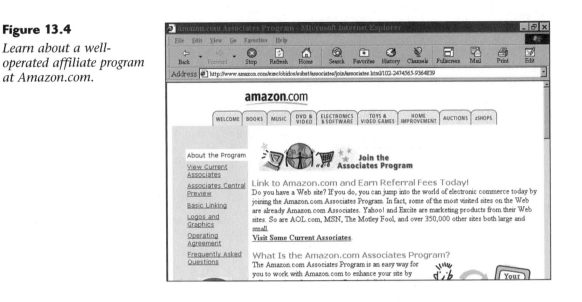

Advertising Offline

Some companies determine that spending huge amounts of money advertising offline is the thing to do to attract a lot of users to their Web sites. These ads can show up as a massive billboard campaign, or full-page ads in *Rolling Stone* or other major national magazines, or even a string of national television commercials.

Are they effective? The first problem with offline advertising is that it is *offline*. That is, you are paying to reach an audience that contains a significant number of people who don't even own a computer. That strikes me as odd. Despite the popularity of the Internet, not everybody is using it. My mother, for example, watches television, reads billboards and national magazines, but has never used the Internet. Those companies that are reaching her through offline advertising are throwing at least some of their money away, at least as far as my mother is concerned.

Naturally, if you place your ads in a computer- or Internet-related publication you will greatly increase your chances of actually reaching somebody who owns a computer and who also uses the Internet.

I guess these Internet companies that engage in massive offline advertising campaigns do so with the intent to reach as many Internet users as possible, knowing full well that much of their advertising audience could care less about the Internet. If we reach enough Internet users with our massive multicity billboard campaign, who cares if some old lady who still drives a car but doesn't even own a computer sees our billboard? Maybe that is what they are thinking.

Heroic History

DoubleClick: Clicks Sellers and Sites

Web site name: www.DoubleClick.net

Founded: January 1996

Service provided: Ad sales and management

Business model: DoubleClick is a leading trafficker in Web advertising. Its most visible face is the banner ads on many of the major sites. Its model is quite simple; it takes money from the advertisers and gives money to the sites that agree to carry its ads, keeping a chunk of it in the process. DoubleClick ads are in place on so many of the major sites that it has an unprecedented capability to track where Web surfers go. DoubleClick maintains a *cookie* (a piece of tracking information) on the hard disk of everyone who views a DoubleClick ad, and can identify that user when they view other sites. This capability has made DoubleClick a source of concern among privacy-oriented Web surfers. The company has sought to address these concerns through a privacy policy that limits when it can attach actual user information to information about a user's browsing habits, as well as through allowing individual users to opt out of its tracking. DoubleClick can offer advertisers very good targeting, due both to its large number of sites in targeted categories (automotive, travel, health, and so on) and its gathered information on the individual surfer. DoubleClick has expanded its offerings through the acquisition of such companies as Abacus Direct (direct-mail marketing) and Opt-In Email.com (email advertising).

Where the money came from: DoubleClick secured $40 million in venture capital in June of 1997. When it went public on February 20, 1998, it released 3.5 million shares for $17 apiece. On January 24, 2000, after a 2-for-1 split, the stock was trading at 106 1/8, an increase of more than 1000%. This gives the company a market capitalization of $9.6 billion. The company trades on the Nasdaq exchange under the symbol DCLK.

Perhaps they are right, too. But for my money I would think that a more targeted advertising approach makes a lot more sense, at least until the time comes when most little old ladies (and everybody else) are using the Internet on a regular basis.

Ads Work

My good and smart buddy Rod is way off on this one. First off, all mainstream advertising includes reaching people who cannot or will not use your product. On a given night, I'm likely to take in ads for feminine hygiene products, for chain stores that are nowhere near here, for software for the PlayStation that I don't have. Web access is not a rare thing these days, and with careful selection of ad placement, a large percentage of the people you reach will at least have the equipment to use your service.

If you stick with computer publications, you'll be hitting a small fraction of your potential audience. If you're running a site for jazz fans, you are far better off advertising in a jazz magazine (where perhaps half of the readers have Web access) than in a computer magazine (where maybe 5% of the readers are interested in jazz).

Major mass-market advertising serves purposes beyond just attracting customers. It also lets potential investors and allies know that you're serious about making it big.

This isn't to say that all advertising is money well spent. There is a reason why the biggest companies and most of the biggest Web sites advertise on TV, in the news magazines, and so on, and it's not because they have piles of money lying around that they don't know what to do with.

Ad Agencies

Hey, remember Darren Stevens? You know, the guy who married Samantha, the wonderful and lovely witch from the television program *Bewitched*? (It doesn't matter which Darren Stevens you remember, because there were two. For me, Darren Stevens was played by actor Dick York, but you might disagree.)

I was always fascinated by Darren's job. He was an *ad man*, a guy who worked for an advertising agency and who made up clever advertising campaigns. That always looked like a cool job to have, don't you think?

Ad agencies are available to help you plan your advertising campaign. They can help you decide where to place your offline ads, if that is something that you decide to do, and will help to design your ad campaigns, as well.

Your yellow pages list local advertising agencies that you might consider retaining. You will learn that there are small, local advertising agencies as well as huge, nationally known advertising agencies. Only your advertising budget can help you decide how big you want to go with offline advertising. You can start by meeting with your favorite local advertising agency and working from there. If you have a serious ad budget, start reading magazines such as *Advertising Age* and *Ad Week* so that you know how to talk the talk and know who the players are.

The Least You Need to Know

➤ Press coverage is great free advertising but is something that you cannot count on.

➤ Both online and traditional offline advertising can be costly yet worthwhile if you carefully target your advertising audience.

➤ Beware spamming people as it will probably cause more harm than good for your business.

Chapter 14

You Scratch My Link, I'll Scratch Yours

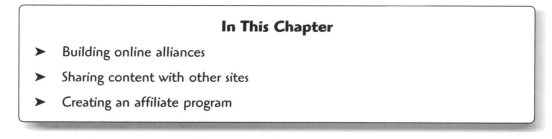

In This Chapter

➤ Building online alliances

➤ Sharing content with other sites

➤ Creating an affiliate program

Yours is not going to be the only site on the Web. After a period of intense research, I've found that the modern World Wide Web features more than a dozen sites! And that's counting only the sites about *I Dream of Jeanie*. I'm only guessing, but it wouldn't surprise me if the number of non-Jeanie sites were as high as a hundred! And of those hundred sites, there might be one that could actually help you!

Everyone Is Friends Online

Okay, that was pretty silly. Obviously, there are more than a hundred Web sites. Web sites number in the millions. If there were only a hundred Web sites, you might think they would each get a lot more attention, but that's not the case. If there were only a hundred Web sites, no one would bother surfing the Web at all. It's the large number of sites covering a large range of topics that has caused hundreds of millions of people to go online.

Web presence is not a *zero sum game*. That's a term that economists (and those who want, for some twisted reason, to disguise themselves as economists) use to describe a situation where one person making a gain means that someone else is making a loss. Instead, the more people who play the Internet game, the more audience and money there are to go around. Because of this, other sites aren't the enemy. Other sites are your friend.

Direct Competition, Indirect Cooperation

Recently, I was shopping for an engagement ring for my girlfriend, Lara. If you've ever done this (I won't even ask why you'd be buying a ring for my girlfriend), you quite possibly found yourself in a big city jewelry district. Go there and you'll find some fierce competition, as the different jewelers compete on price, on the attractiveness of their stores, on selection, on quality, and on how many different languages they can haggle in.

If you think about it, you'll realize that the shops are all cooperating. Even if the owners of the shops never speak to each other, even if they throw donuts at each other when they pass on the street, they are cooperating. By having all those jewelry stores so close together, they make the district *the* place to go for your jewelry, thus pulling your sale away from the stores that are scattered elsewhere. And by offering such a huge selection overall, they make sure that someone who is looking for a golden frog brooch with ruby eyes is almost certain to find it. In contrast, the shopper at an unattached jewelry store may not find the bejeweled reptile she sought, and may instead blow her money on something trivial such as food or shelter.

Of course, the stores are also in competition. The real secret is that competing and cooperating aren't mutually exclusive. If you start an online site offering new sitcoms on the Web, and three other startups offer similar sites, you are in competition with them. However, your real competition is TV stations, and if these four sites get people to start thinking of the Web as a source for sitcoms, it helps all four of you.

All that is *passive cooperation*. It doesn't require anyone to directly make plans with anyone else. Most of the *active cooperation* you are likely to be involved in will be with Web sites that are not offering exactly the same products and services that you are. Instead, you should try to cooperate with sites that share the same audience but have different products. A site that offers Goth music may cooperate with a site that sells Goth comic books or Goth clothing or Goth sandwiches (Black Forest ham on black bread with a smear of gloomayonnaise). Better yet, cooperate with sites that have offerings that have some sort of synergy with yours, such as having a music site cooperate with a music-playing software site, or having an aglet site cooperate with a dictionary site (so that people will know what an aglet is).

(The coolest thing about having cooperation based on synergy is that you get to use the word synergy a lot. Words with more than one *y* in them are cool. Synergy, syzygy, rhythmically, yay!)

DCDC: Direct Competitors Do Cooperate

In the business world, there are actually plenty of examples of competitors cooperating. Much of this occurs in the form of industry associations, where major players in a field cooperate for their mutual advantage. These industry groups work in three common realms:

➤ **Standards**   Groups in engineering and technology fields develop standards to make sure that their products work together or use interchangeable parts, which makes life easier for both the industry and the consumer. For example, the World Wide Web Consortium (www.w3c.org), which sets the standards from protocols on the Web, includes competitors like Microsoft and America Online/Netscape among its members.

➤ **Legal advocacy**   Many industries have groups that exist to encourage legal changes to benefit the organization. The Recording Industry Association of America, for example, represents the major music labels by working to pass legislation that destroys or limits technology that people might use to copy music.

➤ **Publicity and advertising**   Makers of similar products band together to keep their entire product category in people's minds. Who can forget the National Rutabaga Council's ad line, "Got Rutabaga Juice?"

My Visitors Are Your Visitors

A basic form of cooperation is when two sites try to get their own visitors to head to the other site. This way, both sites expose themselves to a host of new people. This means more customers, higher income from ad exposures, and more of those luscious customer counts that make would-be investors dig deep into their wallets.

Rely on Reliability

Be sure that the sites you're cooperating with are reliable. Having links, ads, or other associations with sites that are frequently down will only serve to make you look bad.

Frame Yourself for Stickiness

If you want to make sure that your visitor can come back to your site after visiting a linked site, use *frames*—an HTML feature that divides the browser screen into regions. You can devote most of the screen to the linked site, while keeping a link back to your site in a small strip on the top or at the side, as shown in Figure 14.1.

Ad Swaps

The easiest way to cooperate is simply to do an ad swap. You put an ad for their site on yours, and they do the same. If one site is more popular, it's only fair that the less popular site puts the ad in more locations to roughly equalize the number of ad exposures. (When being cooperative, it doesn't pay to worry about exact counts; a cooperation should be done with at least some attempt at maintaining a sense of friendship.)

You can design ads such as this to specifically address the audience of the other site. Because your ad will appear so often, it's a good idea to change it frequently, to keep the site it's on from looking static.

Inter-linking

If the cooperating sites have mutually relevant content, it makes sense to have material on these sites link to each other. The *inter-site links* (links from one site to another) can appear anywhere you would have *intra-site links* (links from one page to another page of the same site).

Some sites prefer that your links to them announce that the user is visiting another site (Solitairecheat.com: Guide to beating the game), because it serves as an advertisement even if the user doesn't click it. Others prefer they look just like an intra-site link (tips to cheating at solitaire), so that people won't be reluctant to click them.

Content Sharing

Let's say you're running AVastWasteland.com, a site of TV news and reviews. You've got a friend who has an online mystery book store, NovelWaysToDie.com. This is a great chance to cooperate by giving her something: all your reviews of mystery-related TV shows. Does she have any content that you could use in return? Possibly so, but if not, so what? Content-sharing is a win-win situation.

➤ The site using the content gets material that can attract additional viewers and increases the stickiness of the site.

➤ The content provider gets additional exposure for his site name and usually a link to the site, because these things are included on the provided content.

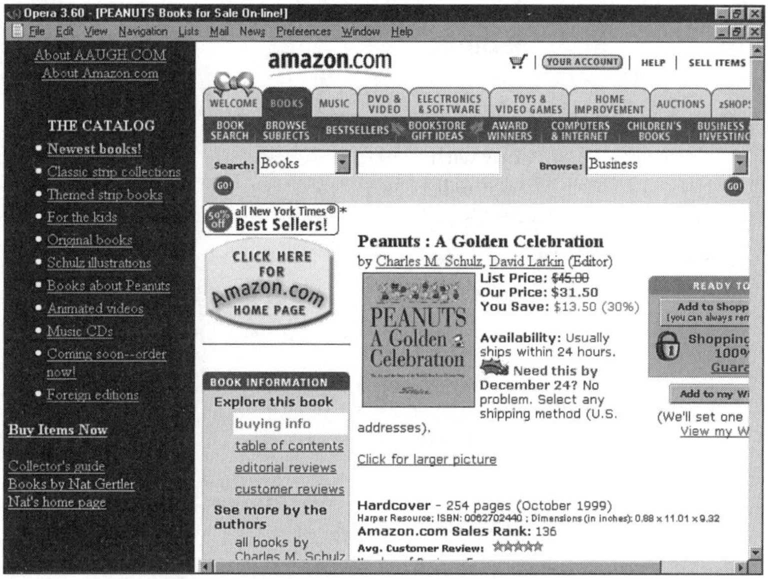

Figure 14.1

While the affiliate-based nature of Aaugh.com requires linking to Amazon.com pages, the index frame on the left side makes sure the surfer can easily return.

Sharing Customer Information

Customer information is a handy and valuable thing, even when it tells you what your customers are doing at some other site. If your friends over at `CheeseWizards.com` tell you that Jim Schumaker has been looking up recipes for Philadelphia cheese steaks, then you know that Jim will soon be a good target market for paper napkins, or a heart defibrillator.

That sort of customer data is most valuable if you have a site that adapts to the individual user, or if you're selling target-marketed advertising space. The advantages of sharing customer data comes only when you cooperate with a site that shares a fair portion of your customer base—which is likely if you're already involved in other cooperative ventures with that site.

Privacy's Primacy

As we've advised elsewhere, you really should have an online privacy policy. If you've promised your customers that you won't share their data with anyone else, you better stick to that. Violating your own privacy policy not only will hurt your relationship

189

with your customers, you might end up with a lawsuit that will cost you your shirt. (As any fashion expert will tell you, having a suit without a shirt just won't cut it.)

Your customers are quite right to have some privacy concerns. After all, privacy is a basic human instinct—and these days, the more information that is distributed about you, the more junk mail, junk phone calls, junk faxes, and junk singing gorillagrams you'll get.

Addressing Your Customers for Them

If PicturesOfPups.com wants to send a special discount offer on an all-puppy calendar to the customers of PuppyYumyums.com, they could just get the PuppyYumYums folks to sell their customer list, and email everyone on the list. This would, however, have a whole lot of downsides:

➤ The customer's privacy has been violated.

➤ PuppyYumYums has given PicturesOfPups more valuable information than they need.

➤ The customers are apt to be mad about getting *unsolicited commercial email* (also known as *spam*) from a company they have not dealt with.

The solution to these problems is simple: Instead of PicturesOfPups sending out the email, PuppyYumyums should send the mail to all their customers making the offer, and directing them to the PicturesOfPups Web site for the details. If done right, not only will no one come out looking bad from this, the customers might actually appreciate PuppyYumyums more for directing them to such a good offer.

To help make sure you stay on the customer's good side, you should give them the option of opting out of mailings when they give you their email address. Then, with every email, give them the option to opt out again, so if they forget they agreed to allow you to email or if they've changed their mind, you don't keep making them angrier with each email. The program you use to handle mass emailings will have some options allowing recipients to unsubscribe from your mailings.

Bribing Your Friends

Intersite cooperation is a lot like marriage: sometimes it's based on friendship, sometimes it's based on mutual interests, and sometimes it's based on cold, hard cash.

An *affiliate program* is a system where you bribe other sites for sending you customers. Other people's sites become affiliates of yours, and receive some sort of commission for customers who order your products or use your services via a link from your service.

Sites of all sizes use affiliate programs. For unknown sites, it's a way of creating a network of boosters. For well-known sites, it can be a way of getting sales people with special knowledge and special audience.

Consider Amazon.com, the big daddy of online retailing. Amazon began as a specialty shop, specializing in books. Books, however, is a huge category. While Amazon certainly had a lot of employees who were knowledgeable about books, they couldn't have people who specialized in every single subcategory of books.

Enter the affiliates (or, as Amazon calls them, *associates*). If someone is interested in kids books about cats, or murder mysteries about cats, or recipe books about cats, they can find a site on that topic. On that site there will not only be reviews and guides, but also ordering links that the customer can use to order the books through Amazon. If you check out the weather at The Weather Center (www.theweathercenter.com), you'll also have a chance to order books about the weather. Suddenly a momentary curiosity about hurricanes can turn into a small windfall for Amazon.

Amazon pays between 5% and 15% for sales that its associates generate. The higher rates are for lower-discount items that are directly linked from the associate site. The lower prices are for items that are heavily discounted, or which are found using a search form on the affiliate site. Fifteen percent or even 5% of the retail price cuts substantially into Amazon's profit for the item. Amazon gets a lot more out of this transaction, as you can see what happens when Miss Sue Finisdore orders a book on sign language for cats from the SingInSign.com associate site:

➤ As long as Sue is on Amazon ordering anyway, she might also order a new cat calendar or a copy of the CD *Music with Too Much Bass* by Lady Power & The Amps. After all, she realizes that the shipping charge for additional items is quite small.

➤ Amazon gets Sue's information in its database. Because Amazon, not SingInSign, actually processes the order, Amazon gets Sue's email address and can reach her for new offers.

➤ Sue gets exposed to Amazon, and might well return there as a customer without any further prodding.

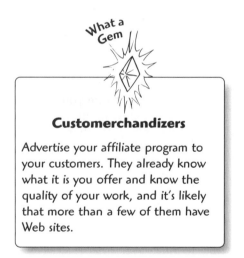

Customerchandizers

Advertise your affiliate program to your customers. They already know what it is you offer and know the quality of your work, and it's likely that more than a few of them have Web sites.

Offering a Lucrative Deal

There are an awful lot of sites with affiliate programs (swing on over to www.refer-it.com, as seen in Figure 14.2, to see lists and reviews of them). To lure quality sites into being your affiliates, you'll need to convince them that you will do well by them. You're competing directly with any affiliate programs offered by other sites offering the same services. You're also competing to a lesser degree with every other affiliate program no matter what the site. In fact, on the sites that are really important to you, you won't be competing with random affiliate programs. If you have an online ice cream shop, the affiliates you really want are the ones that realize that ice cream is a natural thing to sell to their customers, and are trying to decide which ice cream shop to support. Any site that is weighing your affiliation deal against the deals offered by Honest Joe's Online Casino or Pete's Pyramid Program is a site that isn't likely to bring you much in the way of quality customers.

Figure 14.2

For folks who prefer to refer, www.refer-it.com is a key source for information on affiliate programs, and a great place to publicize yours.

Owners of high-traffic sites are pretty savvy about Web business. They know what you have to gain from an affiliate. They know that if your site sells shipped physical goods your actual costs for taking care of the customer are high, and a commission of 5% to 20% is actually reasonable. On the other hand, if you're offering online services when your marginal costs are actually pretty small, commissions of 50% are reasonable, and some sites offer more.

They also know that you're going to be making money off anything else the customer orders at the same time, and also from having this customer on a recurring basis. Some affiliate programs offer a (smaller) cut of everything else the customer purchases at the same time, and even some small cut of everything that same customer buys for the next six months.

If you're going to attract the lucrative affiliates, you'll have to be a respectable site offering quality merchandise. If what you sell is tuna-flavored mouthwash, no one is going to be your affiliate even if you offer 95% commission. Ninety-five percent of nothing is nothing. And if you don't seem trustworthy, not only will the site's visitors not trust you, the site's owner won't either. Sites have been known to stiff their affiliates, so the wise Web site owner steers clear of shady deals.

Setting up an affiliate program does not have to be a major technological challenge. There already is existing software designed specifically for managing such programs, as well as companies that will provide program management. Scoot on over to `www.refer-it.com/main.cfm?screen=info/build/software` for more information on what's available.

Affiliate Afflictions

There are weak affiliates, and then there are bad affiliates. A weak affiliate simply doesn't send many sales your way. That's not something to worry about much; the cost of carrying a weak affiliate on your affiliate list is very low. A bad affiliate is a very different creature. Bad affiliates can make your company look bad, and that can cost you a lot in the long term.

To avoid the problem of bad affiliates, be sure you set firm affiliate policies and make it clear that affiliates will be cut off without commissions for violating them. Your policies should focus on things that can hurt you, such as:

➤ Affiliates must make clear on their sites what their relationship to your site is. They cannot misrepresent themselves as a division of your site, as employees of your site, or as anything else other than partners or affiliates. Otherwise, every bad thing they do taints you directly.

➤ Affiliates may not send out unsolicited email with links to your site or any mention of your site. Many of the recipients of such email will blame you for it. Similarly, affiliates should not be allowed to post off-topic messages on Usenet newsgroups and other discussion groups that use links to your site or promote your name or services.

➤ Affiliates may not place orders through their own links. This policy will keep you from having customers who become affiliates simply to get a kick-back on what they're ordering anyway. This is actually a good policy to enforce weakly;

Commission of Mercy

Charities can be particularly lucrative affiliates. They are expert at reaching out to people and tend to deal with people with money. Connecting your name with theirs can make you look good. Because of this, as well as for reasons of genuine charitable concern, you should be willing to give them a slightly bigger cut. (Check out www.greatergood.com to see a business built on acting as a go-between for affiliates and charities.)

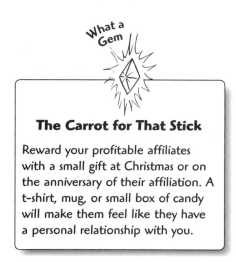

The Carrot for That Stick

Reward your profitable affiliates with a small gift at Christmas or on the anniversary of their affiliation. A t-shirt, mug, or small box of candy will make them feel like they have a personal relationship with you.

193

if HungryJoses.com is sending 40 customers a month to your ice cream store, then you really don't care if Hungry Jose orders a couple gallons for himself.

Heroic History

Refer-It: Affiliating with Affiliates

Web site name: www.refer-it.com

Founded: December 1997

Service provided: Affiliate program information center.

Business model: Refer-it has created an interesting position for itself, because at its core it is a site that Web site owners use to reach out to other Web site owners. Its central purpose is as an information site for those with an interest in *affiliate and referral programs* (programs in which Web sites pay commissions to other sites that steer traffic and sales their way). Its search engine helps users to look through more than 1,000 different such programs, listing the details of the programs and rating them. Refer-it does not charge sites to list their affiliate programs (although it does require that sites provide a link to Refer-it); Refer-it's income comes from advertising. The advertising is primarily bought by companies seeking affiliates; this is an ideally targeted group that is key to many new commerce sites getting noticed, so this is a very attractive advertising situation. In addition to the site, Refer-it also has an email newsletter that site users can receive on an opt-in basis. Its current parent company, Internet.com, runs seminars on affiliate programs aimed at the users of the Refer-it Web site.

Where the money came from: In April 1999, Refer-it was purchased by Internet.com for an undisclosed amount. Internet.com runs 84 Web sites as well as email newsletters, discussion forums, and email discussion lists. Its stock is traded publicly on the Nasdaq exchange under the symbol INTM. As of January 7, 2000, it had a market capitalization of $1.28 billion.

Heroic History

Be Free: Be Paying Your Affiliates

Web site name: www.befree.com

Founded: 1996

Service provided: Affiliate program management systems

Business model: Be Free, Inc. has developed its own software system, which handles all the complex tracking, management, and promotion necessary for any merchant site that wants to have an affiliate program. With two employees, the company developed the BFAST software that is the base of its system. Be Free's first customer was barnesandnoble.com, who needed a robust system to handle what has become one of the largest affiliate programs on the Web. Be Free's offerings expanded in 1999 to include affiliate programs that can be offered through email rather than via Web sites. Be Free makes its money not from licensing out its software, but from keeping the software and licensing out the service. Be Free handles more than 150 merchants and literally millions of affiliate deals. To show that it puts its money where its mouth is, Be Free runs www.affiliaterecruiters.com, which is in effect an affiliate program for people who recruit affiliates!

Where the money came from: Be Free received two rounds of venture capital. In September 1998, it received $10.6 million from a trio of venture capital firms. In April of 1999, it dipped in for another $25 million, from two of the previously investing firms and one new firm. Be Free held its IPO on November 3, 1999, priced at $12 per share. As of January 7, 2000, the price was $72 7/16 per share, giving the firm a market capitalization of $1.9 billion. The company's stock is traded on the Nasdaq National Market using the ticker symbol BFRE.

Don't Just Befriend: Merge!

You're running a seasoning site, SamsSassySalt.com, and you come across the site PaulasPleasantPepper.com. You realize that there are a lot of ways that these two sites can help each other; it's almost as if they were born to be one site. Maybe they should be.

Assuming that these two companies are purely Web based, existing only via their sites, then the merging of sites should be more than just a cooperative venture between two companies. The companies themselves should merge into one larger company. If one company has a lot of financial resources, this can be accomplished by them buying out the other company (for more information on how this takes place, check out Chapter 19, "Become a Sellout for Fun and Profit"). Otherwise, it's generally more of a true merger, with the owners of the original companies splitting ownership and control of the new merged company.

Merger is a very tricky process, because it involves agreeing on the value of what each site brings to the merger. It also may involve merging offices and figuring out what to do with personnel whose jobs may be redundant. Corporate attorneys will be involved.

Alliances Ain't Forever

As I said earlier, inter-site cooperation is a lot like marriage. Sometimes, it really doesn't work out, and you find yourself in court fighting over who has to take the cat.

Like marriage, you should go into a cooperative arrangement not only hoping but clearly expecting it to work well. But you should have some clear agreement (in many cases, a legal agreement) as to what *working well* means, and what happens when it doesn't work out. To avoid anything ugly happening, you may want to set a time limit for the cooperative deal; you can always extend it if everyone is happy with it. Your agreement should also allow you to terminate in such events as:

➤ Your partner gets bought out. (This way, you don't find yourself with a cooperative agreement of your direct competition.)

➤ Your partner fails to make whatever financial payments are provided.

➤ Your partner's site being continually or frequently unavailable or slow (if you're relying on services provided by your partner's system).

➤ The Cubs win the World Series (although this is unlikely to happen, and may be covered by an Act Of God clause).

The Least You Need to Know

➤ Cooperating with other sites is a good way to take advantage of their audience and their expertise.

➤ Cooperation can take many forms, including ad swaps, site-to-site links, sharing content, and mutual promotion of services.

➤ Affiliate programs are a standard way to easily turn a large number of sites into your partners.

➤ If there is a great synergy between your site and your partner's, consider a merger.

➤ Take care that you don't end up with trouble if the cooperation does not work out as planned.

Chapter 15

Expand the Brand

So you've set up the site you've always wanted: an online episode guide dedicated to the obscure 1970s sitcom *My Three Husbands*. You have the episode guide working well, and you have this nifty search program that will help people find exactly the episode they're thinking of. Every single *My Three Husbands* fan on the Web surfs over to your site at least once, and the money you're making from ads for the *My Three Husbands* home video library pays a good chunk of the site's cost. You should be happy, right?

Why Expand?

Valuable Internet companies become valuable not through their immediate profits (even a profitable site such as eBay is valued far higher than the profits would dictate) but through their perceived potential for expansion. There are three dimensions of expansion:

➤ How much you can bring in from each user (whether it's money directly from the user or money from others for serving the user)

➤ What portion of the Internet audience will use your site

➤ How many people are on the Internet

Multiply those three factors and you'll get your total site income. If you stop trying to grow your site in offerings and audience, then the only possible growth you have is from the third factor. Unless your site is already quite strong on the first two factors, you are putting strong limits on your site's success and value. If you wanted your site to have limits, you should've picked up *The Complete Idiot's Guide to Making Seventeen Dollars on the Internet.*

Offering New Services to the Same Customers

By offering a wider range of features (without losing your focus), you encourage the user to come to the site more frequently, to stay longer, and to spread the word more. A site that was meant merely to be visited once can be transformed into one that's meant to become a daily habit.

Compounding Interest

The most obvious form of expansion is to offer more products and services on the same interest, as the site in Figure 15.1 did. Sure, an episode guide is great, but could you put up cast photos and biographies? A "where are they now" section? Trivia quizzes? Interviews with the writers? Those things are easy.

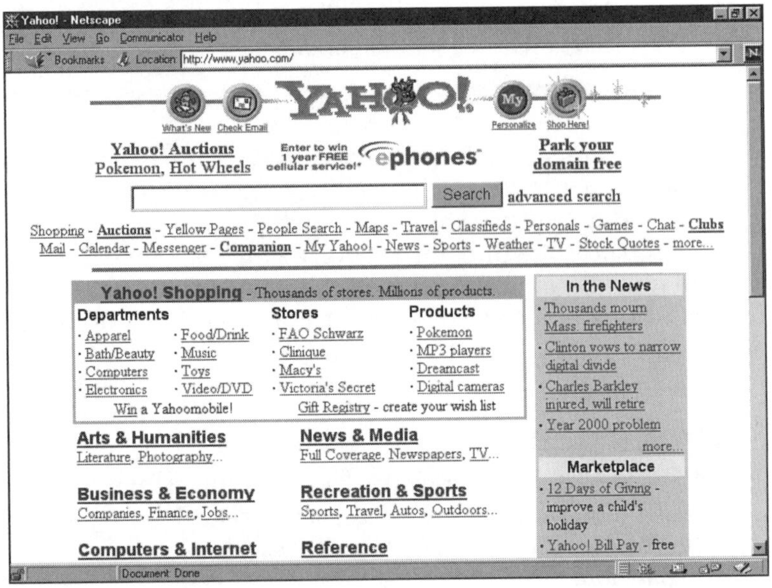

Figure 15.1

Yahoo! expanded from offering just a list of Web sites to offering many of the services that its visitors were looking for.

But that's thinking small. What if you were to license (or even buy) actual rights to the TV show; that's something to plow some venture capital into. You could offer sound clips and even entire episodes to be viewed via RealPlayer (which, for phone modem users, gives a small and jerky picture at best, but if the episodes aren't running on TV, that's better than nothing). Show an episode, and you can have someone on the site for half an hour! And you can put video ads in the program, and other ads on the page around the program! As far as additional services go, this is potentially lucrative. This is eyeball city!

And if the rights you acquire include the right to make derivative products, you could have new fan-written stories that continue the show. You could even create new episodes; sure, actually filming a TV show might be too expensive, but audio-only episodes could be the modern equivalent of the radio show.

And then there are the *atoms*, the physical items you could offer to sell: *My Three Husbands* caps, kitchen magnets, lunchboxes, and even underwear.

Address the User, Not the Interest

A site exists for its users. The users of almost any given site tend to have things in common. If you can figure out what those things are, you can expand your site around your users' lifestyles and keep their attention longer.

What do the visitors to the *My Three Husbands* site have in common? The obvious thing is that they all like the show. This confluence of tastes might seem small, but it can actually start a great basis for a discussion group. Open a discussion group here, and people will discuss more than the show itself. Having found kindred souls, they'll discuss everything under the sun. (In the decade that I've been on the comic book discussion forum on CompuServe, I've sure spent a lot more time chatting about movies, TV, politics, biblical interpretation, and Philly cheesesteaks than I have spent discussing comic books. I know people who have stayed in that group for years after they have quit their comic book hobby, simply because they've found kindred spirits.)

Another thing *My Three Husbands* fans (or M3Holics, as they like to be known) have in common is their age. Most of them will probably have been somewhere between 14 and 24 when the TV series originally aired, as those are the ages when folks are most easily addicted to a TV show. If that was in the mid-seventies, then probably you have a high percentage of folks with kids in college, and you could market an M3H-oriented college survival pack to them. They're in the years where back pain and hair dye become important, so if you could combine the show with those concerns somehow, you'd be addressing your users.

Homogeneity Sells

Understanding what your users have in common will make your advertising more valuable, as advertisers like to target specific groups or specific tastes.

Same ages, similar interests, and an ongoing interest in a show about marriage complexities also suggest a dating service! That's right, these are human beings. Just keep reminding yourself to address the user of your site, and not just the original topic of your site.

Heroic History

RealNetworks: Multimediamania

Web site name: realnetworks.com

Founded: 1994 (as Progressive Networks)

Service provided: Software for sending and receiving multimedia content

Business model: The Real line of multimedia Internet products began with RealAudio, which allowed both recorded and streaming audio to be played, and supported quality compression, which allowed Internet users with standard dial-in bandwidths to hear sounds that, although far from high-fidelity, were well worth hearing. As is standard in such situations, Real would distribute the player/received programs for free. Its money came from selling to sites the software needed to encode and broadcast the RealAudio signal. Soon, it began supporting compressed video, and switched to using the terms RealMedia for the transmissions and RealPlayer for the player. While always maintaining the free basic players, which make using RealMedia on a site lucrative, RealNetworks opened up another income source by offering a deluxe version of its player product for a price. RealNetworks also has created some advertising sales opportunities, with features built into further players. When the MP3 audio compression scheme gained a strong foothold on the Internet, RealNetworks chose to embrace the challenger, producing the MP3 encoder/player RealJukebox. In November 1999, the company ran into some major snafus when it was revealed that some of its products were gathering information about the songs that the users were listening to and sending it to RealNetwork's host, in apparent violation of RealNetwork's stated privacy policy.

Where the money came from: Originally financed by private individuals (including Lotus founder Mitch Kapor), RealNetworks took on venture capital in October of 1996 ($5.7 million) and again in December of 1996 ($17.9 million). The company changed its name in September of 1997 when preparing for its IPO, which came out at $12.50 per share on November 26, bringing the company $38.5 million. The stock split two-for-one in April of 1999. As of January 25, 2000, the stock was trading for just under $143, giving the company a market capitalization of just more than $10 billion. The stock trades on the Nasdaq exchange, under the symbol RNWK.

Repackaging for Different Customers

After you have the basics of your site set up, you should see if you can put a somewhat different face on what you have and pitch it to another audience. Because you already have your expertise, technology, and alliances in place, targeting a second audience should be a lot easier than targeting the first.

Same Cereal, Different Box

Have you ever done your food shopping at House O' Food, brought back a box of House O' Food brand Choco-Orbs, and discovered that they're exactly the same as the UberMarket-brand Cocoa Bearings? And both are the same as Honest Aaron's Artificially Flavored Chocolately Corn-based Irregular Sphere Shapes? Of course you haven't; those names are made up. But the point remains that different supermarket chains all hire the same company to make cereal for them, and just put it in different boxes.

Much the same can be true with Web sites. Take everything that you've done with *My Three Husbands* and instead apply it to that mid-1980s cult show, *Chimp-In-Law*. Suddenly you have another site. You can link it to the M3H site if your want to, or make it appear totally different. You are now in position to reach out to a whole other group of TV fans. And, if you can do it with *Chimp-in-Law*, you can do it with *General Grandma*, with *Home with Habib*, with *Too Many Ghosts*, *Remembering George*, *Lucy and the Losers*, *Dog of My Dreams*, *Rebuilding the Johnsons*, *Stuck in an Elevator*, and every other cult sitcom that might be out there. Soon you'll have a whole network of sites.

Of course, repackaging one TV site into another TV site is putting it in a fairly similar box. Imagine if you took the same sort of information, interview, and discussion format that you developed for the TV sites and instead built it around corporate contract law? You'll be aiming at a very different (and quite possibly smaller) audience, but it could be a very lucrative one. After all, corporate lawyers tend to be well paid, and might well be willing to pay membership fees if they feel the content will be useful. Even if they aren't, they make a lucrative advertising target. Oh, you'd probably have to replace the romantic matchmaking functions with job headhunting ones, but many of the other concepts behind your site actually transfer over.

What a Gem

The Web's Wide World

One of the more obvious types of repackaging is to offer content in other languages. This is fairly easy if you're offering online content, harder if your site sells atoms (as shipping products internationally has its own practical and legal complexities and the costs are often prohibitive for the potential customer).

Same Cereal, Bigger Box

Another way of expanding your site is to expand the focus of the content. Instead of just covering *My Three Husbands*, you can start to cover seventies sitcoms in general, with the M3H site as a subsection of the larger site. And after you have that going, you can expand into sitcoms in general, and then into TV in general, with subsections for sitcoms, dramas, and so on.

What a Gem

Prepurchase with Purpose

Even when you're just starting up, keep possible long-term expansion in mind. You might want to register domain names that would fit well for a few possible expansion directions, just so you have them ready.

Each move like this should be an *expansion*, not just a refocusing; if you start carrying less stuff on sitcoms to be able to cover other TV topics, you'll risk turning off a fair portion of the audience you've already built.

These sorts of moves also should be accompanied by large publicity pushes. You can't count on the people who were coming to the site just for *My Three Husbands* to spread the word for you. Besides, you're likely to want to pick a new domain name. When you do this, try to pick a name that will fit for another few expansions. Every time you change your domain name, you will lose people, confuse people, and most importantly, you will fail to build up visible momentum under any one name. And do keep that old domain address working; people still have links to it!

Super Cereal Multipack

As discussed in the previous chapter, existing sites can be acquired or merged to create a larger community. If you do this, the joined sites should have some larger blanket name—even if each individual site and service has its own name. Remember the point is to convince the users of the existing sites that you're not getting rid of what they love, you're just offering them more.

Reasons to Not Expand

Whenever you expand, you run the risk of moving from a leader of a smaller market to being a generic entry into a larger one. Let's say, for example, that you run a high-quality science fiction bookstore site. The site is filled with knowledgeable reviews of science fiction books, guides to classic books, interviews and online chats with noted science-fiction authors, and so on. The audience for such books is large, but it's limited as well. It would be understandable that you'd want to expand it into a larger, general-purpose bookstore. But it would probably be a mistake.

Heroic History

Buy: Eight Stores in One

Web site name: buy.com

Founded: 1998

Service provided: Superstore

Business model: Buy.com is a major online retail presence with a strong emphasis on discount prices. It addresses the question of expanding the brand by providing eight URLs, each with a specialty focus. If you just want computer hardware, you head to buycomp.com. Software is sold at buysoft.com, books at buybooks.com, videos at buyvideos.com, CDs at buymusic.com, games at buygames.com, stereos and TVs at buyelectronics.com, and surplus items at buysurplus.com. In this way, each individual site can be viewed as a specialty store, but they are all linked through the obvious naming pattern and through the central site, buy.com. In fact, enter any one of these domain names and you'll find yourself forwarded to a domain that starts with www.buy.com. Its financial model is standard retailing; charge more for the product than you bought it for. As is standard with discount-oriented Web retailers, its current discounts are so high that it is likely losing money on every transaction, in a quest to establish retail presence. It also generates some income through ad sales. Buy.com has plans to expand beyond its North American presence to serve customers in foreign lands and languages. It also plans to expand the brand with sites such as buytravel.com (a joint venture in association with United Airlines).

Where the money came from: Buy.com remains privately owned. It has received a series of investments totaling more than $200 million. At the time of this writing, it was preparing its IPO, expecting to issue 14 million shares at an opening price of $10 to $12 apiece. By the time you read this, the IPO will likely have been completed and the shares should be trading on the Nasdaq exchange under the symbol BUYX.

Scaling Up Can Drive You Crazy

When a business expands its services and related engineering and support systems, that is called *scaling up.* Rapid and massive scaling up might be needed for a quickly growing company but it can be very difficult to deal with. If you have any defects in your engineering design, you will most certainly feel the negative effects of a rapid scaling up. This is a very tricky issue for hot, new companies and one that every company will have to plan carefully for. Always remember to design every aspect of your company so that a fast expansion can be easily facilitated or you will find your company tripping over its own shoelaces.

Small Fish in Big Ponds Get Eaten

As a science fiction bookstore, you probably have some direct competition, but they probably aren't that large. It's probably folks that you can hold your own against.

As a mainstream bookstore, however, you'll find yourself suddenly pitted against amazon.com and bn.com, a couple of huge sites for which books are the backbone (although not the only sales source). Unless you have some powerful tricks and powerful promotions and deep pockets, you'll probably not make much headway there.

Your Brand Is Getting Blurry

But there's no real risk, right? After all, you won't lose the base of science fiction customers you already have, will you?

Actually, you might. After all, those customers could have been shopping at other bookstores all along. They came to you because they saw science fiction as your specialty, something you put an effort into doing well. Your site name was a brand name for science-fiction products. After you broadened your specialty, you made it look like you did not care as much about science fiction—even if you continued to do everything you always did in that regard.

This isn't to say that expansion isn't possible. You could expand into science fiction–related DVDs, for example, and only seem to lose your focus somewhat (although those who see literary science fiction as serious and movie and TV science fiction as silly might feel more comfortable elsewhere). Or you could open a completely separate site, focusing on mysteries or romance novels or some other specialty category. You just have to be careful about how you do it.

Amazon Blurred Well

If one wants to look for a counterexample, a case where taking a specialized site and broadening seems to have worked, one need look no further than Amazon.com. Amazon started with a clear specialty: online bookstore. However, it now specializes in books and toys and music and auctions and videos and tools and software and... well, let's face it, it specializes in everything. However, at the time that Amazon started expanding beyond books, people didn't just think of it as a bookstore. People thought of it as the big example of an e-commerce site; the other sites, no matter what they sold, were seen as minor. As such, this expansion played upon that image of it more than on the image of it as a book-seller. And even so, although it has certainly gained a strong foothold in the other worlds, the place where it continues to shine is as a bookstore. It's a very different situation than one today's average site finds itself in.

The Least You Need to Know

➤ For serious growth, a Web site needs to expand its offerings.

➤ You can expand by offering more services to your existing audience, thus profiting from your existing recruiting efforts.

➤ You can expand by offering the same services to different audience, thus profiting from your existing technology and alliances.

➤ You can expand by joining with other existing sites to share customers and services.

➤ When attempting to expand, you do risk losing the special focuses that drew your existing audience.

Chapter 16

You've Seen the Site, Now Eat the Candybar

In This Chapter

➤ Reusing your site content offline

➤ Licensing your site name

➤ Making your brand mean something

So your Web site has taken off phenomenally. In fact, it has grown so fast and so large that you've managed to acquire every other site on the Web! That's right, the Internet is all yours, and everything that anyone does on the Web brings you a profit. But that's not enough. There are still people doing plenty of things off the Internet—eating ice cream, roller skating, thinking impolite thoughts about drummers—and you're not making a penny from it! How are you supposed to achieve tyrannical global domination in this situation?

It's time to expand off the Internet.

Crossing the Online/Offline Line

Online services moving into offline projects are still a small phenomenon, fairly new but growing. It seems to be a very backward sort of move. After all, there is such great furor over the potential online; why would Net-savvy folks be spending time, energy, and money in the brick-and-mortar world?

The real truth is that the online world has not eliminated the need for the offline world, and it never will. Many types of Internet services can have a great amount of *synergy* (mutual advantage through working together) with offline efforts. To rule out offline possibilities just because they aren't online is as silly as not picking up a $5 bill because it's not the $20 you were looking for.

Exploiting Your Value

Your site or service might have exploitable value. Exploitable value tends to come in one of two sorts: a valuable reputation and reusable content. To understand these things, let's think (as I so often do) about movies. It used to be, back in the early days of film, that a movie was a movie. All the income to be made from a movie came from showing it in movie theaters. That's a lot like an online site staying online.

Now, when a *Star Wars* movie comes out, there's a glut of licensed *Star Wars* products. Some of these products have little to do with the film itself. Oh, a *Star Wars* notebook or t-shirt or candybar might be decorated with a picture of some member of the Skywalker clan, but at heart it's just a notebook or a t-shirt or a candybar. The only reason that these things sell better than similar non-*Star Wars* items is that people already like *Star Wars*, and associate the *Star Wars* name with something good. This is exploiting the reputation of *Star Wars* to make money.

After the film is released, however, the actual content of the film takes on a second life. Early on, there's the novelization of the film (plus the audiotape of the novelization of the film), a book reprinting the screenplay, a comic book adapting the movie, and a CD of the music from the movie. Later, the film content will be released to Pay-Per-View, and then licensed for video tape and DVD, then licensed for reshowing on pay cable and on airlines, and eventually the movie is broadcast on free TV. Any of these things might be enjoyed by someone who is experiencing *Star Wars* for the very first time. This is exploiting the content of *Star Wars* to make money.

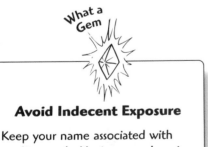

Avoid Indecent Exposure

Keep your name associated with quality goods. Having your domain name on a lame CD or an ugly hat increases your exposure, but can hurt your reputation.

Enhancing Your Value

The other value of offsite licensing is to increase the value of your online offering, usually buy building name recognition. After all, almost any exposure of your name to the public serves as free advertising. If your jazz site distributes the JazzIQ.com record reviews as a weekly column to newspapers, then every time people read the reviews they'll be reminded of your site. If the JazzIQ.com classic jazz CD box sells well at the store, people who buy it will likely head over to your site. And if you get someone to wear a JazzIQ.com baseball cap, you don't just have a fan, you have a walking billboard.

It's nifty to realize that you can be exploiting your brand and increasing its value simultaneously. I was reminded of this the other day when I saw someone wearing a pirated t-shirt featuring a Chihuahua saying "*Yo quiero* Taco Bell." That's right: Without permission, someone had paid money to print up a bunch of t-shirts advertising Taco Bell, and then other people paid the pirate so that they could wear the shirts. Technically, Taco Bell is the victim here, because it was their copyrights and trademarks that were violated, but is that a problem? If the worst thing that happens to your company is that someone goes out of their way to advertise your material at no cost to you, then you're doing well.

Legal Lookout

Get the Rights Right

Paying someone for content for your Web site does not mean you have the right to use that content elsewhere. If you want to reuse content, be sure you include that right in the contract, or cut a separate deal before you reuse it. And be willing to pay again when you reuse the material; if you're getting more than just a Web site out of it, the creator deserves more than just Web site pay.

Expanding to Other Media

Just because your content was born for the Web, nothing says that is where it must end. It can be adapted, expanded, reworked, filtered, and generally chewed up and spit out in a variety of new forms, all ready to make you money.

One of the nice things about expanding to other media is that you are likely to be dealing with an audience that overlaps heavily with the folks that you want at your site. People who surf the Web are very much the same people who read, listen to the radio, and watch TV beyond just the sitcoms. They are an aware bunch.

Books for Special Nooks

My favorite example of someone using the content of his Web site as the basis for a book comes from a site called Web Pages That Suck (www.webpagesthatsuck.com), which was not intended as a commercial site. There, you could read reviews of some horribly designed pages on the Web and link directly to the site. Working from that base, the site's creator (Vincent Flanders) worked with a co-author (Michael Willis) to create the book *Web Pages That Suck*. The book not only explained why various Web pages were bad ideas, but also how to avoid making similar mistakes with your Web pages. This insightful volume became a bestseller, and the site (seen in Figure 16.1) now promotes itself as the Web site version of the book rather than the other way around!

Figure 16.1

*Web Pages That Suck is
actually a Web site that
is useful. Check it out.*

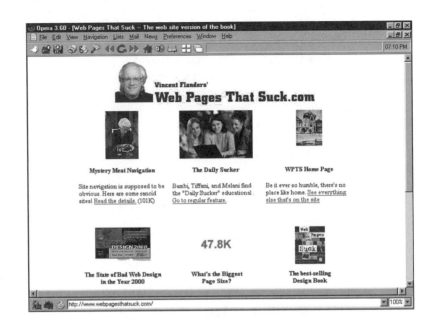

Other types of books that are popping up are books that teach you to use a site.
Sometimes these books are specifically just about a site, along the lines of *The Official
Aaugh.com Guide to Using Aaugh.com*. Other books pre-
sent themselves as more general guides, more along
the lines of *The BuyLotsaStock.com Online Investing
Primer*. Even these supposedly general guides usually
train the reader to use a specific site.

Superfluous Books?

A book on how to use your site
might seem unnecessary. It should
be unnecessary; if your site cannot
be figured out from the site itself,
it's time to redesign the site. But
the book does still serve a purpose.
Some book buyers buy such books
because having a physical reference
is very comforting. It also serves well
because it can be checked quickly
while one is using a page of the site,
rather than having to browse over
to a page of instructions and then
browse back.

If your site is popular or viewed as cutting edge, you
probably won't have much problem finding a publisher for your official book. Check the computer book
aisle at your local store and you'll see examples of
books from a number of publishers that specialize in
computer books. Those are all good possibilities, but
you should also consider publishers that specialize in
the general field that your site represents (business
publishers for an investment site, entertainment publishers for a movie site, nineteenth-century eyeglass
fashion publishers for a nineteenth-century eyeglass
fashion site).

Even if your site is not the leading site, you might be
able to get a publisher by paying the writer yourself
(thus reducing the amount that the publisher is risk-
ing). In any case, you should be able to promise promotion of the book on your site, increasing the book's
odds of success.

If you do put out a guide to using your site, you should get someone who does not work in your company to write (or at least co-write) it. An outsider is more likely to understand the problems that a new user is likely to face with your site; the people who work for you can't see through such fresh eyes. (Of course, this prejudice toward freelance computer book writers might be quickly explained by reading my business card: Nat Gertler, Freelance Love Machine. *Hey, waitaminnit! That explains all the funny looks I've been getting from publishers!*)

Living on Air: TV and Radio

Radio and television are becoming attractive second bases for Web-based companies. Both lend themselves to repeated audience exposure and constant new material. You shouldn't consider a series that is strictly oriented around your site (which would quickly be considered little else than a full-length ad), but rather one that builds around the topic of your site.

The current efforts of e-business sites seem to be focused on getting programs on basic cable television. This focus arises from such factors as:

➤ **Costs**   Basic cable television time is an affordable and simple way to give millions of homes access to your show. (Note that I said *access*; a very small percentage of those people will actually watch the show.)

➤ **Experience**   Producing material for television is likely to be a useful background for many Web sites in the long term. While these days most people access the Web with phone modems, the trend is toward higher-speed solutions, which allow the streaming of medium-quality video over the Web.

➤ **Recordability**   You can expect that most Web-browsing TV users also have a VCR. This creates an interesting and cheap option for starting out: airing it during ultra-cheap late-night dead time, and urging viewers not to stay up for it, but simply to tape it and watch it the next day.

➤ **Respectability**   Television is (for some inexplicable reason) taken seriously. Having a show that's known to be on TV can create respect even from people who have never watched the show.

➤ **Satisfaction**   A lot of the Internet entrepreneurs might be young, but the Web is younger still. None of the founders grew up dreaming of being on the Web; most of them probably wanted to be on TV.

Radio tends to be overlooked, often unfairly so. Consider the advantages that it has:

➤ **Thrift**   Producing audio-only material is much cheaper and simpler than television production.

➤ **Complementary scheduling**   Radio is frequently listened to while driving or while at work, when one cannot usually browse the Web. This is in contrast to a TV show, which the viewer probably watches at home instead of visiting the Web and surfing to your site. (On the other hand, the time slots most frequently used for syndicated material are late at night and on weekends, when you're less likely to get this sort of casual listenership.)

Heroic History

Stan Lee Media: The Man and His Plan

Web site name: `stanlee.net`

Founded: January 1999

Service provided: Superhero stories

Business model: The company is building itself on the name and reputation of one man, Stan Lee. Stan is internationally renowned for his work in superhero comics; working with talented artists such as Jack Kirby and Steve Ditko, Stan wrote and co-created such enduring Marvel Comics characters as Spider-Man, The Incredible Hulk, The Fantastic Four, and The X-Men. While still in the employ of Marvel Comics, Stan renegotiated his contract so that his employment was no longer exclusive. Having gained the right to create characters for others (as well as to use his recognizable name and catch phrases), Stan got into Stan Lee Media. The company's plan is to create new superhero material for the Web, allowing it to develop concepts and build character recognition without going through the currently troubled comic book market. If successful, this will create opportunities for profitable licensing of its characters for TV, movies, toys, theme parks, video games, and so on. The site itself provides opportunities for e-commerce and advertising sales. The company quickly formed alliances with media distribution site shockwave.com, online comic book store NextPlanetOver.com, and theme park ride designers iWerks Entertainment.

Where the money came from: The company was formed with $1.2 million of private money. Rather than taking the company through all the disruption of a standard IPO, a separate company called Boulder Capital Opportunities was created. It was a nonoperating company; it only existed to be a publicly listed stock (trading over-the-counter under the symbol BCOI for about half a dollar per share). When Stan Lee Media was ready to go public, it went through a *reverse buyout*, a process where BCOI technically bought out Stan Lee Media, but with Stan Lee Media ending up in control. Changing the symbol to SLEE, the stock rose quickly. As of February 7, 2000, the stock had zoomed up to 30, giving the company a market capitalization of $365 million.

➤ **Reusability**   If you want to reuse material from your radio show on your Web site, you can transmit fairly high-quality versions over the typical Web connection using standard audio compression techniques (such as MP3 or RealAudio).

➤ **Look-proof**   You can use all your goofy-looking pals on your radio show, because no one looks goofy on the radio.

The previous thoughts all assume that your goal is a factual program built around the theme of your Web site. If your site contains fiction or original characters, you might be able to do much more. The Web is a great place to test out visual concepts, and to build a reputation at a small publishing cost. Consider WhirlGirl (www.whirlgirl.com), as seen in Figure 16.2. Launched on the Web in March of 1997, by February of 1999 it was showing up on Showtime cable TV (as well as on their SHO.com site). If your fiction content is compelling, there's no reason that it couldn't end up as part of a network schedule, or even as a feature film.

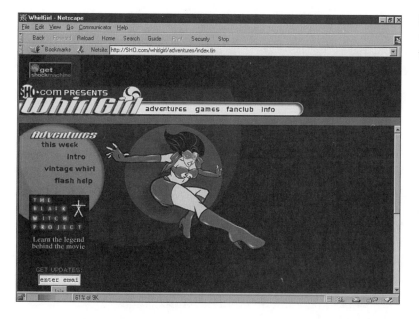

Figure 16.2

WhirlGirl put the whirl in whirled wide Web.

A Mega-Magazine

Of all the other media uses coming from the Web, the most visible is almost certainly *eBay Magazine*. This played very well off the reputation of the eBay auction site (www.eBay.com) as the new force in the buying and selling of collectibles. The glossy magazine was launched in 1999 as a news and showcase magazine for online purchasers and collectors of all sorts (except for those like my Uncle Horace, who collect dust).

215

eBay was smart. Rather than trying to figure out the complex business of magazine creation and distribution on its own, eBay hooked up with Krause Publications. Krause has been putting out collectible and special interest magazines such as *The Comics Buyer's Guide*, *Stamp Collector*, and *Military Trader* for more than 45 years.

Another sign of its smartness is that the magazine is not solely about collectibles. It has sections on computers and technology. These are legitimate topics because all eBay users are Internet users. These sections will attract not only readers, but also big-budget advertisers.

eBay was also smart when it sent the first issue free to every possible registered eBay user. It's a great example of where gathering customer information can come in handy. This is not the only way it promotes the magazine; it's also advertised on the eBay site and the Krause site (that's right, the Web site of the magazine of the Web site). But showing your magazine to your user base of more than five million is a good start!

And it was smart again when it made sure that people at Krause, not people at eBay, had the real control over the content. If eBay was in charge, cynical folks would be quick to cast aspersions on the reasoning behind editorial decisions. If the magazine had an article claiming that interest in old issues of *The Factor* comic book had shot up, people would suspect that eBay was just trying to drive *The Factor* prices up, so that eBay's cut of the sales would be bigger.

Stuff with Your Name on It

After you get beyond putting out media products, you can also put out logo and branded goods of all sorts. In this world, outside names and logos are used to add value to everything from cars to orange juice.

The Bully Bear

The first individual to officially license a product was Theodore Roosevelt, who allowed a stuffed animal to be based on him. This was the first *teddy bear*!

There are two ways to go about releasing products with your label. On one hand, you can hire a manufacturer, take care of the distribution, assume all the risk, and get all the profits. On the opposite mitten, you can license out your name, get a small cut from each sale, and take no direct financial risk.

To license out your name, you'll have to find a manufacturer who thinks your logo will attract sales. That can be a tough hunt. You might want to line up a *licensing agency*, an outfit that specializes in finding *licensees* (companies that buy the license to produce product).

Heroic History

theglobe: Club Your Way to the Top

Web site name: www.theglobe.com

Founded: 1995

Service provided: Online communities

Business model: theglobe.com starts with a core of email-based discussion clubs and personal Web pages and builds a portal upon it. Further services that it provides include a calendar, an address book, stock quotes, and auctions. This all creates a large exposure base for advertising and e-commerce. An impressive string of partnerships and buyouts has allowed the company to take advantage of these opportunities. Company purchases have included Azazz.com, a full-service department store; business Web-hosting company WebJump.com; and Attitude Network Limited, operator of such online game sites as www.happypuppy.com and www.gamesdomain.com. Its allies include CDnow, LowestFare.com, Time Warner/Road Runner, drkoop.com, Fox Sports Online, CBS MarketWatch, hotjobs.com, and Miami Dolphins great Dan Marino (danmarino.theglobe.com). After all, you can't have a great corporation without a great quarterback!

Where the money came from: Founded as WebGenesis, the company picked up private funding (including a $20 million infusion from Alamo Rent-A-Car ex-owner Michael Egan). In October 1998, it held its IPO, and grew a lot of attention as the $9 per share release skyrocketed to $97 on its first day. In the wake of the enthusiasm, the stock was split two-for-one. Interest in the stock waned due to repeated failure to meet revenue expectations, with the price of the split stock drifting downward to $7 13/16 per share as of February 7, 2000. This gives the company a market capitalization of $208 million. The stock trades on the Nasdaq exchange under the symbol TGLO.

Directly Related Products

Assuming your site is about something, you can put your logo on products that directly relate to what your site is about. For example, if you owned JazzIQ.com, you could put out CDs, CD players, maybe even jazz instruments that carry your label. If you're running a health site, you could put out vitamins and health aides.

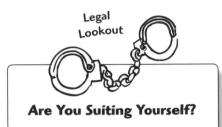

Are You Suiting Yourself?

Licensing your logo to a product can get you involved in any lawsuits which that product faces.

You have to watch out for conflicts of interest. If you start selling Vitamin W under your logo, and an article on your site claims that Vitamin W has been proven to prevent fatal hangnails, questions are raised. Did you just happen to run that article on Vitamin W, or was it part of an effort to drive up sales?

The best way to address this is to acknowledge the conflict wherever it arises. On the Vitamin W article, you should put a little note admitting that your company is involved with a Vitamin W product. It should also note that your site takes steps to make certain that your product-licensing department does not control the content of the site.

Dotcomming a Lifestyle

If your site or service (or some element of it) has a sense of style, an air of hipness or coolness, you might be able to branch into *lifestyle products*. This category includes just about anything that isn't directly related to your primary business but which can attract your primary customers.

The most obvious example of a lifestyle product are t-shirts or baseball caps that prominently display the site logo. If your site has a strong visual component with a real design philosophy behind it, you might be able to extend that visual sensibility to clothing items and accessories that don't display the logo (except on the tag, perhaps) but which reflect the design sensibilities.

The more you know about your audience, the more you understand what elements make up their common lifestyle. If you start up SurfAsphalt.com as a site for skateboarders, you should recognize that there's a strong skateboarder culture. Skateboarders have their own fashion, their own music, their own comic books. Putting out SurfAsphalt clothes and CDs is something that you should strongly consider. On the other hand, if you ran TouchingPoetry.com, then gentle items such as notepaper, perfumed soaps, and potpourri might be the right items for you.

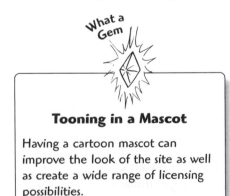

Tooning in a Mascot

Having a cartoon mascot can improve the look of the site as well as create a wide range of licensing possibilities.

No matter what it is you license, remember that quality counts. If a shlocky product comes out with your name on it, at best it will damage the reputation of your licensed product. Even worse, it could damage the reputation of your site. Pick your licensees carefully, and be sure you can check the quality of their designs and of their manufactured goods before you give them the okay to release products.

They Have Stores in the Real World, Too

A number of Web-based retailers are working on setting up brick-and-mortar shops. This might seem a backward step in evolution, but it makes sense for several reasons:

➤ All the money you've spent on promoting your domain name serves double-duty when it's also the name of a chain of stores.

➤ Unlike most Web retailers, most traditional retailers are profitable now.

➤ The stores can serve as a showroom for folks who want to order from the Web, but would like to have a look at the physical item first.

➤ One of the big concerns people have about ordering on the Web is the hassle they have to go through if they have to return an item. People will be more willing to order off the Web if they know that the item can be returned at a local shop.

For Further Info

Licensing is a huge field, with its own lingo and a large number of participants. EPM Communications (www.epmcom.com) puts out a number of interesting publications related to licensing:

➤ *Licensing Business Handbook* shows you the ins and outs of the licensing business. (This book is orderable through www.MillionsOnTheInternet.com.)

➤ *The Licensing Letter* is a newsletter of current events in the licensing world. A one-year subscription (22 issues) will set you back $447. To order, call (212) 941-0099.

The International Licensing Industry Merchandisers' Association (LIMA) has a site at www.licensing.org. The site has a calendar of licensing-related events and trade shows.

The Least You Need to Know

➤ Reusing your content and domain name offline can improve your exposure and generate profit.

➤ Books can explain your site or expand on its content. TV or radio shows should expand further on your site's topic.

➤ If your site attracts people of a certain lifestyle, offer products directed toward that lifestyle.

➤ Quality counts in licensed materials.

➤ Opening brick-and-mortar stores can make double use of your promotion efforts, generate profits, and give people confidence in your store.

Chapter 17

Please Sir, Can I Have Some More Moolah?

The Stages of Investing

In Chapter 10, "The Venture Adventure," you learned some of the basics of venture capital. That was a lot of fun, I know. But did you know that venture capital often comes in various stages? You might be able to get investment moolah more than once. That is because venture capitalists sometimes look to invest in companies when they have reached (or not reached) a certain stage of development.

Let's take a look at the various stages where money might come your way.

The Baby Stage: Seed Investing

The phrase *start-up company* is a helpful one, but it lacks a bit of focus because young companies, like children, pass through various milestones and stages. The earliest portion of a startup's life can bring a type of investment that is deemed *seed investing.* This is the very beginning of your company. At this stage you might be looking to start up in your garage or in a small office, and you are just now getting your first telephone line installed into your business. That's how early into your development you might be.

Seed investment money will be in far smaller amounts than later venture capital, because you will use the money to launch your business. This is a very risky investment for investors, though, as your business is quite unproven at this point. You might not even have your business up and running on the Internet in any fashion at this point. All you might have at this time are some very good ideas.

Individual investors, our so-called angels, can be very helpful at this stage.

The Toddler Stage: Early Investing

At this stage you should have a small office, perhaps, but certainly you already have a presence on the Internet. You'll need additional workers, more space, some lawyers, and more, because your business is doing pretty well and it looks to you like it will be doing a lot better. The trouble is you will need a lot of money at this point to keep the ball rolling.

Both angels and traditional venture capitalists might be interested in funding your company at this stage.

You might also find that a major venture capital firm is interested in investing money in your business at each of the major stages of development when you reach this point. Some money might come now with additional money coming your way later if your company proves itself to the venture capital firm.

Perhaps the company will set some metrics or goals for you so that you will have some clear milestones to pass before you can obtain additional funding from the same venture capitalists.

The Grade Schooler: Expansion Stage

At this point, your company might be on the verge of really exploding into the Internet e-commerce scene. Certainly, various articles about your business have already begun to appear in various Internet or business-related magazines. Maybe the local, or perhaps, national press have dropped by to conduct some interviews.

You need the resources to really ramp up at this point, and might need to scale up your count of employees from a dozen or so to 300 or more. This is the time when some really big investment money might come your way.

The Teenaged Years: Final Stage Financing

While this might not be the last investment money that your company will ever see, it should amount to one of the largest amounts of money that comes into your coffers from investment capitalists. At this point you might need tons of dough to take your company to its Initial Public Offering on Wall Street or help prepare the company to ramp up for a possible sale to a larger company.

Some venture capitalists specialize not only in the various stages of growth that a company might be in, but also in various types of companies. One company might invest only in local startups and another might invest only in companies that share a common interest in a certain type of Internet business, such as email, medical care, or even music.

Give Us Some Examples, Please

Want to know the names of some companies that got started with venture capital? Well, if your favorite computer were an Apple you wouldn't be having such fun with it (mostly because it wouldn't even exist) if it hadn't been for venture capitalists sharing the Apple dream. Maybe you use a Compaq computer instead. Same story there, too, as Compaq is another huge company launched with the aid of venture capital.

Ever shipped a package with Federal Express? Or do you perhaps have an Intel processor in your computer? Or (and please don't laugh) have you ever used a Microsoft product? All these companies got their start with the use of venture capital.

What a Gem

Going Public: An Exciting Investment for Investors

There has been a lot of interest in investment circles regarding funding some hot little company in preparation for it going public. Going public isn't always a goal for a particular company, but you wouldn't think that from all the recent press on this subject. Still, venture capitalists have helped more than 3,000 companies go public during the last 25 years. If the high times on Wall Street continue the way they have been, we would expect this number to greatly increase over the next several years. But remember, having the goal of going public isn't always a condition for obtaining venture capital.

The Venture Capital Process

Venture capital doesn't simply come in the form of an unsolicited check in the mail. Rather, it also goes through various stages. Disregarding angels and other private or (relatively) small investors, let's take a look at the life cycle of a major investment.

The initial stage is when a venture capital firm becomes aware of your company. Perhaps somebody at the company learns about your business by reading a very small article buried in an Internet-related magazine. Or perhaps they stumbled onto your e-business on the Internet by sheer luck. Or maybe you were bold enough to start calling up various investment capital firms. In any event, the first stage is when they learn a little bit about your company and express an interest in learning a lot more.

Heroic History

CarsDirect.com: Surf In, Drive Out

Web site name: CarsDirect.com

Founded: May 1999

Service provided: Retail car sales

Business model: CarsDirect is a prime example of the value of an incubator. This arose from an incubator named idealab!. Bill Gross, founder of idealab!, set the process in motion when he was disappointed with the existing online options for buying cars. Bill has been involved in launching eToys, CitySearch, GoTo.com, and more than a dozen other online successes. So, where others might just get annoyed, he got inspired. Bill, along with Scott Painter (CarsDirect CEO), punched it around and came up with the idea of having a single site at which the user could search through a database of thousands of makes and models. After the user finds just the right car, he can order the car through CarsDirect, and even apply for financing online. In this way, CarsDirect can offer a full range of automobiles to users who might not have every type of dealership nearby. By using fixed, low prices, the site becomes a comfort zone for folks who aren't comfortable with the usual haggling that goes on at new car dealers. After the car is purchased, the customer can either pick it up from a local dealer or have it delivered directly to his driveway. CarsDirect has supported its site with a lot of TV advertising and an affiliate program. CarsDirect pays affiliates $70 for each sale, which is a relatively large amount of money but a small percentage of the sale. You'd have to sell 235 Ferraris to be able to afford one Volkswagen!

Where the money came from: CarsDirect has had a series of private investments. This culminated in the November 15, 1999, announcement when the latest round of funding got them $280 million, a sizable amount by almost any measure.

Before they begin to thoroughly study your business, a *screen process* of some sort will occur. During this period the venture capital firm considers what type of business you are in and compare it to what is going on elsewhere on the World Wide Web. If any huge problems are obvious to them at this stage, they will no doubt take a pass and not consider spending the time and money to study your business any further. But if they like what they initially see, you'll move to the next stage. It might not sound like a big step, but only a few percent of requests for venture capital make it through to the next stage.

Evaluation and Due Diligence

At this stage the venture capital firm will roll up its sleeves and get to work. Interviews will be conducted and reports will be written, but you'll probably never get a chance to read the reports themselves.

The company will really take a close look at the major players at your company. What type of person is the guy who started this company? If you are the owner of the company, they will be very interested in your background, experience, and vision, that is, your essential plan for your company.

What is the essential business concept or plan? This is another crucial element about your business that investment capitalists must understand. It isn't enough that your company's Web site is popular on the Internet. No, there must be a good idea about how the company will make money in the future.

Specialty Funds

Some venture capital firms only invest in companies engaging in certain types of businesses. For example, there might be a specialty fund that only invests in telecommunications. If your business concentrates on telecommunications, you would most certainly want to contact such a specialty fund. You'll have to spend some time researching your own industry to learn what options are out there for you with any such specialty fund investors.

Which brings us to another key element. How soon will this company make a profit if we invest in it? Money is a lot better if you get it sooner rather than later, at least in the minds of all the people that I know personally.

If you make it past this initial investigation, you will move on to the *due diligence* stage.

Due diligence is a fancy phrase for having a third party examine your business under a magnifying glass. After all, these investment capitalists probably don't know you from Adam (or Eve), and they want to be sure they know as much about you as possible before they hand over (maybe) a few million dollars.

Expect the investigation pursuant to the due diligence phase to be quite exhaustive. They'll talk to you, your managers, and maybe your competitors, as well. If anyone out there has information about your business, they might talk to them, from your suppliers to the lady who has been your best customer up until now.

Negotiations and Love Songs: The Final Stages

After you pass the due diligence stage, you will find that the time has come to sit down and hammer out the details of the actual venture capital agreement. You'll need a lawyer (and a darned experienced one) plus other business advisors, as well. Getting the correct professional help will never be more important to you than during this stage of your company's life.

Turnarounds

Sometimes a once successful company will find itself losing money and facing a very bleak future. Sometimes investment capital will be offered to a company so it can attempt to *turnaround* or rather, begin to head into the black once again. However, these funds will usually come with management specialists who have the strength of will to make the hard decisions that often include the termination of various executives and staff cutbacks.

After you obtain your venture capital, you will no doubt have a member of the venture capital firm sitting on your corporate board of directors or otherwise empowered to help you make major decisions that might affect their investment. This is all an expected part of doing business with a venture capitalist.

The King of Internet Venture Capital

Certainly there is room to argue that Sequoia Capital is perhaps the biggest tree in the venture capital forest. Let's end our study of venture capitalists by taking an in-depth look at this fascinating company.

Sequoia Capital began handing out moolah to startups back in 1972. It operates out of its sole office in Menlo Park, California (an area also known as *Silicon Valley*), and it has financed more than 350 early stage technology companies. And that, my friends, is a very impressive number.

According to information found on its Web page (see Figure 17.1), more than 100 of these companies have gone public. And even more exciting, Sequoia Capital invests in every stage of a private company's development.

Which might make Sequoia the best place to ask, "Please sir, can I have some more moolah?" Not to mention asking "Please sir, can I have some moolah in the first place?"

Figure 17.1

Perhaps the world's most famed Internet capital investment firm located at www.sequoiacap.com.

Who Have They Been Handing Out Money to Lately?

Here's a collection of lucky (and no doubt deserving) companies that have recently received venture capital via Sequoia Capital:

➤ Yodlee.com's Web site helps you to consolidate all your various online accounts, from travel to auctions to shopping. Find them at www.yodlee.com.

➤ Want to trade some of your very valuable junk that you no longer want for somebody else's very valuable junk that you do want? You do that, or buy and sell surplus personal belongings at www.webswap.com.

➤ Those of us who believe that Internet access should be free will be very interested in visiting Freei.net, found at www.freei.net.

➤ RedEnvelope.com appears to be a wonderful place to do online shopping for your friends and loved ones. See them at www.redenvelope.com.

Other companies have received Sequoia's money to go public. Here are some recent examples:

➤ MedicaLogic provides electronic medical record products and services. It grabbed $100 million via its IPO. Find it at www.medicalogic.com.

➤ Want to order groceries on the Internet and have them delivered the same day at the same regular store prices, or even lower? Then WebVan is for you. This company netted $375 million from their IPO and can be found at www.webvan.com.

➤ PlanetRx is an online pharmacy that is eager to fill your prescriptions. They grabbed up $96 million from their IPO. Get your prescriptions filled at www.planetrx.com.

Other companies sometimes purchase companies. That can be a real moneymaker for investors as well as those who own the purchased company. For example, Lycos, a huge Internet portal, thought enough of a Sequoia investment company called Quote.com to purchase it. Quote.com provides financial information to its users.

Meanwhile, StratumOne Communications, a developer of semiconductor technology, was sold to Cisco Systems, a manufacturer of computer networking equipment. Once again, StratumOne Communications was a company that Sequoia Capital had invested in.

Heroic History

Quote.com: Stock Answers

Web site name: quote.lycos.com

Founded: 1993

Service provided: Stock information

Business model: Quote.com provides information for individual investors, including stock quotes, charts, company background, news, and more. It licenses this material from Dow Jones, Reuters News Service, Standard & Poor Stock Guide, and more. It offers this content under three programs with very different economic models. It has a standard eyeball-oriented program, providing a range of free information supported by onsite advertising. For this it has more than a third of a million registered users. This also serves as a gateway to its subscription services. For a charge of anywhere from $10 to $129 per month, users get access to premium content and advanced tools. Currently, it has a subscriber base of about 10,000 eager investors. Finally, it offers its services to other Web sites, for a fee. Sites that use Quote.com content include Charles Schwab (www.schwab.com), *Forbes* magazine (www.forbes.com), and NationsBank (www.nationsbank.com). All this has made Quote.com one of the Web's top five investment information sites, and got *Upside* magazine to name it one of 1999's Hot 100 private companies.

Where the money came from: Popular portal Lycos (www.lycos.com) announced its intention to acquire Quote.com, Inc., in September of 1999. The buyout was completed in December of 1999. It cost Lycos $78.3 million, plus Lycos had to assume Quote.com's stock option plan.

How Do You Get Sequoia Capital's Attention?

Sequoia says, "Our favorite investment candidates are companies operating in the electronic and healthcare segments of the economy." (If you just invented a robot physician, it would appear that sending them a telegram is in order.)

You can contact Sequoia Capital directly by sending an email to businessplans@sequoiacap.com. You will need to send a 15–20 slide PowerPoint presentation that describes your business along with your email.

You will also need to send them a copy of your *executive summary.* That's a 15–20 page document that explains the market that you intend to work in, a description of your management team, and more. You will find all the required details at www.sequoiacap.com in its Frequently Asked Questions area.

Despite the fact that Sequoia supplies a method of enabling anyone to contact it, it is quite candid in saying that the best way for somebody to contact it is as follows: "The easiest and most effective introduction is from somebody who knows you and knows us."

Still, the little guy can hope to get Sequoia Capital's attention. Here's what Jerry Yang, the chief yahoo of Yahoo!, has to say, as posted on the Sequoia Capital Web site: "Sequoia invested in Yahoo! when the company was composed of two people and two borrowed computers."

That sounds pretty good, doesn't it?

And if Sequoia believes in you enough to make a major investment in your company, well, you've made the big time. Few things happen to a startup that is as well received by the investing public as being picked up by Sequoia Capital.

The Least You Need to Know

➤ Venture capital can come at different times and in different amounts depending on which stage of growth your company is in.

➤ Some capital investment companies invest in businesses at any stage of their growth and others specialize in startups that are in a specific stage.

➤ Sequoia Capital is one of the most famed venture capital firms in the world and invests in the right company at any stage of its growth.

Chapter 18

Perils and Pitfalls

Internet Criminals and Other Security Issues

There are many disasters that can happen to an innocent e-business, most of which can be avoided via careful planning. But one of the worst things that can happen to any Internet business is to be attacked by an Internet criminal.

One recent case involved an online company called CD Universe. A music retailer, CD Universe maintained a database collection of credit card information for its more than 300,000 customers. Naturally, it was in the best interest for the customers, the related banks, and CD Universe for all this credit card information to be kept highly secure and confidential.

However, on January 9, 2000, the Internet news source SiliconValley.com reported that CD Universe had suffered a security breach. Someone evidently had broken through CD Universe's security and obtained a copy of the database containing each and every bit of information about all those credit cards, or so the intruder had claimed. The criminal demanded $100,000 or he would release the credit card information to the world via the Internet.

When CD Universe refused to pay the money, the intruder released what he claimed to be some of the credit card numbers and other related information on the Internet. He also claimed that he had already used some of the credit card information to make certain illegal purchases.

The criminal called himself Maxim and claimed to be 19 years of age and living in Russia. Investigators concluded that he might be from Russia, Latvia, or some other Eastern European nation. So, the worldwide aspect of the Internet gives crime a leg up on law enforcement, owing to the difficulties involved in working with prosecutors in certain foreign lands.

CD Universe is owned by a company entitled eUniverse. A spokesperson for eUniverse confirmed to members of the press that at least some of the credit card information was in the hands of Maxim. Maxim managed to give away illegal credit card information to several thousand people via an Internet site before authorities shut it down. As of this writing, Maxim is still at large.

Maintaining the highest level of online security is crucial for any e-business to survive. You must be certain that your company has the appropriately experienced experts on staff to prevent what evidently happened to CD Universe from happening to your own company.

If you fail to appropriately secure your e-business from outside attack, you might wake up one morning to find your home page turned upside down, or worse! If your customers feel that they can't safely shop online at your Web site, for example, you could find yourself without any customers at all.

More Security Concerns

While it is very important to make sure that your computer systems are safe from attack from the outside world, you must also be sure that your company is secure from harm from within your own business.

Each PC that you have in your company no doubt connects to an internal network of databases. Your first security step is to make sure that each employee has his own unique password that allows him to connect to your internal network. This password should not be something that he makes up himself but should be one that a special security officer provides. Only the security officer and the individual worker should know what the password is.

The password should not be an ordinary word such as headcheese or even a combination of ordinary words such as madmanmage. These types of passwords are too easy to crack by someone using a password hunting program. Instead, the password should be a combination of letters and numbers and be cAsE SensiTIve. To illustrate this further, an acceptable password could be something like *Ab23FT873*.

All employees must be informed that they cannot release their password to anyone under any condition and that if their password should become known by anyone other than themselves and the security office that they must report it at once so that their password can be changed.

Heroic History

Google: Good Looking

Web site name: www.google.com

Founded: 1998

Service provided: Search engine

Business model: *Search engines* are part of the backbone of the Web. If you want to find out more about Uncle Scrooge creator Carl Barks, for example, you could use any one of dozens of standard search engine sites, enter `Carl Barks` into the search field, and see a list of all the Web pages that had that name on it. The problem was that these lists put in an order based on where on the page the search term first appears and how many times it appears (what search engine folks call *measuring relevance*). With this method, the first site on the list might turn out to be a page from a fourth grader complaining about his dog Carl, while a much more useful biographical site might be far lower in the list. Two Stanford Ph.D. candidates came up with a better idea. They rank sites on the basis of what other sites link to them. If a lot of important sites have links pointing to the biography site, then Google figures that the biography site is itself important. A complex mathematical method is maintained for judging what sites are important on the basis of what other sites point to them. By combining this ranking of importance with the usual ranking of relevance, Google is far more likely than other search engines to put the site you really want to find at the top of the list. Google makes its money through selling advertising on its site, and through licensing its search services to other sites who either want to offer a full-Web search service or who want a high-quality engine for users to search just their own site.

Where the money came from: Google is currently privately owned by a list of impressively Web-savvy investors. It received $25 million worth of equity funding in June of 1999.

Restricted Access and Other Issues

Each employee should have access to databases, programs, and other computer-related functions only if such access is called for by their job description. Your computer engineers will be able to design your system in such a manner. That way, salespeople won't muck around with your sensitive programming functions, and engineers won't take a gander at your sensitive sales records.

PCs should have up-to-date antivirus software installed. Your employees should not open files sent to them as email attachments unless they are aware of who is sending the attachment. Even then, viruses can sometimes be inadvertently sent from friendly parties. For example, a virus can be attached as a hidden attachment to email without the knowledge of the sender or the receiving party. You will accordingly require the services of an employee who can design an excellent antivirus protocol for your company.

Virus designers seem to enjoy coming up with new ways to cause trouble for us all. Your antivirus employee must keep abreast of all the new ways that a virus can be delivered to your computers via email. There are ways to restrict such viruses to your PCs and keep them out of your main computers. Your engineers should design such a system for you.

Keeping the Building Secure

All employees should sign a *nondisclosure agreement* on their first day of work. Your lawyers will draft this document, which will essentially protect your company from having any employee disclose your business secrets.

All visitors to your offices should also sign a separate type of nondisclosure agreement in the form of a sign-in log. Each visitor would sign, date, and affix the time of entering/leaving the building on this document so that you can track the identity of each nonemployee who enters your offices.

You might consider restricting visitor access to certain areas of your offices. (You might even consider restricting *general employee access* to certain areas of your offices, as well.)

Visitors should be asked to wear a visitor badge. "Hey! There's a visitor. I better not gossip about our incredible and highly secret project until he's outta here."

Visitors should also be escorted at all times by an employee of the company. The nondisclosure agreement that the visitor is asked to sign should clearly state that any confidential information that the visitor receives during his visit must be kept confidential. The agreement should carefully define confidential information so that it includes all technical and business information that the visitor might come across in the course of his visit.

Your visitors might include outside contractors, possible business partners, or spouses and relatives of employees. All nonemployees should wear a visitor badge, be escorted by an employee at all times, and sign a visitor log/nondisclosure agreement every time they enter the building.

I Think the Cleanup People Swiped My Laptop

Those laptop computers certainly seem to entice people to pick them up and spirit them away to far away lands, don't they? All your company's laptop computers should be locked up safely at night or they could be stolen. The laptops are valuable, sure, but the data that is held within the memory of the laptop might be far more valuable than the computer itself.

All the internal offices of your company should be locked at night and even during the day while they are not being used. This security precaution should be particularly true for any of your company's executives. This makes it more difficult for sensitive information to be stolen.

Shredding all your discarded paper documents should be something that is second nature to all your employees, as well.

Your Friend, the FBI

Sometimes e-businesses receive scary email from crackpots. These unwanted bits of electronic correspondence can take the form of out and out threats to do you or an employee physical harm.

Never ignore threats that you receive via email (or by the phone or regular old postal mail, either). Any successful e-business runs the chance of attracting the attention of some crazy person who is capable of harboring a dangerous delusion about you or your company. Remember, a successful e-business could deal with millions of different people each month and out of those people a handful could be highly dangerous psychopaths (unless, of course, your site is ToolsForPsycopaths.com, in which case it might be more than just a handful).

If you or any of your employees receive threats via the Internet you should contact the Federal Bureau of Investigation. The FBI takes such electronic threats very seriously, and they will prosecute any case that should reasonably be prosecuted.

You can contact the FBI via the Internet at www.fbi.gov (see Figure 18.1), but I would suggest that you telephone the nearest office if you wish to report threatening email. Here's another really cool service that the FBI provides (beyond helping to protect you from dangerously insane people): The FBI produces CyberNotes.

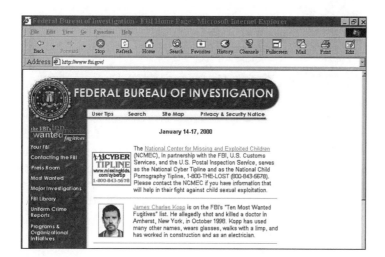

Figure 18.1

Report Internet crime to the FBI. Visit its Web site at www.fbi.gov *for more details.*

According to its Web page, CyberNotes is published every two weeks by the *National Infrastructure Protection Center (NIPC)*. Its mission is to support security and information system professionals with timely information on cyber vulnerabilities, hacker exploit scripts, hacker trends, virus information, and other critical infrastructure-related best practices.

Subscribing to CyberNotes

The FBI's CyberNotes comes in PDF format and you can download a PDF reader and subscribe to CyberNotes all for free at `www.fbi.gov/nipc/cybernotes.htm` (as seen in Figure 18.2).

I've examined one of the recent editions of CyberNotes and found it to be chock-full of helpful information. The report starts out with a comprehensive list of bugs, holes, and patches relating to various types of equipment or software. In each case, the type of vulnerability to a remote malicious attack is explained. In each case, the risk attributed to attack is listed as low, medium, or high.

The report continues with a listing of recent *exploit scripts* and techniques. If your own company would like, you are invited to provide your own short description of scripts that are for some reason vulnerable to outside attacks. You can allow the FBI to release your discovery to the world at large, to a list of people that you define, or ask the FBI to keep it to itself. Such script information should be sent to the FBI via email at `nipc@fbi.gov`.

Figure 18.2

You can get the FBI's free virus protection newsletter at `www.fbi.gov/nipc/cybernotes.htm`*!*

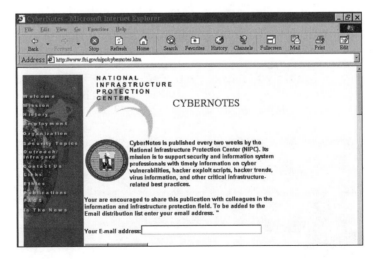

Each issue of CyberNotes contains a list of trends that has appeared during the previous two weeks. If new variations of the Melissa virus are continuing to appear, then they will tell you. Worried about intruders compromising your machines to install distributed systems used for launching packet-flooding Denial of Service attacks? (Hey, its Greek to me, too, but somebody around here should be worried about this stuff!) If so, the FBI has some important information for you. It's all right here in CyberNotes.

Viruses and Trojans

You've probably heard something about computer *viruses*, those sneaky little programs that can burrow into your software and do all sorts of damage, or at least annoy the heck out of you. CyberNotes keeps an updated list of computer viruses.

These viruses are pretty nasty. One of them, W97M.Prillisa.A, infects Word 97 documents as it attaches itself to email messages, thus spreading itself all over the world. It triggers up to 50 emails being automatically sent out to people who you have previously communicated with. The email bears your own name (or rather, the user name of the email account) and carries the cheerful greeting "This document is very important and you've GOT to read this!!!."

When the document is executed, the virus is now triggered within the computer of the receiving party. Once there, it again resends itself, overlays colored shapes onto the open document, and sets up your computer so that the next time you start up your system, all your software and files will be trashed. Ouch!

Trojans are a slightly different creation. They enter a computer and sometimes conduct hidden and evil tasks. For example, the *girlfriend trojan* enters your PC and lets people steal information such as passwords or even takes control of your computer and sends your browser to any World Wide Web location that it wants. (Somehow I think I missed an opportunity for a bad joke at this point. Please make whatever bad joke you feel comfortable with at this time.)

CyberNotes keeps you informed about all the current trojans. Meanwhile, serious antivirus protection programs can be obtained from the Norton Company. See its Web site at `www.symantex.com/nav/index.html` for further details.

Look Out for Virus Hoaxes!

There are many pranksters who spread lies about nonexisting computer viruses. Innocent believers pass on the scary stories from person to person until a large number of people are freaked out and scouring the Internet for some sort of antivirus software that doesn't exist to protect your PC from a virus that likewise doesn't exist. You can arm yourself against these hoaxes by visiting a helpful Web site maintained by the Department of Energy's Computer Incident Advisory Committee. There you will learn about all sorts of virus hoaxes. You will find them at `ciac.llnl.gov/ciac/CIACHoaxes.html`.

The World Has a Lot of Laws—Try Not to Break Any

It's a wonderful thing when an Internet site attracts users from all over the world. It's less of a wonderful thing if a significant number of your users are breaking some local law while they use your site.

Antivirus Fear Tactics

Antivirus software companies make money by keeping people paranoid. They commonly exaggerate the impact of viruses, and have a long history of making bad predictions about how bad the next virus attack will be. They also overestimate the abilities of their software, which generally work fine at catching yesterday's viruses but are useless against tomorrow's new attack. This isn't to say that you should go without antivirus software, but you should also check out the Computer Virus Myths page at www.kumite.com/myths/ to get a good dose of reality.

Consider for a moment the plight of online casino gambling. For many people, gambling is a relatively harmless form of entertainment. But historically, gambling has been tightly regulated by most states in the U.S., and usually gamblers have to drive or fly quite a distance from their homes to reach their favorite gambling mecca, such as Las Vegas.

Presently, some crafty e-business people have been offering gambling via their Web sites. Interested gamblers can play various video-style games from the privacy of their own homes and lose (and maybe even win) real money. Credit cards are used to establish a line of credit and your losses are deducted from your credit card account. Any winnings are supposedly credited to your same credit card account. Users can also bet on various sporting events.

Of course, gambling is tightly regulated by all sorts of laws in the United States, both federal and state. So, is online casino gambling illegal? It's a complicated issue.

Most, if not all, of these Internet-based casinos are operating from some offshore location such as an island in the Caribbean where their activities are legal. But a whole lot of my fellow Americans find time to do some gambling at their online casinos. This has led to a lot of legal debate and even some offshore arrests of e-business people by our federal authorities.

Why? Because a lot of people in the United States oppose the expansion of gambling. The current legal tool used to attack Internet Casinos is the 1961 Interstate Wireline Act, a federal law that prohibits placing bets via telephone lines and other pre-Internet communication technologies, unless authorized by the state in which the gambler lives. But what about the case of an online gambler using a satellite connection to reach the Internet? There is some debate going on regarding that issue.

To clear the murky legal waters, some congressmen would like to pass a law that prohibits Internet gambling in some fashion. The bottom line for the Internet casino owners is that they have their hands full with various legal problems.

By the way, if the entire idea of gambling on the Internet has you searching underneath your couch cushions for loose change, you might be interested in picking up a copy of *The Complete Idiot's Guide to Online Gambling*. We *bet* you'll like it.

Heroic History

Hotmail: Free Email, Expensive Company

Web site name: www.hotmail.com

Founded: July 1996

Service provided: Web-based email

Business model: Hotmail is the leading provider of *Web-based email*, email accounts that let you check your mail by visiting a Web site and use the Web to compose and send email. This sort of email offers the user a number of advantages. Unlike the email you have through your ISP or place of employment, you won't have to change your email address if you change jobs or move. You can check your email from any Web browser anywhere, which makes it great for those who travel without toting around a laptop. People who are looking for some discretion have an email address that their spouse or employer doesn't have to know about, and that cannot easily be tied to them. It's also handy for those with families whose ISPs only offer a single email account. Hotmail also promotes its antispam filters, and has been active in the legal fight against spam. Email service is provided for free, working off the "selling eyeballs" model. Hotmail has proven very popular, with 40 million registered accounts as of July 1999. The service did run into some problems during 1999, however. In August, a security flaw became known that allowed anyone knowing the trick to access the content of any Hotmail account, a flaw that drew a lot of negative publicity. A while later, Hotmail was redesigned in such a way that access required browsers that supported *Java*, a programming language understood by most modern browsers. This unfortunately reduced the number of browsers capable of accessing the service, which reduced the service's value for travelers.

Where the money came from: On the last day of 1997, Hotmail was bought out by software megalith Microsoft. The terms of the acquisition were not disclosed, but folks smart enough to think Hotmail up and implement it can be counted on to have extracted a tidy sum in the deal.

As you begin to plan your own Internet business, you must carefully consider whether or not you are offering a service that might actually be illegal for your clients to use. There is still a great deal of legal ground to cover regarding the Internet. For the first time in our history, state borders and even international borders have become easy to cross, at least electronically via the Internet. Perhaps what we are really seeing is something that history books a century from now will call the first step that humanity took toward establishing a one-world government.

You enter into some international legal risk merely by making your site accessible to the world. You enter into further legal risk when you start doing business with individuals or companies in other nations. Don't head into international marketing until you are ready to face the laws of other countries.

A Failure of Scalability

One of the worst things that can happen to an online business is to fail to plan for rapid growth. All your computer systems and connections to the Internet must be able to be rapidly expand as your business grows. If you are doing the right things to enlarge your e-business, you might find the number of users coming to your Web site to grow exponentially seemingly overnight. Nothing will break your systems faster than unexpected, unplanned-for client growth. Too much traffic coming to your site can cause unwanted side effects such as a failure of services. Such lack of *scalability* is a crying shame. Make sure that your engineers and programmers have carefully built appropriate scalability into your Web designs.

The Christmas Stocking Problem

It's easy to assume that the only problem scalability causes comes from your Internet hardware and software, but that's not the case. Consider, for example, the problems of ToysRUs.com. Christmas 1999 was clearly going to be a time of major growth for Internet retailing, and many companies made a big push to get your gift-buying dollar. ToysRUs.com was in on the push, publicizing its Web site and offering some good deals. Its publicity was successful, and many folks streamed to the site to order goodies to put under the Christmas tree. The computers generally held up fine; there was a glitch or two, but those happen. The problem was that the company didn't have enough items in stock to fill the orders, and was having manpower trouble keeping up with the demand for what it did have in stock. Had the company noticed its stocking and manpower problems in time and reacted appropriately, it would have stopped taking orders and simply turned away some customers with a slight disappointment of not being able to shop there. Instead, it took orders and failed to deliver the products before Christmas. ToysRUs.com tried contacting the customers when it could, warning them that the presents wouldn't be in on time, and offering the customer a large gift-certificate to make up for the difficulty. This came as little solace to customers who had promised their kids something special under the tree.

The store lost the trust of customers, who will probably spend the big gift certificate and never visit that shop again. Even worse for the company, however, was that the news media grabbed onto the story, telling the world about the missing presents. Suddenly, ToysRUs.com had a bad reputation not only with people who had shopped there, but with the public at large. With so many toy stores on the Web, people will have no problem taking their business elsewhere.

Some Final Tips to Help Keep You Out of Trouble

The Internet is a culture. You need to understand this culture so that you don't open a business that will be shunned by most of the Internet. Your business should offer plenty of free services, or a service that is just so incredibly useful that people will jump at the chance to pay for it. It is very important for you to understand what sorts of things are considered cool in the eyes of Internet users and what sorts of things are considered to be insulting.

For example, you might want to send repeated advertisements to your customers via email. That would probably be very uncool unless your emails were written in an entertaining fashion, contained helpful information, were sent only sparingly, and included a method in which your clients could effectively tell you to stop sending this stupid spam!

Regarding your e-business itself, I have a few words to say. Move swiftly! Internet speed is something close to the speed of light. If you have an idea for a Web site that nobody else is doing, move swiftly. If you have an idea for a new feature for your Web site that nobody else is doing, move swiftly. Delays can be costly. Don't let another Web site steal your thunder by being the first to offer your service or feature.

Finally, consider this. I estimate that about 80% of the businesses operating on the World Wide Web offer its services exclusively in the English language. Yet only about 20% of the world speaks English as their first language. There seems to be plenty of room for growth in non-English based e-businesses. Perhaps that is something that you should carefully consider before launching your new e-business.

Check In Often with Internet.com

Internet.com operates a very helpful Web site called the Electronic Commerce Guide. There you will find some very helpful articles on the latest ways you can keep your e-business out of trouble. You can locate the Guide at ecommerce.internet.com. While you are at it, you should plan a visit to its home page (www.internet.com) so that you can keep abreast of the most recent Internet news and issues.

Being Too Swift Is Not Too Swift

One mistake that is often made by a new site is publicizing itself to the public before the site works properly. The other day, I found a link to singleshop.com, a site that organized the content of a number of Internet stores, which it claimed made it more convenient to find what you want. It offered a $20 rebate on the first purchase made through its service, and as I like free stuff as much as the next guy, I tried it out. Its interface was awkward and its catalog program just didn't work properly. It was very difficult (and sometimes impossible) to find items that I knew were available from the stores it claimed to index. By the time I put in all the effort it took to order two CDs, I knew that my time wasn't worth that 20 bucks. Later, I learned that it took the company days to put my order through to the store, leading me to suspect that it was doing the order by hand rather than automatically. Thanks to this promotion, it'll have paid a lot of people $20 to learn that its system is slower and more awkward than shopping directly at a Web store. Be prepared to do a big mainstream publicity push for your site the moment it's ready—and not a minute sooner.

The Least You Need to Know

➤ You must maintain the highest level of security possible regarding both your computer systems and physical offices.

➤ The Federal Bureau of Investigation prosecutes Internet crime and provides e-business operators with helpful antivirus information.

➤ It is important that you plan early for scaling up needs presented by a rapid growth of your e-business.

Part 5

The Big Payoff

Congratulations! You have a business! An active Web site with lots of visitors, product being sold, and a long-term business plan that has the business losing money every quarter for the next decade! Isn't that just what you wanted?

Actually, no, it wasn't.

If I know you, you wanted money. Big money. The kind of money that lets you build that mansion with hot-and-cold running Perrier, with the swimming pool in the shape of Martha Stewart, with so many rooms that your in-laws could move in and it would be three years before you noticed.

In this part of the book, we show how attractive Web businesses can be turned into actual spendable cash.

Chapter 19

Become a Sellout for Fun and Profit

In This Chapter

➤ Selling your existing Internet business

➤ Sites that might buy your site

➤ Having your e-business as a public corporation

Every business should be considered to be for sale at all times, at least in the mind of the owner. Really, it's all a matter of price, isn't it? You should always cheerfully consider any and all reasonable offers to purchase your business when you are confronted with them.

While somebody might drop in unexpectedly one day with an astounding offer of big bucks for the sale of your business let's take the bull by the horns and see how you can generate a sale of your e-business.

Evaluating Your Privately Held Internet Business

When considering selling an e-business, you need to determine the expected value of that business. How much should you ask for it? There exist several tried-and-true methods of determining the value of your privately owned Internet business.

You should obtain the assistance of a certified public accountant or other suitable professional to help you evaluate your business's valuation. However, let's look at some of the common methods used:

➤ *Book value* is when your liabilities are deducted from your assets, which results in a figure of what your assets might be worth. This method ignores several key factors, such as the value of your patents and trademarks, and as such, isn't probably something that will pinpoint with accuracy the valuation of your company. Instead, it is a starting point, or rather, a point of reference.

➤ *Adjusted book value* is a more refined approach, and a bit more accurate, as it considers the fair market value of your company's assets and liabilities. Both of these methods are called *balance sheet* approaches to obtaining a valuation of your business's worth.

➤ Another method is to compare what similar businesses have recently sold for. Another method involves studying what revenues your company might earn in the future. Again, if your business is an ongoing one, you should seek out professional assistance to determine the probable value of your business. Of course, the final answer is always that your company will sell for the price that somebody else is willing to pay for it.

Can't Find Your Assets with Both Hands

Evaluating *financial assets* (money in the bank, stock, other people's debts) and so on, is generally quite easy. These things have set values. Evaluating your *physical assets* (your computers, a warehouse full of bottles of PattyWater, that ugly fern in John's office) is a little harder, but there is a market for such items and either the price they could be sold for or the cost to replace them can be evaluated.

However, in many Internet-based businesses, financial and physical assets are a fairly small part of the value of the whole company. The real value is tied up in intellectual property and intangibles, and those are hard things to put a money value on. Don't make the mistake of assuming that because it's hard to pin a dollar figure on something, it's not worth a lot of dollars. Here's just some of the harder-to-price values that your company might hold:

➤ **Your users**   You might not have found a way to make a single penny off anyone who uses your site, but if you have a vast base of people visiting your site regularly, then your site is worth many millions. It's worth that much because someone else can merge your site with theirs and have the chance to sell their services to your users.

➤ **Your technology**   The software you've created and the patents you have on your technology can be valuable even if your business is a flop. If they do something that is particularly useful and can be used to add key features to the sites of others, your business might be bought out just for them. If your business is successful, then they are a key element to your success.

➤ **Your reputation**   If your site is well-known and people think well of it, that makes your company worth more than if you were somehow getting the same amount of business with a bad reputation. The company buying a site with a good reputation is hoping to have some of that glow reflected on them.

➤ **Your employees**   While you can't actually sell your employees (not since the Programmer Emancipation Proclamation of 1992), having a base of talented and loyal people is an item of value. In these days, there's a talent shortage in the Web world, and having a talented group of computer geeks can sweeten the deal. (On the other hand, a purchasing company will be worried that your workers might be eager to rush for greener pastures after the buyout, leaving them with a newly purchased site and no one who knows it well enough to maintain it.)

➤ **Your domain name**   Sometimes, the real value of your company is that your domain name is just right for someone else's idea. If this is your most valuable asset, then your site wasn't as much a success as it should have been—but a good domain name can be part of the mix.

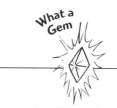

What a Gem

Dumping Your Domain

If your business doesn't take off, you might want to just sell off your domain name. You might also have some spare domain names that you bought in case you might use them, but have decided not to. There are sites designed to help you auction off (or just plain sell) your domains. Check out the following: www.greatdomains.com, www.DotBroker.com, and www.DomainNamesBuySell.com.

Sighting the Right Site

Most of the Web sites that are bought for millions of dollars are bought by other sites or by companies that run a large number of sites. It is quite possible that an interested site will approach you. However, you don't have to sit around twiddling your thumbs waiting for them to come to you. Instead, you can go bowling! Or, if you want to make productive use of your time, start approaching sites to see if they might be interested in buying you out.

Sites that might find your site worth buying include

➤ **The competition**   Those same S.O.B.s that you've spent the last couple years trying to drive into the ground might be just the folks to buy you out. They'd love to have your customers, would gain advantage from your content, and would be pleased as punch to have you out of the way.

➤ **A compatible site**   The service you offer does not exist in a vacuum (unless, of course, you offer a vacuum repair service). There might be other sites whose offerings do not overlap very much with yours, but which are aimed at the same audience. If your site offers a fax-sending service, you might want to hook up with a fax-receiving site, or one that offers other forms of telephony, or even a site that sells items to home office users.

➤ **Portals**   Sites like Yahoo! (www.yahoo.com) and Lycos (www.lycos.com) try to be all things to all people, and thus make attractive potential suitors.

247

Make a point of attending major industry conferences, both for the Internet industry and for whatever special interest your site addresses. You never know when you might encounter a well-funded startup that could use what you have, or an established business looking to expand.

Finding Buyers

Major investment banker firms have acquisition and merger specialists who can provide you with many services, including helping you find a potential buyer for your e-business, if the firm is interesting in becoming involved with you on that level.

You could also advertise in appropriate newspapers or magazines and offer your business for sale, or find a business sales broker who might represent you. These are all tried-and-true methods for selling any business.

BusinessBrokers.com offers several services that you might be interested in if you have a business to put on the market. From business valuations to helping you find potential buyers for your business, you will find them on the Internet at www.businessbrokers.com. They specialize in privately held businesses valued between $100,000 and $10 million.

But, we're Internet-crazy people, right? Why not offer your business for sale on the Internet, to millions of potential purchasers, and let them fight it out among themselves? (We want to make money and have fun!)

And, as it turns out, there are some pretty cool places on the Internet where you can offer your e-business up for sale.

Selling Your e-Business on eBay.com

The famed Internet auction site eBay.com offers up a whole bunch of different items for sale. For the most part the sellers are private parties. Some unusual items show up for sale on eBay and I'm starting to see them auction off some high-ticket items, such as businesses worth more than $1 million.

As I write this chapter, I notice that eBay is featuring some businesses for auction today. Let's take a look at what's going on in the wild and wooly world of Internet auctioneering.

Ever thought of buying a long established satellite television company? Well, me neither. I am more of the brand-new, unproved satellite television company sort of guy. Anyway, the business in question is being offered at a $195,000 starting bid.

Maybe owning an antique shop is more up your alley. I saw one offered today, located in Phoenix, Arizona, and offered for a starting bid of $75,000. Established Internet businesses do show up for sale on eBay, as well. I noticed one just today. It is called Trackstar, and according to the advertisement on eBay, it is the number two–rated missing person locator in the country. I don't know whether that claim is true or not, but the site is located at www.missingperson.net. It is being offered at a $650,000 starting bid.

Heroic History

Priceline: Price-Picking Pioneers

Web site name: www.priceline.com

Founded: July 1997

Service provided: Online sales

Business model: Priceline takes the world of online retailing and turns it on its head, making major vendors act like flea market dealers. In a normal online shopping experience, you would find the item you want, see what it's priced at, and then decide whether it's worth it. At Priceline, you go there, tell Priceline what you want and how much you want to pay for it, and Priceline checks the vendors that it deals with to see if anyone is willing to sell it to you for that price. Consider airline tickets (which was the first product that Priceline handled). If you want to travel from Los Angeles to St. Louis and are willing to pay $200 for the round trip, you enter all that information and the dates you want to fly into Priceline. Priceline's computer puts your bid in to the airlines, and if it finds one that can take the deal, it will sell you the tickets. (Never mind that the plane leaves at 2 a.m. and sticks you with a four-hour layover in Minneapolis in the dead of winter; you agreed in advance that you'd buy the tickets if it could find them. And you will also never find out that you could have gotten the same ticket for a $150 bid.) Priceline now uses this same bidding model to sell hotel space, cars, and groceries. They've also set up *Perfect YardSale*, a price-naming service that will compete with eBay for sellers wanting to get rid of their old junk and buyers who decide they need more old junk. A series of patents protects the sales method that Priceline uses.

Where the money came from: Priceline went public on March 29, 1999, offering up shares at 16 bucks apiece. (No, you couldn't name a lower price and see if it would accept it. In fact, if you wanted to buy it on the first day of public trading, you had to pay at least $73.) The stock soared as high as $165 per share. As of February 10, 2000, it was trading at $57 1/8, giving the business a market capitalization of $8.4 billion. Priceline.com trades on the Nasdaq exchange under the symbol PCLN.

If you want to sell your established Internet business, maybe you should consider giving eBay's auction services a shot. If you do, there are a few things that you should know. (Actually, these rules are the same for selling anything on eBay, not just businesses.)

You need a credit card to establish a seller's account on eBay. Your business will need to be offered for a 3-, 5-, 7-, or 10-day auction period.

You can set a minimum price for your business. If a bidder has met your asking price, then you have sold your business. Try to back out of a sale and you could very well get sued, plus it's a violation of your agreement with eBay. During the course of the auction, any bidders (or potential bidders) can email you directly. It would be in your best interest to answer questions posed by legitimately interested parties when they contact you.

If you have a successful bidder, then the two of you must contact one another within three business days and work out the transfer of your business. If the bidder flakes and doesn't contact you, and you can't contact him, then after the three-day period has elapsed you are free to contact the second-highest bidder to see if he is still interested in buying your business. But he has no obligation to follow through with the purchase.

eBay offers more than one type of auction. You can establish a *reserve price* if you won't sell your business below a certain price. This is different from setting a minimum bid. Bidders will know that there is a reserve price but the actual reserve price is kept a secret from them. The bidder will win the right to purchase your business if he meets or exceeds the reserve price and has the highest bid.

If nobody meets the reserve price, then the whole deal is off and you don't have to sell your business. Want a little secrecy in your life? If so, you might like to sell your business on eBay via its *private auction* services.

In a private auction, the buyers' email addresses are kept secret from the public and only you, the seller, know who purchased your business. This could be a good thing to do when you sell a business, because your buyer might not want his competitors to know what he's up to. Sneaky, huh?

Visit eBay.com for more details on how you can auction off your e-business on the Internet.

You Sold What?

Just putting your company up on eBay isn't going to attract buyers. The people there to pick up Beanie Babies and Woodstock PEZ dispensers aren't going to want to buy BusinessMonitoring.com. You have to publicize the sale with press releases and advertising.

Selling Your e-Business on Millionaire.com

I like *Millionaire Magazine*'s style. Its companion Web site, Millionare.com (seen in Figure 19.1) is very snazzy. You'll find it at `www.millionaire.com`, and when you go there you'll notice that it also has an auction service. Its auctions have a distinctly different twist to them when compared to eBay's auctions. Millionaire.com specializes in luxury items. I tell you, the whole enterprise simply smacks of class in all respects. (Okay, that ought to get me invited to some swanky *Millionaire Magazine* parties. Just write to me in care of the publisher of this fine book.)

It auctions off domain names, too. Some of the ones that I have seen there are pretty pricey, with opening bids running in the multimillion dollar range. It also offers expensive real estate, as well.

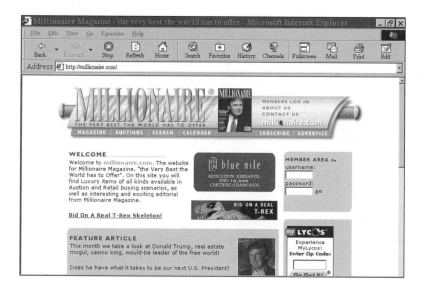

Figure 19.1

Check out the luxury items for sale at auction at Millionaire.com!

I didn't notice any businesses for sale, but I did notice one item that was pretty unusual. Millionaire.com (in association with Lycos) was auctioning off a T-Rex fossil, and asking for bids to start at $5.8 million. Now while that fossil isn't precisely a business in itself, I did notice something intriguing about the sale.

Potential buyers had to register to make a bid and disclose personal information including financial information. Why? So the seller wouldn't have to deal with a bunch of yahoos giving him fake bids and trashing his auction.

You will have to contact Millionaire.com directly if you are interested in auctioning your e-business on its site. It has standards, after all. You will find an online form to complete at `www.millionaire.com/sub/auctions/auction_email.asp`. You can use that to tell it about your business (or other luxury item) that you want to sell on Millionaire.com.

Heroic History

CDNOW: Investing in CDs

Web site name: cdnow.com

Founded: 1994

Service provided: Recorded music sales

Business model: CDNOW was founded by a pair of twins (Matt and Jason Olim) working out of their basement. They've done for CD and tape sales what Amazon.com did for books, offering a far larger selection than one can get at the local store, with very competitive prices. (One major difference: where Amazon fulfills its own orders, CDNOW takes orders for another company to process.) CDNOW attracts music fans not only because of its large selection, but because of its wealth of information. Pull up a CD listing, and you'll not only see the title, price, and song tracks (like you'd be able to see just looking at a sealed CD at a typical store). You'll see the full credits of the CD, with links for reviews, a biography of the artist, and a list of recommended similar artists. You can also listen to sound samples from the tracks of this CD. This can make it a fun site to spend time bopping around, making it likely that the user will stumble across some CD he wants to order. It has started offering custom CDs, allowing users to build their own mix of tracks from a library of licensed music. CDNOW also offers music and nonmusic video gifts. To grab the international market, the site is available in eight different languages. The company's accounting practices raised some eyebrows when it was revealed that if someone bought a $20 CD using a $5 coupon, it would be counted as a $20 sale and a $5 marketing expense, rather than a $15 sale.

Where the money came from: CDNOW Inc. went public on February 10, 1998, closing its first day of trading at $22 per share. In July 1999, it announced a merger with Columbia House. As of February 10, 2000, the stock was trading at $10, giving the business a market capitalization of $304 million. The shares trade on the Nasdaq market under the symbol CDNW.

Selling Your Public Corporation

Public corporations are subject to a host of federal and state laws, and this is certainly true when a public company is sold. If your e-business is a public company, it is doubtful that you would need a book to guide you in the sale of your business. (No, you'd have a dozen gray-suited attorneys to guide you, while they also feed you grapes and tell you how handsome, rich, or manly you are.)

In any event, here are some things to consider. When any buyer wants to purchase more than 5% of a public company, he must disclose certain information to the Securities Exchange Commission and to the company that is being sold. If the potential purchaser of the 5% (or larger) interest in the company intends to liquidate the business, sell off its assets, or make any other substantial changes after he gets control, he must disclose this in advance.

Like I said, it's complicated. One of the most interesting things about public corporations is that the controlling shareholders (the *owners*, as it were) often take steps to keep their company from being sold against their will.

Huh? Remember, a public corporation is generally for sale all the time. You can buy shares of stock, right? If somebody can figure out a way to buy enough shares of stock to gain voting control over the corporation, he can have a lot of control over the future of that corporation. Hence the 5% law that I mentioned. Naturally, not all the shares of stock in a corporation are available for sale at any given time, but somebody might find a way to buy a controlling amount or at least team up with other shareholders and build up a controlling interest in that manner.

A *merger* is generally a stock for stock transfer of ownership. The company that is purchased ceases to exist and is absorbed into the purchasing company. There are a lot of laws that affect this sort of purchase, as well.

Enough laws to fill more than one book. If you own a public corporation, your corporate attorneys will be guiding you should you want to sell your closely held public corporation.

In this book we often mention *going public*, so it is important that I tell you that if you do take your corporation public, selling it is a very complicated affair. But then, nearly every aspect of running a public corporation is very complicated. Don't worry! If you've gone public you'll hopefully have enough money to afford the very best attorneys.

The Least You Need to Know

➤ The value of your site includes tangible assets, intellectual property, and intangibles such as good will.

➤ Competitors, compatible businesses, and portals all make good potential purchasers for your site.

➤ Privately held businesses can be sold on the Internet at various locations or through traditional business brokers.

YEEEHA!!!!

Chapter 20

Little Bitty Pieces of Company: Stock and Stock Options

In This Chapter

➤ What you need to know about stock and stock options

➤ The different types of stock options and how they vest

➤ Tax issues surrounding stock options

➤ Insider trading: lucrative, yet illegal

What Is Stock?

Stock means that you own a portion of a company. If you own a share of stock, that means you own a portion of the company that issued the stock. Let's pretend for a minute that I am a company, rather than a devilishly handsome author of books about the Internet, and I have issued a grand total of 100 shares of stock in my company, which could only be called Handsome Rod, Inc.

Let's further pretend that I sell you 10 shares of Handsome Rod, Inc. You now own 10% of Handsome Rod, Inc. See, nothing to it? Of course, most companies sell a much larger number of shares of stock than a mere 100 shares, but you get the picture. Each share represents a portion of ownership in a particular company.

Stock generally comes in two standard types: *common stock* and *preferred stock*. (Hey! Don't let your eyes glaze over quite yet, this is really pretty easy stuff. Let's try a relaxation technique that I learned in Tibet. Take a deep breath. Breathe in, hold it, breathe out. Okay, great. You look very relaxed now. Let's move on.) Common stock and preferred stock share one characteristic: They both indicate that you, as a shareowner, own a particular portion of a particular company. Common stock differs from preferred stock in one important way. Common stock grants the investor the right to cast a vote in the annual Board of Directors election. You don't have the right to cast this vote when you own a share of preferred stock. With common stock you get one vote for each share you own. With preferred stock you don't enjoy the ability to vote.

But there is an advantage to having preferred stock, even though you don't get the chance to cast a vote for your favorite Board of Directors candidate. Dividend payments are usually higher for preferred stock than for common stock and are generally paid before common shareholders receive their dividends. It's called preferred because the company prefers that you keep your nose out of the company's business, and bribes you to see that you do.

You now know more about stock than, I would venture to guess, 99% of your neighbors. Go ahead, take a walk outside later and ask around. "Hey, Lady! Yes, you walking the dog. Do you know the difference between common and preferred shares of stock?" I bet you a bag of jelly beans, your choice of flavor, that few of the people you come across will know the answer to that simple question. Don't you feel like a real smarty pants right now? Go ahead and enjoy it.

A Brief Look at Going Public

Companies that *go public* issue shares of stock that you can purchase on one of several national stock exchanges. The United States Securities and Exchange Commission is a federal agency that closely regulates the initial public offering of stock and the sale of stock thereafter.

Companies that go public usually first appear on the Nasdaq (National Association of Securities Dealers Automated Quotation system), which is also known as the over-the-counter market. There are rules about how many millions of dollars of assets (and other financial stuff) a company must have to obtain a listing on the Nasdaq. The American Stock Exchange usually lists companies that are much larger than those on Nasdaq and those companies that are listed on the New York Stock Exchange are even larger and richer than those listed on the American Stock Exchange. There are also several other stock exchanges in the United States, such as the Chicago Stock Exchange and the Pacific Exchange. You will find a link to all the United States Stock Exchanges and Associations at www.sec.gov/others.htm.

Why do companies go public? Because they can make some major money if the offering does well. But there are downsides to going public. Public companies have to compose quarterly earning statements and annual reports, which are made available to the steely, unblinking gaze of Joe Investor (and me and you and Aunt Sally, too). These reports take a great deal of time, effort, and money to complete. And sometimes the mandatory portions of the reports can be embarrassing or otherwise contain statements that the companies would rather not have mentioned, such as "Oops, we took another silly $10 million loss this quarter. Better luck next time!"

Anyway, we'll be discussing going public in much more detail in Chapter 21, "Sell Your Cake and Eat It, Too: Going Public." It will be exciting, I promise. Why? Because it deals with money, money, and more money, and that's why you bought this book, right? No shame in that.

Taking Stock of Stock Options

Think of a *stock option* as being a contract between yourself and the company you work for. This particular contract will give you the right to purchase a certain amount of the company's stock. The really neat thing is that the agreement will state how many shares you can purchase and will also set a certain price for the shares of stock. The purchase price is called the *exercise price*. Naturally, you will want to get an exercise price that is as low as possible. Buy low, sell high, right? That's what you want to achieve here. You want the stock option to mean that you are getting a special bargain rate on stock that you hope will gain a great deal of value over a reasonable period of time. In short, you want to have the best opportunity to turn a tidy profit.

You'd not be getting much of a bargain if the exercise price ended up being the market price on the day you used your stock option. Nope, what you want is an exercise price that is as low as possible, so that, if the stock rises in value over time, you will be able to turn a tidy profit.

The Motley Fool Web site is a great place to learn about the stock market. See Figure 20.1 to see what its home page looks like.

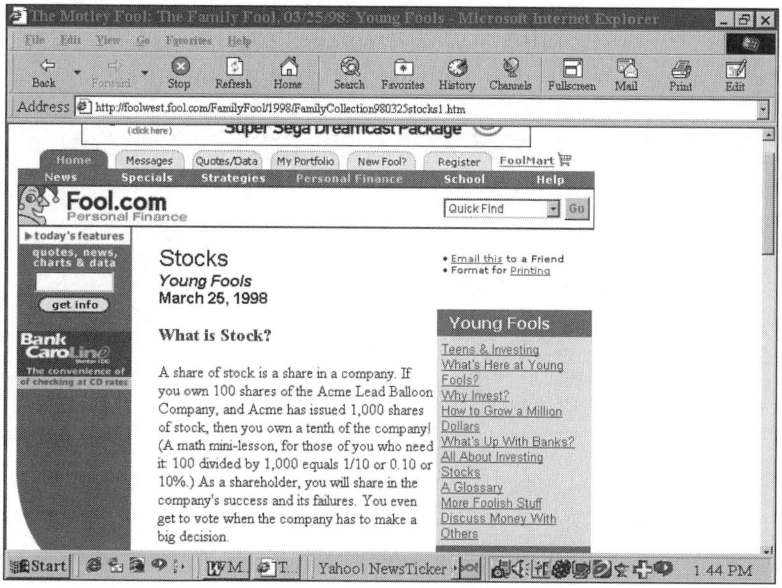

Figure 20.1

The Motley Fool: Investment information in foolish hats at www.fool.com.

What a Gem

The Motley Fool: Fun, Not Folly

The Motley Fool Web site is a great place to obtain a wide range of information about the science of investing, all delivered up in highly entertaining fashion. Pop over to this foolishly wonderful Web site to learn to pick up tips for your personal finances, to get educated in the basics of investing, to read the latest business news, and much more. You will find the Motley Fool Web site at www.fool.com.

Why Having Stock Options Can Be Really Cool

Because your contract gives you the right to purchase the shares at a certain, guaranteed price, you can make a likewise guaranteed profit when you sell the stock later—if the stock rises in value after you buy it. In fact, depending on how well your company does, you might find yourself buying stock at far below the market price when you exercise your option to make your purchase. That's the best of all possible worlds!

But, here's something else that's really cool. If the shares go down in value before you exercise your option to buy the stocks, you haven't lost any money. How come? Because stock option contracts don't require you to purchase stocks if you don't want to. It's an option.

This probably sounds like a deal that is too good to be true, huh? If so, don't fret, don't worry, and don't be upset! You are wondering why the heck a company would offer such a stunningly generous bounty to an employee. Don't worry, I won't hold you in suspense.

The federal government's Security Exchange Commission's Web page offers a bounty of information about the stock market. See Figure 20.2 to get a glimpse of what its page looks like.

Figure 20.2

The U.S. Securities and Exchange Commission keeps stock issuers in line using a combination of laws and really nasty stares.

Heroic History

E*Trade: Stocking Up on Profits

Web site name: ETrade.com

Founded: 1982 as a provider of online quotes and trading services in the days before the World Wide Web was invented. The Web site was created in 1997.

Service provided: Online brokerage

Business model: E*Trade's primary income comes from charging service fees for investors buying and selling stocks via its online brokerage. It competes with traditional full-service offline brokerages by charging lower per-trade fees, while providing less hand-holding. It has a customer base of more than one million independent investors. Additional income is gained by selling eyeballs to advertisers (potentially lucrative given that it receives more than 600 million page views per year), and by having forged an alliance with Amazon.com, which will profit it through the sales of shippable materials. Through acquisitions, E*Trade has gotten into online banking and into business-related software.

Where the money came from: The company went public in November 1997. The stock price was in a general decline for about the first year, reaching a low of 12 ¼ in October 1998. During the following year, however, the stock grew strongly, with two 2-for-1 stock splits. As of December 29, 1999, the stock was trading for 28 ¼, giving the firm a market capitalization of almost $7 billion. The company trades on the Nasdaq exchange under the symbol EGRP.

Why Do They Give Options Away?

Because smart companies see the wisdom in giving rewards to important employees, they give them stock options. This is especially true for brand-new Internet start-up companies that might be cash poor during their early days and that want to obtain talented workers who are willing to take a gamble. The workers gamble their time, efforts, and talent in the hope of striking it rich in stock options.

Sometimes these enterprising workers are people who joined a start-up company in the very early days, when the company was basically dirt poor. Sometimes the employees come on after it looks like the company is well on its way to success, but the workers have special backgrounds and experience that makes them especially valuable to the company.

Fictional, But Plausible, Examples of How This Can Work

Let's examine the fictional but not outlandish story that I call "The Happy Adventure of Milo and the Highly Successful Internet Startup." Our story begins with Milo, an unhappy attorney working for a minor government agency who never got so much as a free holiday turkey, let alone a highly valuable stock option package, despite his many years of faithful service to his master, uh, employer. Besides, the people he worked with thought he was strange because he was always reading computer magazines during his breaks and talking incessantly about the Internet. "The Internet won't lead to anything of value," they often told Milo.

Milo decided one day to look for greener pastures. Because he had purchased the highly informative book that you are holding in your hands (cheap at twice the price), Milo knew that he might be able to find success by locating employment with a worthy Internet startup.

Luckily for him, he noticed a small article buried deep in a computer magazine that mentioned a little Internet-based company called GroovyHawaiianShirts.com. He was surprised to read that the nascent little business was located in his very own town.

Desiring to learn more about the business, Milo called the owner and asked him out to lunch. He learned that the company had only $20,000 in the bank, and two employees: the owner, a rather brilliant fellow named Fred Visionary, and his partner, a pocket-protector sporting engineer called Spike.

Mr. Visionary feels that his company has a good chance for success. "What could be better than an Internet company that covers the entire Hawaiian shirt market? We offer vintage shirts, new shirts, material to sew your own shirts, shirt stain remover, books about collecting Hawaiian shirts, and Hawaiian coffee."

Mr. Visionary is impressed with Milo's energy, ideals, ideas, and general business experience, but he is most impressed with the fact that Milo happens to be wearing a Hawaiian shirt.

Milo is accordingly offered the position of Vice President of Procedures and Contemplations. When Milo comes to work on Monday, he learns that the job description for this particular position is limited to answering the phone and taking messages.

However, Milo isn't bummed out about the lack of prestige regarding his job description. In fact, he is really quite excited about the stock option package that he found on his desk the morning he reported to work. Milo has been offered the chance to purchase 100,000 shares of stock at a fixed price of 10 cents a share. He will be allowed to purchase the stock over a period of four years. After the day that Milo completes his first year of employment he will be entitled to purchase 25% of his promised stock, or 25,000 shares. Each year that follows he will be entitled to purchase another 25,000 shares until he has bought all 100,000 shares.

Things Quickly Pick Up for GroovyHawaiianShirts.com

A week after Milo is hired, a well-dressed person from a major investment capital company walks into the cramped office that Milo shares with Mr. Visionary and Spike. Mr. Visionary is not upset that this person isn't wearing a Hawaiian shirt because, after an hour of discussion, Mr. Visionary has a check for $10 million of investment capital in his hand. Six months later the company has gone public with the most successful IPO in history. In four years, Milo finds his stock to be worth $100 a share, for a grand total of $10 million. His purchase price for the shares totaled $10,000. Even after taxes, Milo is a very rich man.

Of course, another plausible scenario here is that Milo's company, well, loses its shirt a month after he starts his job and he finds himself looking for another job. But as long as we are dreaming, why not have happy dreams instead of scary ones?

Fine Print About How Stock Options Are Granted

Generally speaking, the Board of Directors will grant stock options to the company's employees. This means, of course, that the CEO's Auntie May, as nice as she might be, doesn't have the right to grant you stock options nor does the CEO on his own, although he certainly will carry a lot of weight with the Board, especially because he will probably sit on the board as Chairman.

The terms and conditions regarding your stock option agreement are embodied in the form of a written contract. You will want to read this contract very carefully and even have your lawyer go over it with you. Typically, if you are terminated from your job before your first-year anniversary of employment, you will not gain any shares of stock at all. This deals with the issue of vesting, which I will explain in detail a little later in this chapter.

Exercise Prices: Not Just Gym Fees Anymore!

The *fair market value* of the shares is generally the price that is set for your stock on the day that you are given your stock option agreement. Naturally, a start-up company with $20,000 in the bank and no other assets will not have a very large value reasonably placed on their shares of stock. In the days prior to a company going public, the Board of Directors will make its best estimate on what the stock is worth. It will base this estimate on the company's economic situation at that time.

After a company goes public, the value is easy to determine because it is based on what the market value of the stock is, that is, what people are actually paying for shares on the open market.

Charles Schwab operates one of the best online stock market Web sites in the world. See Figure 20.3 and then go visit its home page for more information.

Figure 20.3

Charles Schwab's online brokerage enables you to buy and sell stocks without ever dealing with human beings!

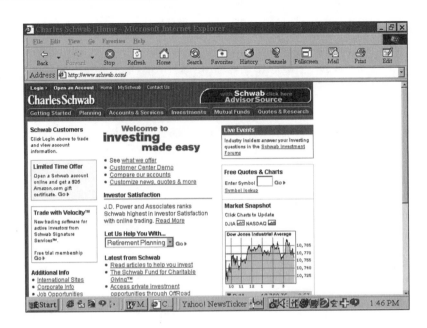

Buy and Sell Stocks Online!

It is now easier than ever to trade shares of stocks on the Internet. All you have to do is set up an account with a brokerage house and away you go! No more telephone calls to your broker putting in your buy or sell requests. Instead of trying to conduct business on the telephone, you will be able to quickly perform your transactions from your own computer. Charles Schwab & Co. maintains a very popular site where you can do your online trading. Give it a look at www.schwab.com.

Vesting: You Don't Need a Suit to Do It

When our friend Milo was given the option to buy his first 25,000 shares of stock on the first anniversary of his hiring, that meant that those 25,000 shares vested on that happy date. Even if Milo quits or gets fired after the vesting date, he still has the right to buy those shares pursuant to his stock option agreement. Typically, the stock option agreement will allow the employee several years in which to exercise his option to purchase the vested stocks before he loses the right to do so. (And, remember, you can take a pass and not buy the shares when they vest but can put off purchasing them for sometimes up to as long as 10 years after your vesting date arrives. It all depends on the terms and conditions of your stock option agreement. Because of this, even if you have an option to pay $10 per share for a stock that is only worth $5 on the day of vestment, that option isn't worthless. Next year, if the stock goes up to $20 per share, you can still buy it at $10.)

The balance of the shares will vest according to the specifics of the contract involved. For example, it is common for shares to vest on a monthly, prorated basis after the completion of the first year of employment.

Opting to Sell Your Options

After you have purchased your stock, the day will probably come when you will want to sell your stock. There are many rules that apply regarding this. Typically, you will only be able to sell your stock during certain trading periods called *windows*. This is because various laws control when an employee working for a company can sell his stock. These rules exist for the protection of the investors in the general population—those not somehow employed or enjoying a business relationship with the company.

The general counsel for your company or some other advisor for your company will usually be able to alert you as to when you can actually sell your stock.

It is very important to remember that you should always seek the advice of an attorney regarding any questions you might have regarding stock options or any other issue pertaining to your employee benefits.

ISOs? NSOs? You Dunno?

An *ISO* is an *Incentive Stock Option*. These are the types of stock options that are usually granted only to employees of the corporation issuing the stock. *NSO* is short for *Nonstatutory Stock Option* and can be granted to employees as well as directors of the corporation or even outside consultants who have been hired to assist the corporation in some manner. The stock options that you might receive will be either ISOs or NSOs. How will you know? They will be identified as such in the stock option contract that you get from your company.

The Taxing Subject of Taxes: The ISO Is So Better!

The tax that you pay on money made from the sale of ISOs is delayed until you sell, trade, give away, or in some manner dispose of your shares. You are responsible for paying the taxes on NSOs when you exercise your option to purchase the NSOs. So, if you are like most people and want to put off paying those taxes as long as possible, ISOs are for you.

But there's more: You will pay a different tax regarding your NSOs than ISOs depending on whether or not the NSO shares are vested when you purchase them. Remember, *vesting* means, essentially, the time when you can first purchase the shares pursuant to your stock option agreement, such as when you have completed your first year of employment with the company.

When you exercise your option to purchase vested NSO shares, the tax that you pay is the difference between the fair market value of the stock on the date when you exercise your option and the exercise price. So, if the fair market value is $100 and the exercise price is $1, you will pay taxes on the $99 profit.

The Section 83(b) Election and More NSO Tax Stuff

If you purchase unvested NSO shares, you are taxed on the difference between the fair market value and the exercise price of the stock on the day that the stock vests. So, if you purchase your unvested NSO stock at the fair market value of, say, $10 per share but the stock is worth $100 later on when it vests, you will pay tax on $90. Easy, huh? But there's one more wrinkle. You can choose to have the tax calculated based on the taxable income on the date of your exercise to purchase the unvested NSO stock. This is known to tax lawyers and accountants as the *Section 83(b) election* (which shows how little imagination tax folks have; I've called it *The Great Financial Switcheroo*). Your company will also be compelled by this law to withhold taxes on the taxable income regarding your NSO if you are employed by the company, just as they deduct money from your paycheck for taxes.

With an NSO you will pay taxes based on the fair market value of your stock as calculated the day you buy the shares and the actual price at which you are allowed to purchase the stock. (Huh? Are your eyes shutting? Are you going to sleep? Here, have some GroovyHawaiianShirt coffee.)

You see, the stock might well be worth more on the day that you buy it than the price you get to pay for it. So, the tax is based on the difference, as established by the market value, on the day that you buy the stock. Easy, see?

The money that you have made (that is, the difference between the two prices) is treated like income you might have been paid as an employee and taxed like it was a salary or a fee you might have been paid as an independent contractor. So, if you are an employee of the company, you should expect them to withhold enough money to pay your taxes regarding the profits that you have made when you exercise your option to purchase your NSO shares.

Remember this: If you buy unvested NSO shares, the difference is that you pay your taxes based on the value of the stock on the day it vests *unless* you elect to calculate your taxes on the date of exercise pursuant to *The Great Financial Switcheroo*—er, Section 83(b). It would be remiss of me not to suggest at this point that you contact your friendly neighborhood tax attorney for further information on these subjects.

Even More Reasons ISOs Are Better, Taxwise

When do you owe taxes regarding ISO shares? Only when you sell them, trade them, give them away, or otherwise get rid of them in some fashion. Not only that, but you will pay taxes on your profit from the sale of the shares as if it were capital income, rather than standard income, such as the salary you make as an employee or fees paid to you as an independent contractor. That's usually a far better deal for you.

If you make money from the sale of your ISO shares, that is deemed a *capital gain*. If you lose money, it is considered a *capital loss*.

If you hold your ISO stock for a period greater than a year, you will pay a *long-term capital gain* tax, which is currently at a maximum rate of 20%. If you elect to hold your shares of stock for a period less than a year, you will pay *short-term capital gain* taxes, which is currently figured at a maximum rate of 39.6%. Either way, please consult with your tax advisor regarding full details and to help you plan which way to go, assuming you've got some ISO-related profits coming your way, you lucky person!

The other cool thing about ISOs is that capital losses can be used to offset capital gains, decreasing the tax you have to pay. Isn't Uncle Sam cool?

How Does the Alternative Minimum Tax Work?

Certain people, who shall remain nameless here because I don't know their names, complained to the IRS that certain other people, specifically some of the very rich, had large incomes and paid virtually no taxes. This made other people, who had far less income, very upset because they were paying larger tax bills than some of the lucky rich people who were essentially skating by with a very modest tax burden.

The IRS agreed that this wasn't particularly fair, so they came up with the Alternative Minimum Tax. People with a great deal of tax-exempt or even tax-deferred income would have to pay at least some minimum amount of tax. The point of this is that when you exercise your Incentive Stock Option you might find yourself affected by the Alternative Minimum Tax law, depending on when and how you dispose of your shares of stock. Consult your tax advisor to be sure. (Please note: that's consult, not insult. Telling your tax advisor that she has a funny haircut will not help.)

Holding Periods Are Not Cuddling Times

There is an unpleasant little thing that we have to talk about now. It is called a *disqualifying disposition*. If this ends up applying to you, it will mean that you will have to pay much higher taxes on your ISO profits than if it doesn't apply to you.

You can avoid having your sale of shares being labeled a disqualifying disposition by obeying certain *ISO holding periods*.

This means that you cannot sell, trade, or otherwise dispose of your shares of ISO stock within a period of one year from the date that you exercise your stock option, and you cannot dispose of the shares within two years from the date that your company gave you your option grant. If you fail to honor either of these time periods you might find yourself subject to the disqualifying disposition rules.

How About an Example, Mr. Book Writer?

Fair enough. Let's assume that on October 7, 2000, you were granted an Incentive Stock Option agreement that gave you a vesting date of October 7, 2001—one year to the day after your grant date.

After the first year passes, you hold on to your stock for another full year before you dispose of your shares. Because of the time period that has elapsed between your grant date, your exercise date, and the date of disposition of the shares of stock, you have met the requirements to avoid a disqualifying disposition.

Why? Because you have not disposed of your shares within two years of being given the ISO grant and you have also not disposed of them within one year of exercising your right to purchase your shares of stock.

Any capital gain that is produced by the disposition of your shares of ISO stock will be treated as a long-term capital gain, which should put you in the best possible tax situation. Remember: Consult with your tax attorney or other qualified tax counselor for in-depth, personal advice in this area.

Insider Trading: A Big No-No

You don't look like the kind of person who wants to go to prison. Insider trading is just the sort of thing that can lead to prison. But, don't fear, I am going to tell you about the types of activities that are generally considered insider trading so that you'll be sure to stay out of trouble, okay?

It is against the law for you to buy or sell shares of stock if you possess material, private information about the company that has issued the stock. By private I mean information that has not been made public. In short, a secret that could reasonably cause someone to either buy or sell stock in the company.

If you are employed by a company you could very well know *inside* information that investors would love to know. If you give such information to a friend of yours, that isn't fair to all the other investors, or would-be investors, who would also like to know that particular secret. Insiders and friends of insiders of any specific company shouldn't have an unfair advantage over investors who are members of the general public.

Violating insider trading laws is very serious. Past violators are now insiders—inside the penitentiary.

Trading on Material Nonprivate Information

Let's assume that you are a director, officer, or somehow employed by a particular company. Or you could be a salaried employee, perhaps, or even a contractor or consultant. Or you could simply be a member of their household, such as a family member or roommate. If so, then the following would apply to you.

You can violate the law regarding insider trading by becoming involved in a sale or purchase of stock in your company during certain periods of time if you possess important private information about the company.

For example: If you know that some big news is going to be released about your company that would likely cause the value of your company's shares to drop, and you quickly sell off your own shares before the news gets released to the general public. That would be wrong. That would also be a crime. Unless you get a jury that likes your haircut or is, perhaps, asleep during your trial.

Your company will no doubt have a written policy establishing when you can trade your shares of stock and you will want to be sure that you clearly understand this policy. Later we'll be discussing trading windows, that is, the appropriate period of time when you can sell your shares of stock. I promise it will be exciting, too.

Cowless Tipping

If you learn some important (and secret) information about your company that would reasonably influence an investor to buy or sell your company's stock and you tell someone outside your company about it, you might have engaged in *insider tipping*, which is illegal. The Securities and Exchange Commission can still hold you responsible even if you do not personally profit from any sale or purchase of shares that come about because of your tipping. This can result in huge penalties, such as being fined or going to jail. You could also get fired by your company for violating its in-house policy against insider tipping.

Types of Material Nonpublic Information

Following are a few examples of the type of information that should not be released to any individual member of the investing public until it is released at the same time to the world at large.

Let's say you knew that your company was going to announce in its quarterly report it was going to make a huge, unexpected profit. Or, even a huge unexpected loss. Yup! That's a perfect example of material nonpublic information.

How about stock splits? Investors get really interested when they learn that a stock is going to split. That's another good example. How about news that your company is going to buy another company? Sure, that's another perfect example.

If some genius in your company has invented a wonderful, secret new invention that your company will probably make a zillion dollars on, would that be a good example of insider knowledge? Of course!

Let's say that you knew that your company's product was causing everybody who used it to have serious, and unexpected, health risks. That's the sort of thing that a company could be sued over, right? Another example of insider information.

Heroic History

Telebank: Banking Without Lines

Web site name: www.telebankonline.com

Founded: 1989 as a bank without branches, only phone access

Service provided: Online and telephone banking

Business model: Telebank makes its money as any bank does, by investing the money that people save with them. While it began as a telephone-only bank in the days before the World Wide Web, its manner of thinking was very much in the style that would lead to success on the Web. Its lack of need for branches and traditional tellers meant that it was operating with a much lower overhead than traditional banks. Because of this, it could afford to offer higher interest rates on savings than the vast majority of banks, and thus attracted money-conscious savers (and it's hard to imagine a saver who isn't money-conscious to some degree). When it created its Web presence, this improved its ease of access and attracted the Web-savvy saver. It became the premiere pure-play Internet bank, with more than 97,000 accounts and $2.1 billion in deposits as of September 30, 1999.

Where the money came from: The company began limited stock trading in 1994, with stock issues in 1998 and 1999. During 1999, Telebank was acquired by E*Trade in a stock trade. The estimated value of the trade at the time it was announced was approximately $1.8 billion.

Companies frequently provide their employees with education about insider trading, including training seminars, videotapes, and written educational materials. Insider trading can result in criminal or civil sanctions against both the insider who is trading and his supervisor, under certain conditions.

Because of the seriousness of the insider trading laws, be sure that you get the counseling you need so that you do not accidentally cause some serious trouble for yourself. "Hey, Fred, you ought to buy some shares of stock in my company because the guy down the hall from me came up with a great new invention" might be enough to land you in prison or at least get you fired. Be careful. Be sure you fully understand the rules in this important area of corporate life.

The federal government is very careful about seeking out insider trading. It constantly watches over the market to look for unusual trading activity that might be evidence of possible insider trading. So, and please don't get mad at me for suggesting this, don't ever think that you can get away with insider trading. It simply isn't worth it.

Trading Windows: Portholes to Prosperity

When you have stock in a company where you are employed, there are usually certain time periods when you cannot sell your stock. In fact, these time periods might be more common than the times when you can sell your stock. These periods when you can sell your stock are called *trading windows,* and will be announced to you by your company's legal advisors. For example, you might not be able to trade your shares for a certain number of days after your company has issued its quarterly report. Your company will advise you when these trading windows will be open.

Wealth of Knowledge

Splittin' for Good

A *stock split* is when a company decides to increase the number of shares that exist by saying that every one of the existing shares is swapped for two (or more) new shares. It doesn't change what percentage of the company you own. This is usually done because the stock price has gotten so high that it's hard for small investors to buy. By doing a two-for-one split, the company cuts the price of a single share in half—although the announcement of the split frequently leads to raising the price.

What is the reason for this rule? So that you, as a company insider, can't benefit unfairly regarding inside knowledge about how well, or poorly, your company is doing. Here's the bottom line: Your trading of company stocks will have to be cleared by the company prior to your being allowed to trade your shares of stock. This is done to keep both you and your company out of legal hot water.

Special Rules for Directors and Officers

Section 16 of the Securities Exchange Act of 1934 requires that directors and officers of a company comply with certain additional rules that affect their ability to purchase and sell shares of the company's stock within a six-month period of time. Directors and officers might not be permitted to engage in certain types of transactions at all. If you are a director or an officer in your company, you will want to obtain clear legal guidance from your attorney regarding how Section 16 affects you.

Helpful Web Sites

Following are a few Web sites that will help you navigate your way around the world of stocks and options:

➤ The U.S. Securities and Exchange home page can be found at www.sec.gov. You will find a great deal of helpful information there.

➤ The American Stock Exchange home page is located at www.amex.com. Meanwhile, you will find the New York Stock Exchange and Nasdaq pages at www.nyse.com and www.nasdaq.com, respectively.

➤ If you feel the need to research insider trading laws and other interesting federal legal material, why not surf over to uscode.house.gov/usc.htm? You will find a very easy-to-use search tool there.

➤ Corporations Law can also be researched at the "Securities Lawyer's Deskbook" which is provided by the University of Cincinnati's College of Law. That Web site is found at www.law.uc.edu/CCL/intro.html.

The Least You Need to Know

➤ Stock options can be a very valuable way to be rewarded by your company.

➤ Taxes on stock options vary depending on how long you hold the stock before you trade it.

➤ You might be limited from trading your shares whenever you want to do so; you should comply with the trading windows offered.

➤ Trading shares of stock based on insider information is a serious crime.

Chapter 21

Sell Your Cake and Eat It, Too: Going Public

In This Chapter

➤ What it means to go public

➤ What types of experts are required

➤ How the Securities and Exchange Commission gets involved

➤ What the benefits and disadvantages of going public are

Why Do Companies Go Public?

The simple answer is that it can bring in a great deal of money—money for the company and for the founders of the company. By offering shares of stock in a company to the public, a company can attempt to obtain financing for many important needs. I say attempt because not all Initial Public Offerings are successful, of course.

However, there are downsides to going public. First of all, it costs a great deal of money to pull it off. After a company goes public, there are certain requirements to disclose various types of financial information. The profits or losses of a company become a record that is open to the public. Most of us would rather keep our finances secret, of course, but a public company must give up that bit of privacy.

Other types of business information must be released as well, but all public companies are allowed to keep certain information secret such as secret formulas or other proprietary information. Essentially, the general business aspects of the company become public record. Consult with your attorney to see what information your own company will or will not be compelled to release should you become a public corporation.

Investment Bankers: You Can't Go Public Without Them

Investment bankers are crucial regarding the launch of a public corporation. Sometimes referred to as *underwriters,* the investment banker is a specialist who arranges to sell the stock of a corporation to the public.

More than one investment banker might be required and there will generally be one investment banker who will manage the others.

Investment bankers come at a high price, too. The rule of thumb is that they get paid about 10% of each share of stock sold. In practice, you might find that the actual percentage that the investment bankers demand might be higher and you also might find that you don't really have a lot of room for negotiations as to the percentage that they demand. You could try and act as your own investment banker, but that would probably not be a wise idea. They can demand a high price for their services because an experienced investment banker earns it.

Lawyers and Other Needed Professionals

You will need some attorneys if you are going to go public. They will want to get paid for their services. Attorneys are very funny about that. If you don't pay them, they will be grumpy.

Your lawyer costs for taking your company public can vary a great deal, based on the size of your corporation, how long it has existed, and other factors. In any event, attorney costs could run up to $200,000, although they could be much lower. Your attorney will no doubt be able to cheerfully tell you how much his firm would probably end up charging you to help take your company public.

You'll need accountants, as well. They'll set you back about $20,000 but that figure can vary a great deal, too.

And, don't forget your printing bill. Yes, there is a lot of printing that has to be done when a company goes public. Your actual *offering*, a written statement about your company's impending Initial Public Offering, will be printed along with other various documents. You can't simply use the local print shop, either. Nope, you'll have to use one of the major *financial* printers because your printing must follow many special requirements. Expect your printing bill to clock in at about $50,000. But, once again, that bill could be higher or lower depending on your own company's requirements.

Cooley Godward LLP, Lawyers

Cooley Godward is a very experienced national law firm that handles Initial Public Offerings and much more in the area of corporate law. It has offices located in Boulder, Denver, Kirkland, Menlo Park (Silicon Valley), Palo Alto, Reston, San Francisco, and San Diego. You will find it online at www.cgc.com, as seen in Figure 21.1.

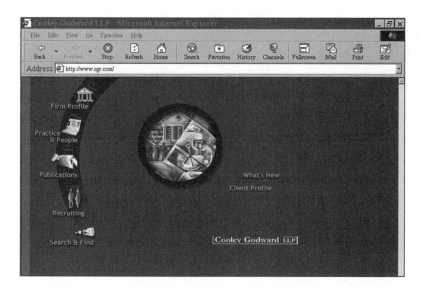

Figure 21.1

The Cooley Godward LLP law firm is especially noted for its work in the area of Initial Public Offerings.

Your attorneys and accountants must be extremely experienced at the necessary steps regarding taking a corporation public. You don't want your nephew who just got out of law school to act as your lead legal counsel. You do want to hire a firm that has a proven, successful, track record in this area. That goes for your accountants, as well. You must have extremely experienced professional help for this undertaking.

Your financial printer has to be a seasoned expert, too, such as Bowne & Co. (as seen in Figure 21.2). Your law firm should be able to guide you to an appropriate financial printer.

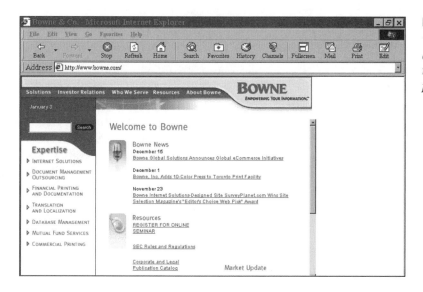

Figure 21.2

The Bowne Corporation is certainly one of the nation's leading financial printers.

Heroic History

E-Stamp: You Can't Email Everything

Web site name: e-stamp.com

Founded: 1994

Service provided: Downloadable postage

Business model: Postage can be a pain in the neck. Keeping stamps on hand or recharging your postal meter just adds complications to the day. On the other hand, you can go with E-Stamp, a system that you can use to pay for postage over the Internet then print your own postage stamps right onto the envelope or mailing label using your word processor and printer. To use the system, you have to purchase an *electronic vault,* a little device that hooks on to your PC and stores data about how much postage you have remaining. When you order postage online, that information is downloaded into the electronic vault. When you use your word processor to print out a stamp, E-Stamp software tracks that printout and updates the vault. E-Stamp sells the electronic vault (with all the relevant software) for about $50. Its real money comes from tacking on a *convenience fee* to the price you pay for postage. This fee generally runs at 10% of your stamp purchase. E-Stamp is the pioneer in this field, being the first company that the United States Post Office allowed to sell postage over the Internet. While there is competition lurking, there are also a lot of opportunities for expansion both within this country and to other countries.

Where the money came from: E-Stamp had raised $11 million from private investors before September 1997, when it got some new investors. Microsoft and AT&T each obtained a 10% equity stake in the firm, for an undisclosed amount. E-Stamp Incorporated went public on October 8, 1999, with an announced price of $17 per share. While the price surged as high as 44 7/8, by January 24, 2000, the price had calmed down to 18⅝. This gives the company a market capitalization of $728 million. The stock trades on the Nasdaq exchange under the symbol ESTM.

Advisors Are People Who Know Important Stuff

Taking a corporation public is a complicated project. Any CEO of a corporation going public will have a lot of headaches to deal with. There is a great deal of paperwork and many legal requirements.

Finding a good advisor from a top-flight consultant firm can greatly ease the pain of going public. You must have lawyers, accountants, and underwriters of course, but advisors are an option.

But a good advisor (also called a *consultant*) is someone who has already gone through the entire process of taking a corporation public. Maybe he's done it several times. Wouldn't it be nice to have someone like that to talk to every step of the way?

Your law firm will gladly help you to find a top-notch advisor should you feel the need for such a service.

You might find the need to hire consultants in various other areas, as well. Be careful. Hiring consultants that you don't actually need can be a waste of money. Consultants can also rack up quite a bill, so be sure that their professional time is carefully managed.

How much will it cost to hire a consultant? That is something that you will have to negotiate. Hourly fees and flat fees are commonplace. You might also offer to hire your advisors as salaried employees.

Wait! Have Your Remembered to Incorporate?

You can't take your company public until you have incorporated it. Most public companies have incorporated in the state of Delaware because they have some pretty cool incorporation laws there. Your attorney will explain all the reasons that Delaware is so popular among corporations.

Bowne, Masters of Financial Printing

Bowne and Co. offers high-tech financial printing that goes beyond simply printing your required financial documents. It can print documents in any required format and probably do more financial printing than any company in the world. It specializes in securities printing and has been in business for more than 220 years. See its corporate Web page at www.bowne.com for more information.

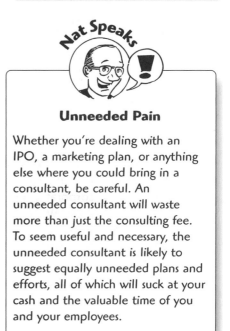

Unneeded Pain

Whether you're dealing with an IPO, a marketing plan, or anything else where you could bring in a consultant, be careful. An unneeded consultant will waste more than just the consulting fee. To seem useful and necessary, the unneeded consultant is likely to suggest equally unneeded plans and efforts, all of which will suck at your cash and the valuable time of you and your employees.

If you are already incorporated, you should understand that there are some pretty significant differences between a private corporation and a public corporation in terms of legal stuff. You'll have to update your legal paperwork such as your articles of incorporation and your bylaws. Once again, your attorney will guide you regarding amending your corporation's legal paperwork.

How Much Stock Can I Sell and Still Retain Control of My Company?

You might be thinking that you have to keep ownership over at least 50% of your stock to maintain control of your company, but that isn't the case at all.

It is the *voting* stock that makes the difference here. If you control, directly or indirectly, the majority of the voting stock, then you control the company.

Some founders of public corporations remain in control of their company with much less than a 50% ownership in the total shares of stock because they effectively control 60% or greater of the stock through their influence over the other shareholders.

However, this is a very important issue. Please consult with your attorneys and financial advisors regarding how you can best maintain control over the corporation that you have founded, if that is an issue that is relevant to you.

Meet the Securities and Exchange Commission

The *Securities and Exchange Commission*, also known as the *SEC,* is a federal governmental agency that monitors the activities of public corporations, including all aspects of a company's Initial Public Offering.

They aren't the only government people who watch over public corporations. Your own state will also have state laws that can control the activities of public corporations. Sometimes state laws even have priority over federal laws. Your attorney will guide you regarding the SEC and the laws of your state.

Other federal laws that apply to public corporations include the Securities Act of 1993 and the Securities Exchange Act of 1934. These laws were passed to stop various abuses of the public in regards to securities and public corporations. In fact, the SEC regulations themselves change on a more or less regular basis. Your attorney, once again, will offer to keep you abreast of all current laws that will affect your soon-to-be public corporation.

The Registration Statement

When a corporation offers shares of stock to the public there is a federal requirement that a *registration statement* must be filed. All relevant information about a public offering must be filed with the SEC. The registration statement is a complicated affair and must follow specific formats. Your professional advisors will have to be very experienced at composing registration statements to be sure that it is done correctly.

276

The registration statement will disclose much about your company. It will contain information that is both positive and negative, so that it amounts to a complete and fair document that would reasonably allow a reader to make a clear evaluation of the likelihood of success that the company might enjoy after it goes public.

If your management team, for example, is unproven, then such information should appear in the registration statement. The document will also contain specific financial information and business information, and will identify the company's top management people.

The filing and subsequent review of your registration statement will include meetings with the SEC staff prior to your filing of the document. It will review the registration statement and inform you of any problems that it sees so that you can correct them.

The SEC, after checking your registration statement, will send you a *letter of comment* that outlines any deficiencies that it found in your registration statement. You can then discuss these problems with the SEC and modify your registration statement accordingly.

Your lawyers handle most of the problems regarding the filing of your legal documents with the SEC. The SEC can delay you from going public if you don't satisfy its requirements. So, having good, level-headed, legal counsel is crucial. In any event, it might take two months or more to successfully file your documents with the SEC even if things go smoothly or much longer if you have repeated problems with your filings. An experienced attorney can make all the difference in the world regarding having your filings promptly approved by the SEC.

The Quiet Period

Federal law does not allow normal corporate publicity during the registration period and the time of the Initial Public Offering. Your company will be given a strict time schedule showing when the quiet period begins and ends. Why? Because the SEC wants to be sure that the company doesn't unfairly pump up the public's interest in the forthcoming stock offering.

Certain preoffering public statements are allowed, though. A touring *road show,* complete with videos, slide shows, speeches, and more will travel throughout the U.S. and even abroad in an effort to excite potential major investors to invest in the Initial Public Offering.

The SEC regulates how these road shows proceed, and requires a complete reading of the *prospectus*, that is, a formal statement that has both the negative and positive elements regarding the upcoming public offering.

The road show allows the investment community to weigh the pros and cons of the upcoming public offering. They sound like a lot of fun to most people—the CEO and other corporate heavies get to jet all over the world, hitting all the major cities—but, all in all, they are exhausting affairs and nothing like a vacation, except for the travel.

After You Go Public, Even More Documents

All sorts of reports must be filed after a company goes public. Some are legal documents, and some are for the public, but they never seem to end. A corporation can spend between $50,000–100,000 each year just to print all the required documents.

Annual reports, quarterly reports, forms about material changes in your company, and much more are required as your fiscal year moves along. Lawyers and accountants are needed to prepare all these reports in a timely manner. If you forget to file a form on time, you will most certainly hear from the SEC.

Heroic History

You: Making Millions

Web site name: Got it picked out yet?

Founded: 2001

Service provided: Helping Internet users and inspiring investors

Business model: You hooked up with a team of folks. One of you had a great idea, and the others were all good at all the little steps it took to make that idea real. The programs got programmed, the Web page got designed, and then you launched it. Early press and advertising drew a few curious users, and then they began to spread the word. Soon you had a going concern—not profitable, perhaps, but popular. You faced every challenge with wisdom and power. Other services were happy to ally themselves with you, in hopes of building an audience for everyone. Copycats arose, but you continued to lead not only in reputation but also in innovation.

Where the money came from: Venture capitalists who thought that your idea was great and would prove of towering important in the future. Users who needed your services and your products right now, and were willing to shell out for them. Advertisers who found the demographics of your site far too tempting to pass up. Larger sites that knew that your innovation and their reputation could lead to something even greater. A stock offering that everyone was eagerly awaiting. Is this happening to you? It will almost certainly happen to many, many people in the coming months. There will be many small teams with big ideas, the right idea at the right time. Will you be part of one of those teams?

The End of the Story

Complicated to the extreme, the taking of a company to an Initial Public Offering is a demanding bit of business. The rewards for the founders of a successful corporation can be astounding.

It is up to you to consult with your attorneys, accountants, and advisors to determine whether or not your own company should go public. The timing of taking a company public is also something that must be carefully considered. Any deficiencies in your filings with the SEC can delay your public offering and greatly damage your timing and even result in having to reschedule your IPO.

Consequently, you must certainly have the best-trained and most experienced professional help that you can obtain to ensure that your IPO proceeds smoothly.

The Least You Need to Know

➤ Going public means offering shares of stock in your company to the general public.

➤ You need to hire experienced lawyers, accountants, and advisors to prepare your Initial Public Offering and to advise you after you have taken your company public.

➤ While you might make a great deal of money for your company if you go public, there are many filing requirements before and after you have had your Initial Public Offering.

➤ You will be required to release a great deal of financial and other information about your company if you go public.

279

Index

F

T

U

V

X-Z